POLITICAL YOUTH, TRADITIONAL SCHOOLS

POLITICAL YOUTH, TRADITIONAL SCHOOLS

National and International Perspectives

Edited by
Byron G. Massialas
Florida State University

Prentice-Hall, Inc., Englewood Cliffs, N.J.

Library of Congress Catalog Card Number: 73-169133

ISBN: 0-13-685578-4

10 9 8 7 6 5 4 3 2 1

Printed in the United States of America

Prentice-Hall International, Inc., London
Prentice-Hall of Australia, Pty. Ltd., Sydney
Prentice-Hall of Canada, Ltd., Toronto
Prentice-Hall of India Private Limited, New Delhi
Prentice-Hall of Japan, Inc., Tokyo

To Students for Educational Innovation (SEI)
for challenging the
Establishment with skill and determination.

Contents

Preface

This book is about youth, their schools, and their relation to the polity.

The studies reported in this volume generally seek to establish the role of the school in developing a milieu in which youth may understand and develop sensitivities toward their political environment. The studies, which deal with different school levels, focus on what are considered traditionally to be the important components of formal education—the curriculum, the teachers, the instructional process, the textbooks, the classroom, the school organization—and they try to ascertain, through empirical research, the extent of their influence on the political socialization of youth.

The results are quite revealing. The schools in all of the countries where they were studied have failed miserably to provide a politically relevant education—an education that not only encourages but cognitively and affectively enables one to become an active participant in the political process, rather than an uncritical and apathetic spectator. In many cases it appears that youth became politically mature and efficacious in spite of their schools. The young person received his political education from his peers, from the mass media, from youth organizations or other contacts, all outside formal schooling.

Given the conditions of our world, many of which foster gross inequalities, hate, racism, and overt aggression of man to man, the spontaneous quest of youth to become involved witnessed in the past few years should be most welcome. Yet the general attitude of educational institutions as represented by teachers, administrators, and school boards is quite negative. They seem to feel that students should not bring the problems of society into the school because these problems do not belong within the legitimate and "time-honored" domains of formal education. Much of youth's challenge to the educational establishment centers on this concern, namely, that the school has stayed outside the mainstream of society and has, therefore, remained aloof to society's problems and unresolved issues. As a result, what is presently offered in the school is basically obsolete, irrelevant, and has no social or political significance. On the whole, the studies included in this book support the above claims.

To make the schools functional, the authors of this volume argue, educators must accept and understand the idea of a new political activism for youth. This new activism is characterized by direct involvement in the political process both in the school and in the community, as well as by a radical change in all school programs and activities to be in line with the inalienable right of students to examine openly and reflectively in the classroom the significant social issues of the time. The critical analysis of controversial social issues in an open school climate, coupled with students' actual participation in the governance of the school, become the overarching goals and the *raison d'être* of the school. The "Inquiring Activist" is the sought-after product of this school. We trust that this volume will help open the way.

BYRON G. MASSIALAS

POLITICAL YOUTH, TRADITIONAL SCHOOLS

The School and
The Political World
of Children and Youth

1

AN OVERVIEW

Byron G. Massialas

Q: Do you think you can trust government?

A: Yes, I do.

Q: Why?

A: Well, because like if people elected them or something that means most people think they can trust them, so that's why they're elected.

(Fifth grade girl, rural school)

Q: Do you think you can trust government?

A: Never.

Q: Why?

A: Because . . . they . . . take more than half the money from my mother and more than half the money from my father. Now all they do is just keep it, they haven't cleaned up Detroit, they just send people to the moon and make jails and everything.

Q: Do they care about you and your family?

A: They don't care about nobody just about the moon.

(Sixth grade boy, inner city)

Q: Do you think the United States can trust other countries?

A: It depends on what countries they are. Some countries, yes. The Soviet Union, no. I mean, some countries you can. Some countries like the Soviet Union could invade us right now. I mean they're a country you can't trust. Some countries, yes, you can really trust them.

Q: What countries can you trust?

A: Oh ah, Australia, that's one you can trust. We go there all the time. That's one you can trust. Right now, this year and that, Vietnam. Ah, Denmark, Sweden, Ireland, ones like that.

Q: What are some other ones? You said you couldn't trust the Soviet Union. What are some other countries that you couldn't trust?

1

A: Yugoslavia, ah Germany, ah let me see, one half of Vietnam.

Q: What about the Soviet Union, why can't we trust them?

A: We can't trust them at all. I mean, they're just a state, I mean a country, that likes to have war. We think that they just love war; if they had freedom they would probably die. It's just that their custom is war all the time.

(Sixth grade girl, rural school)

There are at least four ways in which the school may relate to the political system: (1) through the political socialization of children and youth (e.g., the process of developing cognitive understanding and attitudes toward the political world); (2) through the selection, recruitment, and training of political leaders (e.g., the mechanism for the screening and political training of those who will join the country's elites); (3) through politically integrating a community or society, and bringing about ethnic unification among different people occupying a given territory; and (4) through the organization of special interest or pressure groups, such as teacher or student organizations, which attempt to influence political decisions and demand certain things from the system. This book concentrates on the first function, although at times it is difficult to separate one function from the other.[1]

The school—curriculum, textbooks, instructional methods, school clubs, classroom milieu, students, teachers, administrative structure, and the like —may implicitly engage in the transmission of basic political orientations. These can be (a) cognitive (the ability to analyze and interpret data about political institutions or behavior), (b) affective (the development of positive or negative attitudes toward the symbols of authority), or (c) evaluative (judgments based on the application of certain standards to the performance of political roles).

It is generally held that basic political orientations are formed very early in life, especially between the ages of 3 and 13, and unless a very powerful environment impinges upon the individual (or a cataclysmic event such as the assassination of the President or a major war), he tends to maintain the same orientations throughout his life.[2] More recent work, however, suggests that considerable political conceptualization does take place during the high school years.[3]

The political orientations that children develop largely determine the political culture that will prevail. Cultures in which there is a relatively high degree of citizen involvement (civic cultures) are generally comprised of people who view themselves as politically efficacious. That is, they feel that they can, through their own efforts, influence political decision-making. Nations in which the people have very little concern for changing the government through their own efforts tend to have parochial political cultures;

[1] The other functions of the school are developed in Byron G. Massialas, *Education and the Political System* (Reading, Mass.: Addison-Wesley, 1969).

[2] Robert D. Hess and Judith V. Torney, *The Development of Political Attitudes in Children* (Chicago: Aldine, 1967).

[3] M. Kent Jennings and Richard G. Niemi, "Patterns of Political Learning," *Harvard Educational Review* 38(3):443–67, Summer 1968.

in these nations the citizen expects virtually nothing from the political system. Systems that provide open mechanisms for rapid change and are responsive to the demands of their citizens appear, in historical perspective, to have more chances for political survival and continuity than those systems that have no institutionalized means of change.

In order for a political system to survive, it must secure reasonable support from its citizens. Support for, or criticism of, the system is provided by various socialization agents, such as the family, the church, the peer group, or the school. For instance, the schools may socialize children to accept, without question, the policies of the government and to develop benign attitudes toward the authorities. Traditionally, the policeman was an object of respect and awe among teachers; children generally reflected this attitude and accepted policemen to be major "community helpers." The idea that all policemen are good or are to be depended upon has been internalized by most young children.

Conversely, the schools may impart critical (examined, informed, evaluative) orientations toward the regime. Schools may socialize youth to understand how the system operates—its formal and informal processes, its gatekeepers, its sensitive spots—and to develop corresponding strategies to influence the operation of the system. By stressing the rights and privileges of citizens (rather than just their duties and obligations), schools may stimulate youth to organize and articulate certain wants to the government in the form of responsible demands. Sometimes, as in several recent cases of student activism, these demands are directed against the administration of the school, which to some students represents the symbol of political authority of the larger community.

In many countries, (for example, Turkey under Adnan Menderes and South Korea under Syngman Rhee), governments have been toppled through student-initiated action. In France massive student protests in the spring of 1968 almost brought about the collapse of the de Gaulle regime. In the United States the incidents at Kent State and Jackson State in 1970 gravely accentuated the conflict between youth and government over the continuation of an unpopular war in Vietnam. Elsewhere, students expressed through their actions, both spontaneous and organized, varying degrees of concern and interest in the affairs of their government.

The Results of Political Socialization

Political socialization is generally the process of acquiring and changing the culture of one's own political environment.[4] Political socialization may be measured through the use of indexes, the most important of which are (1) political efficacy; (2) political trust; (3) citizen duty; (4) expectations for political participation; (5) political knowledge; and (6) other-nation or

---

[4] Note the inclusion of change process in the definition. This constitutes a departure from the way the term has been used traditionally. Learning the ways of the system but influencing it to change moves away from a static and fixed interpretation of political socialization.

world concept. The performance level in each of these indexes often provides a good indication of the country's political culture—parochial, subject, civic, or mixed. In the parochial culture the individual has practically no expectations for political change. In the subject political culture the individual may accept or reject the legitimacy of the government, but his affective relationship with it is passive. The civic culture attempts to provide for citizen participation. A parochial political culture theoretically has a traditional political structure. A subject culture has a centralized, authoritarian government. A civic culture has a democratic political structure. Often culture and structure are not congruent, thus creating serious problems for the political system. Also, it is virtually impossible to find pure types of any of the political cultures mentioned above—usually they are mixed types but have certain dominant tendencies.

Let us review these indexes briefly, since they will be used throughout the book. *Political efficacy* is a person's ability to understand the functioning of the government and to feel that it can be changed; the efficacious person feels that he or other citizens have the power to influence political decisions. *Political trust* refers to the feeling of confidence (or lack of it) that one develops toward the government and its officials. One may score high on the index of political trust if one views the government as caring about the personal lives of the citizens. Conversely, one may score low on political trust if one thinks government officials (e.g., the President, members of Congress, or even the school principal, if the school is thought of as a miniature political system) do not care about nor listen to the wishes of the people. The first two interviews in the opening pages of this chapter focus on the political trust of children. The first child appears to be trustful toward government, whereas the opposite is true of the second child. Each of the children offers reasons for his trust or mistrust. *Citizen duty* is the sense of obligation one feels toward his government, usually expressed through voting in an election or obeying the laws and regulations. Citizen duty could also be interpreted to mean obligation to present dissenting views. To the extent that dissent is part of the political culture, it can be considered as a political obligation that citizens have to their country. *Political participation* refers to either expected or actual involvement in political activity, such as political discussions or political rallies and meetings. *Political knowledge* refers to the cognitive understanding that one has of the operation of the political system (both its structure and process) and to the capacity that one has to evaluate critically the system's effectiveness. *Other-nation concept* refers to perception of the relationship of one's nation to the world community. The extent of ethnocentrism among children in a given country would be a measure of this concept. All of these concepts have been stressed in traditional civic education projects (e.g., the Detroit Citizenship Education Study[5]), but until recently very little has been done to translate them into actual behavior for purposes of measurement and evaluation. How does the school generally relate to all of these political outcomes?

[5] Arnold Meier, Florence Cledry, and Alice Davis, *A Curriculum for Citizenship* (Detroit: Wayne State University Press, 1952).

THE POLITICAL ROLE OF THE SCHOOL

Studies conducted in the United States and abroad generally support the notion that the more education a person has the more efficacious he becomes. For example, he who has a college education is more likely to have a higher sense of political efficacy than he who has no education at all. A question asking whether or not one can do something about a local regulation that one considers unjust or unfair elicited an affirmative response from 60 percent of those who had only a primary school education or less. The same question elicited an affirmative response from 82 percent of those with some secondary education and 95 percent of those with some college education.[6]

Of the five nations studied, the Americans and British emerge as the most efficacious, followed by the Germans, Mexicans, and Italians. In all countries perception of ability to influence the government, both on the national and local levels, varied with the amount of education a person had—the more education, the higher the expectations for active citizenship. Age, sex, social class, intelligence, personality, ethnicity, and religion were also important factors in understanding patterns of political efficacy of children in different nations. Several chapters in this book deal in depth with some of these variables.

In the five-nation study already mentioned, it was found that when the individual is given the opportunity to participate in school decisions, either by protesting against an unfair regulation or by taking an active part in classroom discussion, his political efficacy is increased. That is, the individuals who remembered participating in school decisions had higher scores on the index of political efficacy than those who did not. This finding is reinforced by Ehman in a later chapter in this book.

THE ELEMENTARY SCHOOL

The major political function of the elementary school is to foster compliance with governmental rules and authority. The formal curriculum and instructional programs generally over-emphasize compliance with the government and uncritical loyalty toward the system. Political parties and partisanship do not receive much attention in the curriculum or from the teachers responsible for it.[7]

Suburban vs. Inner-city Schools

It appears, however, that schools differ in their influence on the political socialization of children. Children attending suburban elementary

---

[6] Gabriel A. Almond and Sidney Verba, *The Civic Culture* (Boston: Little, Brown, 1965), p. 162.

[7] Hess and Torney, pp. 212–25.

schools tend to have a higher sense of political trust than do children attending inner-city schools. (For an example, see second and third dialogues above.) As Glenn indicates, to the question, "Do you think people in the government listen to what the people like you, your family, and neighbors want the government to do," 67 percent of the suburban school children in the sample responded in the affirmative as compared to only 47 percent of the children from the inner-city school. Also, children from inner-city schools felt much less efficacious than their rural or suburban counterparts in being able to influence the government. To the statement, "People like me and my family can change what happens in the government," 69 percent of the children in the inner-city school responded negatively, but only 53 percent of the rural and 49 percent of the suburban school students responded in the same manner.[8] It appears that various factors within and outside the school make the inner-city child perceive his role in the political system in a different light from the suburban or the rural school child.

It is interesting to note that as children advance through the elementary grades they become more politically efficacious but their feeling of political trust decreases. This phenomenon is more observable among children in suburban schools than among other children. It appears that in addition to general developmental factors among children, the school curriculum may contribute to the sense of political efficacy and trust of children. The Hess and Torney research is suggestive of the connection between the two sets of factors, but the available research does not establish explicit relations.

The impact of the formal curriculum, in general, and that of textbooks, in particular, may be inferred by looking at children's notions of how one goes about changing the government. As Glenn shows, children, especially those in the suburban school favor traditional or textbook ways of changing the government. For example, 58 percent of children in suburban schools, as opposed to 33 percent of children in inner-city schools, thought that writing a letter to the President was the best way to change the government. Not surprisingly, given the nature of the traditional curriculum of the school, only a very small percentage of children in the suburban and inner-city schools (11 percent and 8 percent, respectively) advocated such non-traditional ways of changing the government as taking part in a demonstration or protest.[9] The relation between how children feel about ways of political change and what the most popular civics texts advocate is certainly not coincidental. The chapters by Goldstein and Glenn treat in depth some of the observations and findings discussed in this section and suggest new ways of looking into the influence of the school on this age group.

---

[8] Allen D. Glenn, *"Elementary School Children's Feelings of Political Trust, Political Efficacy, and Political Change"* (Ph.D. dissertation, University of Michigan, Ann Arbor, 1970). See also Glenn's chapter in this book.

[9] Ibid.

THE SECONDARY SCHOOL

School people have for years claimed that formal citizenship education programs in the high school (e.g., civics, U.S. History, government,
"Problems of American Democracy," etc.) contribute to the development
of good citizens. The few studies available in the field generally contradict
this claim—they find very little or no relationship between civics education
and the six political socialization measures to which we pointed earlier.[10]
More courses in social studies or civics will not produce better results.
What appears to be more important than the number of courses offered is
whether or not controversial issues are introduced and whether or not these
issues are discussed in a classroom climate that is conducive to critical
inquiry. When students analyze issues objectively and are given the opportunity to generate and defend their own ideas about social events, they perform relatively high on all important political socialization measures. This
observation applies to both black and white students. The chapters of both
Ehman and Heggan in this volume provide new insights into civic education in two different countries and into the political beliefs and values of
secondary school age youth. The work by Shantz focuses on the content of
the political attitudes and knowledge of youth in junior high school.
Billings' chapter deals directly with the activist orientations of the black
high-school age group and compares them with those of the non-activist
group. Although the activists are more inclined to do so, both groups view
violence and direct confrontation as defensible ways to change the system.

As we pointed out before, the available evidence indicates that most
classrooms and the textbooks used in them in the United States and abroad
are not conducive to inquiry into social and political issues. That most
textbooks and materials foster apathy toward and an uncritical compliance
with the system is well-documented in the literature.[11] Teachers are also
unwilling to probe into social issues in their formal classroom settings. We
find for example that the majority of secondary school teachers (52.5 percent) spent between 0–10 percent of their teaching time discussing social
issues. Only 3 percent of the teachers give to social issues between 50–75
percent of their instructional time. Also, teachers in the sample (comprised
mainly of teachers of biology, English, and social studies), although often
willing, are not adequately equipped to deal with issues in the spirit of
inquiry. For example, in a simple task of separating fact from opinion, 44
percent of the teachers indicated that the following statement is fact or
mostly fact: "The American form of government may not be perfect but

[10] Kenneth P. Langton and M. Kent Jennings, "Political Socialization and the High
School Curriculum in the United States," *American Political Science Review,* 62
(September 1968) 852–67; Lee H. Ehman, "An Analysis of the Relationships of
Selected Educational Variables with the Political Socialization of High School
Students" *American Educational Research Journal* 6 (November 1969) 559–89.

[11] C. Benjamin Cox and Byron G. Massialas, eds., *Social Studies in the United
States: A Critical Appraisal* (New York: Harcourt, Brace and World, 1967)

it is the best type of government yet devised by man."[12] Teachers who had a high belief in traditional sociopolitical values were strongly inclined to identify this opinion statement as fact. In the total sample we find a good portion of teachers to have quite traditional attitudes. About one-third of the teachers scored very high on the scale measuring belief in traditional sociopolitical values (BTSV). Some of the statements upon which the BTSV Scale was based were: "Obedience and respect for authority are the most important virtues children should learn;" "the main purpose of social studies courses is to teach students to be good and loyal citizens."[13] In view of these findings it might be useful to know, perhaps during the four years of college, how teachers-in-training score on this or similar scales so that they may be advised to pursue appropriate careers.

A great deal has been said about the generation gap that purportedly exists between parents and their children. Some studies indicate that there is no such gap—that the offspring share the basic value orientation of their parents. There are, however, some indications that certain discontinuities do exist between generations. Levenson, for example, showed that high-school seniors define the good citizen in different terms than do their parents.[14] There is a higher propensity among students (46.6 percent of the group) to point to participatory criteria of citizenship than among parents (34.2 percent of the group). Parents, much more than students or teachers, define the good citizen in non-political terms—he helps others, goes to church, is a good neighbor, etc. Obedience criteria are also important to parents. Teachers, on the other hand, seem to be much more compatible with the students on the definition of the good citizen. As a matter of fact, the 1,213 teachers in the national sample used present a much more activist picture than either the students or the parents. In spite of their participatory orientation, students much more than their parents and teachers, identify criteria of allegiance (e.g., saluting the flag and performing other "patriotic" rituals) as being descriptive of good citizenship. Perhaps twelve years of school and explicit attendance to political symbols through rituals have had some effect on this group of students (14.6 percent), who point to the allegiant qualities of citizenship. Persistent repetition of such behavior (one civics or history text after another, or one classroom setting after another) must have affected this small group of youth. On the other hand, it is interesting to note in the evidence cited the major changes in youth over a 40-year period. From 1925 to 1965 the proportion of youth

[12] Byron G. Massialas, with Nancy Sprague and Jo Ann Sweeney, *Structure and Process of Inquiry into Social Issues in Secondary Schools,* Volume I (Ann Arbor: The University of Michigan, 1970). (Research performed pursuant to U.S. Office of Education Contract OEC 3–7–061678–2942.)

[13] The details of the BTSV scale are given in ibid. Also available in the report is the *Michigan Social Issues Cognitive Category System,* an observation instrument designed to measure the extent to which the teacher utilizes inquiry skills in dealing with social issues and the extent of student involvement in classroom discussion.

[14] George B. Levenson, "The Public Responsibilities of Private Men" (Ph.D. dissertation, University of Michigan, Ann Arbor, 1971).

identifying participatory criteria as desirable qualities of citizenship almost doubled, whereas the reverse is true for non-political criteria. It seems that during this period, youth, in spite of their textbooks, parents, and teachers, became politicized. The nature of the politicization, of course is somewhat indeterminant, especially when we look at it from the perspectives of Berkeley, Columbia, and Kent State. Is the politicized student of 1965 good enough to cope with the demands of the political system of the seventies? Are the kinds of participatory mechanisms used during the early sixties appropriate for the seventies? These are the questions that emerge from Levenson's work. Hopefully the reader will obtain the necessary perspective from reading the chapters of this book to be able to answer these questions for himself.

COLLEGES AND UNIVERSITIES

During the past few years university students have entered the arena of politics in a most direct way. Whether in Berkeley, Columbia, the Sorbonne, Tokyo University, or, more recently, Kent State and Jackson State, students have shown in a dramatic fashion that there are ways that the system can be changed. Students in the United States influenced the government to change some of its policies, for example, in official attitudes toward Vietnam, in introducing and enforcing civil rights legislation, and more recently, in initiating a constitutional revision to lower the legal voting age to 18. In many cases the school or university by denying students the opportunity to participate in decisions affecting them replicates the conditions prevailing in the larger political system and thus become the object of attack. The young generally feel they are left out of crucial political decisions, and this attitude may prompt them to lose faith in government at all levels. The following statement given by a 25-year-old veteran of the Vietnam war, now a freshman at a large urban university, recaptures some of the attitudes of the young vis-à-vis the system:

> Everything about the American system is contrived to dehumanize the individual. It's this structure that allows wars to be fought [and] people to go hungry, and everybody ignores the suffering of others because they're so concerned with their own material needs. There's a new culture starting that rejects these things and my objective is to protect it from those who are trying to annihilate it—the police departments and the people who control police departments. I'm getting more radical in my attitude. . . . It bugs me to see freshmen so completely systematized with locked minds that they don't question the major issues. . . . I want to see people who thrive on constant change and challenge authority, who dare to struggle. You have to take chances to get things. . . . I want to see people become exhilarated and wholly appreciative of the beauty and significance of all other people, to break down the stratification so the only way you know what a man is is to talk with him. . . . There's no appeasement that can be given me. If they legalize marijuana, I'll want the right to walk nude down the streets and if

they give me that, I'll want the right to make love in the front yard, and if I get that, I'll want—what I really want is for people to question everything.[15]

Although research on university student activism is still in formative stages, some observations can be made. First, prevailing university conditions have a great deal to do with students' political activities. Both in the United States and abroad there has been great dissatisfaction with the modern university—with instructors, curriculum, living quarters, limitations on student participation in decisions, etc. Many students feel they are treated "like numbers in a book" and resent the loss of personal contact with their teachers and administrators. The concept of the multiversity, i.e., a university system that has many campuses and several thousand students, seems to symbolize the feeling that the university is an impersonal, "bureaucratic" institution which does not and cannot develop the appropriate human and intellectual conditions to motivate students to engage in true learning experiences.[16] While general university conditions contribute in one way or another to student activism, general social conditions are also important forces to consider. Examples which demonstrate clearly that conditions of social inequality, discrimination, suppression of fundamental rights and freedoms, and war, precipitate student protest movements can be drawn from many countries in the world.[17] Often the university is looked upon as the agent of the larger system—a system which is perceived as imperialist, racist, and under the influence of the "military-industrial complex."

The chapters by Blackburn and Lindquist, Hanf, and Barakat deal directly with college students—with the way they perceive themselves in the political system and the forces operating in education institutions that are for or against increased student participation in decision-making.

INTERNATIONAL POLITICAL SOCIALIZATION

International political socialization has two general meanings. First, the term refers to the process of transmitting knowledge about and attitudes toward the international community of men. For example, what kinds of cognitive understanding about and affective orientations toward other peoples do children develop? In what way does the school contribute to the development of these orientations? Second, the term refers to the process of transmission of political orientations in different national settings. Questions asked in this context are: Are German children as strongly influenced in developing politically relevant behavior by educational institutions as are English children? Are Italian children as cynical toward certain aspects

---

[15] Charles Patrick, "Voices from the Campus—1970", *The Floridian*, October 25, 1970, p. 23.

[16] One of the better known multiversities is the State University of New York. In 1970 this university had 69 campuses with 190,000 students and a $450 million operating budget.

[17] See special issue on "Students and Politics" in *Daedalus*, Vol. 97, No. 1 (Winter 1968).

of political life as Lebanese children? Let us look at some relevant findings from comparative studies.

CONCEPT OF OTHER NATIONS

Among youth in Western Europe there is a strong movement away from strictly nationalistic orientations to identification with larger systems (for example, an integrated Europe).[18] In 1964–65 the overall percentage of youth, ages 13–19, who were for European unification was as follows: In the Netherlands, 95 percent; Germany, 95 percent; Britain, 72 percent. A poll of adults in these countries taken earlier indicated a strong feeling for unification but not as strong as that of youth. The age group of 55 and over is markedly less European than all others. The differences between adults and youth are due to the early socialization patterns in the different age groups. Although the research suggests that the prospects for a "United States of Europe" are good, it does not attribute to any particular agent any significant influence in this development.

A study of children's attitudes toward foreign peoples in 14 countries revealed that Bantu and Brazilian 14-year-old children were the most ethnocentric.[19] American, Canadian, Japanese, and French children were the least so. Lebanese, Turkish, Israeli, and German children formed an "in-between" group in terms of ethnocentrism. When asked to name other peoples who were similar to them all groups with the exception of Bantu children considered Americans to be "like us." (Americans were within the first three choices). The British and the French were also considered by several of the national groups to be "like us." The Chinese and Africans were most consistently considered "not like us."

As children grew older they increasingly considered the Russians "not like us." The characterizations given to the various reference groups are also revealing. In general, the Israelis were thought of as good, religious, peaceful, intelligent; the Japanese as poor, intelligent, bad; the Turkish as good, peaceful, ambitious, religious, patriotic, clean.

The views of the sixth-grade girl in the opening pages certainly reveal her attitudes toward other people. It is interesting to see how she has been able, in her own mind, to categorize nations as good or bad. A detailed analysis of children's views of other nations in two cultural settings is given in the chapter by David Statt.

It is difficult to interpret these and other results concerning the development of stereotypes in children. Some of the factors are embedded in the national backgrounds of the children, the cultural values under which they are brought up, demographic factors such as age, sex, and social

---

[18] Ronald Inglehart, "An End to European Integration?" *The American Political Science Review*, 61, No. 1 (March 1967), 91–105.

[19] Wallace E. Lambert and Otto Klineberg, *Children's Views of Foreign Peoples* (New York: Appleton-Century-Crofts, 1967).

status, and the impact of the various socialization agents. It is interesting, however, to note that the majority of six-year-olds receive their information about foreign peoples from parents, television and movies, and direct contact. Older children, ages 10 to 14, identify major sources of information as television and movies, books, school course work, textbooks, and magazines. Parents, teachers, and friends are not often mentioned as sources of information among the older age group.

Although it is extremely difficult to trace the origins of ethnocentrism to any of the sources of information that young children point to (there are so many other mediating factors involved), it *is* revealing to see how other cultures are treated in formal school work. Studies are not plentiful in this area, but the ones we have (mostly studies of textbooks) indicate that standard texts tend to perpetuate misconceptions and national stereotypes and are ethnocentric in their treatment of other cultures. American civics and history texts, for example, usually present the United States as the champion of freedom, goodwill, and rationality, whereas other sovereign states are either aggressors or second-raters.

Traditional elementary and secondary school textbooks (most of which describe and then either praise or condemn, rather than critically analyze, political institutions and actors) provide the worst means to introduce students to an understanding of government and the role of the citizen in decision-making.[20] Authors and publishers of texts, not only in the United States, but abroad, tend to underestimate the ability of young people to order their own learning experiences and to develop plausible explanations of political and social phenomena.

SUMMARY

In the preceding pages an attempt was made to set the framework for the research reported in the book. Earlier empirical studies on the role of education in citizenship were referred to, relevant findings were reported, and a few new hypotheses were formed.

It is very difficult to draw definite conclusions about youth and citizenship since there are so many factors operating and so few study controls that can be applied. The earlier studies showed some relationship between formal education and citizenship, but the relationship does not apply equally to all levels of education and to various programs and educational agencies. The studies included in this volume were conducted recently and begin where previous work left off. All of the studies reported try to provide more empirically based claims than previous studies. In this connection they go far beyond anything ever attempted in civic education during this century. Such works as Howard Wilson's, *Education for Citizenship* (1938), the Citizenship Education Project of Teachers College, Columbia (1952),

---

[20] Byron G. Massialas, "Citizenship and Political Socialization," in *Encyclopedia of Educational Research*, (4th ed.), ed. Robert L. Ebel (New York: Macmillan, 1969), pp. 124–41.

and Stanley Dimond's, *Schools and the Development of Good Citizens* (1953), all considered classic when published and instrumental in changing civic education programs in the schools, provided very little, if any, actual data from youth on their citizenship values. Such projects brought more attention than before to citizenship on the part of educators and the public, but they offered virtually nothing in the way of adequately measuring the behavior and feelings of students toward the social and political systems or of explaining how the behavior and attitudes came about.

In addition to providing a broader base than before to claims about education's role in citizenship, the studies in this volume move into areas where very little or no research has been available. For example, the area of political socialization of blacks is studied by both Billings and Ehman. Goldstein analyzes the way curriculum guides and textbooks deal with blacks. Ehman's study provides longitudinal data—something that has rarely been done in this field. Many of the chapters, including Ehman's, provide qualitative educational data from the classroom. This is certainly a major departure because many of the national studies in the past relied exclusively on gross quantitative measures, e.g., number of courses, years of education, etc. Another area where very little has been done in the past is the relationship between the organizational structure of the school on the political beliefs and attitudes of youth. The chapter by Wittes discusses this area and provides some interesting insights into the type of school power structure that would correlate with a high sense of personal participation in school decisions. The chapter by Blackburn and Lindquist extends the concern over the academic power structure but looks at it from the point of view of faculty participation in decision-making. The particular issue discussed (around which the political process in academia was centered) is the nature and extent of student formal participation in the governance of the institution.

In addition to the new areas of study indicated above, the book includes a strong international and cross-national component. The chapters by Lewis, Heggan, and Cave provide in-depth analyses of aspects of youth political socialization in Sierra Leone, Colombia, and Soviet Uzbekistan, respectively. The chapters by Statt, German and Farnen, Hanf, and Barakat offer political socialization findings from two or more countries—their work is truly comparative.

The seminal work in the international area, especially with elementary and secondary-school age groups, reflects the growing interest of educators and social scientists throughout the world in finding out and explaining the political behavior of youth. These individuals operate under the assumption that one learns one's own political culture best if one studies the political cultures of others.

Elementary School Curriculum and Political Socialization

2

Robert J. Goldstein

This chapter reports the results of an examination of some aspects of selected social studies curricular materials used today in United States elementary schools (herein defined as grades 1–6). Special stress will be placed on the type of information contained in these materials that appears designed to influence children's attitudes toward the United States, its government, and citizenship responsibilities. I have also included a condensed discussion of the type of information the curricular materials contain relevant to black people, social class, and foreign countries and peoples. Although the development of attitudes toward these latter subjects has not generally been considered within the realm of "political socialization" studies, I maintain that any definition of political socialization that excludes them conceives the political extremely narrowly.

Although studies of children's attitudes toward the topics examined in this paper strongly suggest that the elementary school period is more crucial than later school periods with regard to the formation of basic attitudes, previous curriculum studies have concentrated almost exclusively on secondary rather than elementary school materials. The purpose of this chapter is to fill that gap and to study the elementary school curriculum specifically with the findings of political socialization research in mind.

The curriculum materials examined in this study include 30 social studies textbooks used in grades 1–6 (five per grade) and 15 curriculum guides which outline for teachers of elementary school social studies in 15 different cities the sequence of instruction and content.[1] The texts, on the

This chapter is a condensation of the author's master's paper written in and available through the Department of Political Science, University of Chicago.

[1] The guides cited in the References, pp. 31–33, will be referred to by city and the texts by name in the body of the paper. In many cases, the texts examined were special teachers' editions which include additional information, summaries of text material and points to stress for teachers. Citations that include the notation TE

whole, are more lengthy and detailed, and, of course, are used in more localities than the curriculum guides, but there is no way to tell the specific manner and sequence of their use in the schools; the guides vary in length and detail from those that only outline content and major goals, to those that include a detailed exposition of content and goals. The latter are used in only one locality, but they provide a definite sequence and content of instruction for that locality at least. The goals and content stressed in the guides presumably create a framework for the use of textbooks in each locality.

An attempt was made to select a representative sample of curricular materials being used in the United States today. Therefore, only guides and texts published since 1963 were selected. An attempt was made to choose curriculum guides from cities diverse in size, geographic region, raical composition, and socio-economic characteristics and to include textbooks published by a wide variety of major publishing houses.

ATTITUDES TOWARD THE UNITED STATES, THE U.S. GOVERNMENT, AND CITIZENSHIP

The material contained in the curriculum guides and texts for the early elementary school grades (approximately grades 1–3) that appears relevant to children's concepts of the United States, the U.S. government and citizenship is basically of two types: material concerning "citizenship" and "government" in the home, school, and local community and material on national "symbols" such as the flag and patriotic holidays.

Much of the material on "citizenship" in the home and school appears to have little direct political relevance. The children are encouraged to develop such traits as friendliness and cooperation, to share in home tasks, to take care of their rooms at home and at school, to care for personal and school property, and to practice other tasks that show a sense of responsibility and concern for others as well as oneself.

Much of the material on citizenship and government in the community is of possible direct political significance. Virtually all of the curriculum guides and many of the texts used in the early elementary school grades place a heavy stress on the services offered by communities and community workers, such as fire and police protection, libraries, parks, schools, sanitation and health services, etc. Some of the guides and texts deal with these services in the context of a discussion of local government and nearly all indicate that the services are paid for by all citizens through taxes or that the workers involved are "city" or "public" workers. Thus, public services are usually identified as such, and the school may be a factor in the ability of young children to differentiate between the public and private sectors. The fact that taxation is used by many of the curricular materials as a concept linking the individual with governmental services

---

indicate that the information is obtainable only in the teachers' edition and not in the regular (student) edition.

suggests that taxation may become an important symbol of government to young children. Perhaps the most important point to be made about the treatment of community workers is that they are viewed in a very favorable light—they are generally presented as "friends" and helpers who provide essential and helpful services, and children are encouraged to cooperate with them. Thus, in what is usually their first contact with curricular material relevant to government per se, the children receive a very favorable impression, and the services provided by government (local government in this case) are often very tangible. The first grade text *Your School and Neighborhood* sums up the attitudes that most of the texts and guides express, following its discussion of city workers like police, firemen, and garbagemen:

> Many people work in our city. They work together to take care of us. They make our city a safe place. They keep our city clean and healthy. They make our city beautiful (p. 45).

The favorable treatment accorded to all public employees is particularly evident in the case of the policeman. Whereas other workers such as the fireman and the teacher also get a great deal of attention and are presented in a positive light, the policeman seems to receive both the most favorable treatment and perhaps the most treatment in terms of space of any public figure in the early elementary school curricular materials. The most important point made about him is that he helps people and keeps them safe. Among the activities policemen are depicted as performing in some of the texts are watching children as they go home from school, taking injured children to the hospital, stopping traffic so a cat and her kittens can cross the street, helping to find a missing automobile, and bringing home a lost boy. Altogether, the policeman receives substantial treatment in five of the 15 texts used in grades 1–3 and is mentioned or discussed to some extent in five others; he is discussed to some extent in all of the 15 curriculum guides during the early grades, many of which suggest that students either visit a police station or invite a policeman to speak to their class.

In addition to the favorable treatment of local governmental services and personnel, one point of obvious political relevance included in almost all of the guides and many of the texts during both the early and later elementary school years is that school, home, and community rules and laws should or must be obeyed. Many of the materials add that rules and laws are necessary and helpful, and provide a safe and orderly life for all. Thus, the St. Louis guide tells children:

> Wherever people live together they must have rules to guide them. A set of rules, called laws, helps protect people and helps people share the advantages found within the community. Laws also make people share responsibility in the community. Laws are for the benefit of everyone (pp. 56, 58).

The only material included in the early elementary school years that seems designed to inculcate a feeling of patriotism for and transmit information about the United States and the U.S. government as opposed to local government and the local environment is in the treatment of "symbolic" material such as the flag and national holidays. Virtually all of the guides and about half of the texts used in grades 1–3 include some information about the flag and/or national holidays. The purpose of this material is clearly partially informational, but seems mainly designed to inculcate feelings of love and loyalty for the United States. Treatment of the flag usually consists of historical material, rules for display and use of the flag, and material concerning the Pledge of Allegiance; points that are especially stressed are that the flag represents the country and should be respected, and that the flag salute is a "promise to be true to our nation" (St. Louis, p. 42). The material included in some of the texts and guides relating to flag etiquette seems especially designed to create a feeling of solemn reverence for the flag. Thus, the teacher's edition of the first grade text *At Home* says that although first grades cannot grasp the full significance of the flag salute, the fact that one teacher succeeded in establishing an "atmosphere of reverence" and a "love for his country" was evidenced when one child replied, when asked what the pledge of allegiance meant, "I don't know, but it's sort of like a prayer" (pp. 24–25).

The treatment of patriotic holidays usually includes such holidays as Thanksgiving, Veterans' Day, Independence Day, and Washington's and Lincoln's birthdays. The purpose of the treatment of these holidays appears to be similar to that concerning the flag. Although very few of the guides and texts spell out in great detail what material is to be included in the studies of Lincoln and Washington, those that do indicate that a highly favorable and stereotyped image of these presidents is transmitted.

There are a few scattered references in some of the early elementary school materials to other "great" presidents and some mention the current president. But by far the bulk of the treatment of the president in the early elementary school years is personalized to Washington and Lincoln, and except for general comments that these presidents were the leaders of the country, there is no information on presidential duties in general. The discussion generally occurs only in the context of holidays and is not extensive. Both the flag and the policeman appear to receive more attention than the president. At the same time, no other figure or institution associated with the national government receives any significant attention in these grades. The early elementary school curriculum, then, may reinforce the highly salient and positive image that young children have of the president, but it seems very apparent that much and probably most of the information young children possess about the president's qualities are obtained elsewhere or generalized from what they know of Washington and Lincoln.

To sum up, most of the material relevant to the United States and its government in early elementary curricular materials seems designed to inculcate feelings of love and loyalty; relatively little factual information about the country or government is presented. Thus, the child who gains all of his information from the curriculum could probably write no more about being a good American than the Chicago child who wrote this sample composition:

> I am a good American. I love my country. I help my country. I obey laws and regulations. I try to be a good citizen (Chicago, I, p. 231).

During the late elementary school years, the focus of the curriculum guides and texts shifts from the home, school, and community to the U.S. government and the United States as a nation. The major point to be made about the treatment of the organization and operation of American government is that this material is generally very skimpy and strictly formal. Of the 25 or so texts and guides that discuss the U.S. government, for example, only the Gary, Indiana, guide (pp. 339–42) and the fifth grade U.S. history text *Our Changing Nation and Its Neighbors* (pp. 143–53; TE, pp. 60–62) discuss the role and importance of political parties. In fact, if one were to assume that children learn only what the texts and guides tell them, the children who use the two or three texts and guides that contrast the Russian one-party system with the American two-party system (i.e., *Nations of Other Lands*, p. 88) during their study of Russia would learn this facet of the U.S. government for the first time. *The Story of Our Country*, in its descriptions of the results of the constitutional convention, is typical of the rigidly formal treatment of government organization contained in most of the materials:

> The congress was to make the laws. The president was to be the head of the nation and see that the laws were obeyed. The courts were to settle disputes and judge people (p. 177).

Children are told in the curricular materials that the president and the congress represent and are elected by the people; however, the materials contain no information at all that suggests that governmental officials may be interested in personal gain or responsive to pressure groups with vested interests rather than to the public or their own beliefs as to what is best for the country. Clearly the limits of the school curriculum may help to explain children's lack of sophistication about political parties and pressure groups, and their relative lack of cynicism in viewing politics and government.

Just as local government is presented as providing helpful—and only helpful—services in the lower elementary school grades, so the federal government is pictured in the upper grades as a rather benevolent Santa Claus in both its domestic and foreign policies. Domestically, the federal government is shown as providing helpful services, such as construction of roads, dams, and parks, wildlife conservation, national defense, and protection of consumers, farmers, and workers. In its foreign policy, the government is portrayed as selflessly fighting for freedom and benevolently aiding and trading with other nations all over the world. The United States is repeatedly described as a world leader and the leader of the "free world." A few texts make explicit what some others imply: that the United States bears responsibilty for the maintenance of freedom around the world. Thus, the fifth grade *Our Changing Nation and Its Neighbors* tells children that the United States believes

> we must help free nations remain free when they ask for help. This belief has taken us into many parts of the world where the freedom of people has been threatened. We believe that protecting freedom is in our best interest. Control

of large world territories by groups who are opposed to freedom of action and thinking can be a threat to our way of life (p. 376).

The United States is pictured as maintaining friendly and benevolent relations with all non-communist nations. "Under the guidance of U.S. experts, many nations are making life better for their people," *Living as World Neighbors* explains (p. 481).

The curricular materials repeatedly point to U.S. aid to and defense ties with Europe, and aid programs such as the Peace Corps when discussing relations with Asia and Africa. When U.S.-Latin American and U.S.-Canadian relations are discussed, there is a heavy stress on themes of friendship and cooperation, with mention of specific cooperative endeavors such as the St. Lawrence Seaway, the Pan American Highway, and the Organization of American States. Of the 20 or so curriculum guides and texts that discuss Latin America, only the Denver guide includes a frank discussion of the present difficulties in Latin American relations. (Two texts do discuss past U.S. interventions in Latin America and resultant Latin American resentment, but they imply these were events of the past and that there are no serious problems today; all of the other materials basically present a picture of pure sweetness and light in U.S.-Latin American relations, past and present.) The Denver guide states that the U.S.-Latin American relationship has been one of "alternative interest, neglect, cooperation and conflict" and lists among the causes of difficulties "the now hot, now cold interest displayed toward Latin America, claims of political, economic and military 'yankee imperialism,' U.S. preoccupation with events in Europe and Asia, our country's seemingly taking Latin America for granted, our country's frequently being blamed for many of the problems of Latin America and at the same time expected and requested to provide aid." The Denver guide adds that most Latin Americans view Americans as "materialistic at the sacrifice of spiritual and artistic values," that they are "wary of our size and power" and sometimes unaware of our intentions, and that they "tend to be on their guard when dealing with us" (VI, pp. 71-72). Of the 15 or so texts and guides that deal with Canada, only *Our Changing Nation and Its Neighbors* includes any material indicating that some Canadians distrust or fear the United States now, or did so in the past. United States treatment of the Philippines seems to be used in many of the curricular materials as an archetypal example of U.S. benevolence in its foreign policy. Improvements made by the United States in the Philippines during its rule there and its "preparation" of the Philippines for independence are repeatedly cited (i.e. *Living as World Neighbors* tells students, "Schools were built and illiterate children learned to read and write and were taught the meaning of democracy," p. 489). Of the 15 texts and guides that discuss U.S. treatment of the Philippines in this vein, only two mention that the inhabitants wanted independence before the United States gave it, and only one makes any reference to Aguinaldo's insurrection.

It is apparent, then, that the favorable treatment of national and local government in the elementary grades may help to account for the favorable view that elementary school children have toward government and governmental authorities. There is generally no recognition that governmental actions involve any costs to anyone except for taxes, that they are often the subjects of fierce controversy, or that the government may have erred in any foreign or domestic policies in recent memory.

The United States, as a country, is presented in the texts and guides as a strong and great nation, rich in natural resources and advanced technology, and as a leading democratic nation in the world. *The Story of Our Country* says the United States is a "great and powerful nation" and asserts that "Americans have found ways to overcome the effects of geography. They have made powerful machines that are not stopped by rivers, deserts or mountains" (pp. 6, 12). The Chicago guide tells students that the United States has an "abundant supply of natural resources" that has contributed in great measure "to the development of the U.S. as a leader among the nations of the world" (II, p. 139). *In These United States* terms the United States a "land of plenty" and "the greatest manufacturing nation" in the world. It tells students, "no other nation produces nearly as much as this country does" (p. 36). The Gary guide says the United States' "capacity to manufacture and produce economic goods is unlimited" (p. 135). A number of the curricular materials describe the United States as beautiful in addition to being rich; the term "beautiful" is frequently used in descriptions of Washington, D.C., in such a way that the child is likely to gain greater respect for governmental institutions (i.e., *In All Our States*, p. 161). The fifth grade U.S. history text *Your Country and Mine* perhaps best sums up this type of portrayal when it terms the United States "beautiful, strong and great" (p. 194). It is clear that such descriptions are likely to reinforce the positive but nonreflective image young children have of their country.

As the discussion of the treatment of the U.S. government and foreign policy above and the discussion of the treatment of blacks and social class below make clear, there is a definite downplaying of material that reflects "badly" upon the United States or its government or that indicates significant (especially recent) internal conflict. A few examples may help to illustrate this point. Although all five fifth grade U.S. histories examined discuss the causes and battles of the War of 1812, only two mention the fact that some Americans both wanted to and tried to annex Canada. These same two texts (*In These United States*, pp. 148–51; *Our Changing Nation and Its Neighbors*, pp. 156–63) are the only ones to mention the strong opposition of the northeastern states to the war. Only three of the five texts discuss the rise of labor unions (*Your Country and Mine*, pp. 181–82; *Our Changing Nation and Its Neighbors*, pp. 386–87; *The Story of Our Country*, pp. 336–38). Although all three frankly discuss the low wages, poor working conditions, and long hours that led to the formation of unions, all imply that such poor conditions no longer exist and/or that labor and management no longer have serious disagreements. Only one of the five histories discusses the Alien and Sedition Acts (*Our Changing Nation and Its Neighbors*, pp. 148–50), and, incredibly, only one discusses the depression and the New Deal, although even this text omits mention of any controversy over the New Deal (*The Story of Our Country*, pp. 340–43). In fact none of the texts discuss major ideological disagreements in the nation since the Civil War. The only text that mentions political parties discusses the ideological disagreements between Jefferson and Hamilton that gave birth to them, but attributes their present importance to providing a check on the power of those who run the government; the closest it comes to mentioning any ideological element in their present existence is the statement that the two-party system "helps to provide a government that serves the interest of most of the people rather than only a few." (*Our Changing Nation and Its Neighbors,* pp. 143–53). In general, the texts include little information about recent developments, although they are replete with details about the colonial period and the period leading up to the Civil War.

Along with the shift from concentration on the home, school, and neighborhood to a concentration on the United States that comes during the later elementary grades, comes a shift from "citizenship training" that is largely non-political in character to citizenship training that shows much greater politicization. This parallels the increased politicization displayed with age by elementary school children, as shown by their answers to questions concerning what a good citizen does. The child in late elementary school is told the good citizen understands and appreciates the American "way of life," is proud of his country, and understands and tries to perpetuate "democracy" (defined in such terms as respect for the individual worth and rights of all citizens, recognition that responsibility comes with rights, and respect for democratic processes). But aside from general statements urging support for American democracy through becoming well-informed, voting, and supporting laws, the materials generally offer no guidance for effective political action on the national scene. Children are not told to write their congressmen or join political parties; they are given no information about pressure groups and generally get no information about how political processes work that would enable them to affect national politics. Instead they are given vague statements such as:

> The freedom and opportunities of the nation were won and protected by many men and women of the past. Americans have the responsibility to see that these efforts continue and that freedom and opportunity are shared by all citizens (*The Story of Our Country,* p. 370).

ATTITUDES TOWARD BLACKS AND SOCIAL CLASS

Despite the clear evidence that elementary school children are aware of and make unwholesome racial and social class distinctions, the curriculum materials, on the whole, fail to devote adequate space to or include material of satisfactory frankness dealing with counteracting these discriminatory feelings. The curriculum guides generally avoid dealing with race or social class at all. Twelve of the 15 curriculum guides studies either made absolutely no mention of black people, made only the most incidental references to blacks (i.e., the only item relevant to blacks in the St. Louis guide is a suggestion that fourth graders read the biography of a black who invented a machine connected with shoe manufacturing), or made reference to blacks entirely or virtually entirely in the context of the Civil War during fifth and sixth grade treatments of U.S. history. None of these guides includes any material on the life of the black as slave, post-Civil War discrimination, the civil rights movement, the present condition and problems of blacks, or any other material that might be designed to give children factual information about blacks or to counteract prejudicial sentiments. The other three guides—Springfield, N.J., Chicago, and Gary—show at least an attempt to include a sympathetic and positive treatment of blacks, although none of them is satisfactorily comprehensive. The Springfield guide is the only guide that includes a study of race and clearly asserts that the Negro is basically the same as other races. It is also the only guide that suggests an open-ended study of the present condition of blacks; it lists present-day attitudes towards civil rights, including the "effects of continued discrimination in a democracy" as a topic to be discussed in grade five, and advises the teacher to "discuss disadvantages in discrimination," such as preventing persons from showing their potential.*

The Gary guide includes a four-week unit during fourth grade on the American Negro—the only guide to include such a unit. This unit describes in rich detail—far more so than any other guide—blacks in America, at least until Reconstruction. The only references to recent times state that the United States is still trying to solve problems resulting from attitudes developed during the slavery period and to bridge the gap between Negro's constitutional rights and "the actual discrimination to which he is still subjected" (p. 162). There is no elaboration of this, no discussion of the civil rights movement, and no mention of recent civil rights leaders, although blacks such as Crispus Attucks, Frederick Douglas, George Washington Carver, and even W. E. B. DuBois are suggested for study. Among the statements included in the comprehensive treatment of the pre-Civil War Negro are that the life of a slave varied somewhat "in the degree of hardship and cruelty" but was a "hard one at best;" that some slaves planned and carried out insurrections; that the content of the Negro spiritual is a "testimony to the slaves' desire for freedom," and that the white South had to "convince itself that Negroes were an inferior breed to justify their practices to themselves." The Gary treatment of Reconstruction is far more positive to blacks than standard treatments of the subject; it emphasizes that the hardships blacks suffered were due to their denial of education and wages during the period of slavery and stresses establishment of schools, business, and publications by Negroes who did not find a "welcome in the already established institutions of America" (pp. 157–62).

The curriculum guides' treatment of social class is even more lax than the treatment of blacks. With the exception that material dealing with occupations often stresses that all occupations contribute to society and should be respected, the guides generally totally avoid dealing with social class and show no awareness that some pupils and some Americans are poor (or even that people have different amounts of wealth) and that the poor are objects of serious prejudices apparently shaped during childhood. For example, although all of the guides include a significant amount of material for the early grades on living in the family, and many of them specify mem-

---

* Pages in the Springfield guide are unnumbered; thus, citations are impossible.

bers of the family and their roles (with mother and father pointed out and *father's* job as breadwinner noted), only one guide (Chicago) mentions that some families have only one or even no parents, and only one guide (Mobile, Alabama) indicates that some parents are unemployed. Similarly, although most of the guides include a study of how Americans obtain their basic needs of food, shelter, and housing, only two guides (Chicago and Mobile) give even the slightest hint that some families may not have their needs adequately fulfilled.

If the curriculum guides, in neglecting to include information that takes cognizance of differences in status and resulting class prejudices among Americans, are implicitly middle-class then almost all of the texts examined that deal with American life are *explicitly* middle-class in the pictures and stories they contain. The characters in almost all of the texts used in grades 1–4 both black and white, live in middle-class apartments or homes, in middle-class towns, go to clean, modern schools, and shop in middle-class stores. Any material relevant to lower-class children and the fact that differences in wealth occur are generally omitted. The general trend of the texts is perhaps best caricatured by the third grade text *Living in America Today and Yesterday*, in which a family living in a middle-class town in the east drives across the country and helps build a new middle-class town in the western desert.

Most of the books used in grades 1–4 that deal primarily with American life demonstrated an attempt to *pictorially* show the American Negro as an integral part of American life and as basically similar to other Americans rather than as a sterotyped figure. However, these books include virtually no *textual* information about blacks. A few of them depict a limited and clearly inadequate proportion of black characters, but most of them have blacks sprinkled throughout quite frequently, often in natural interactions with whites, and include Negroes as main characters in some of the episodes, although whites are shown far more frequently. Although the pictorial depiction of blacks and whites as similar and interacting might help break down stereotyped views held by white students, the total lack of textual material dealing with blacks vitiates the impact of the pictorial material: indeed, without textual material to impress racial messages on the mind of the student, the pictorial material may be so far removed from what the typical white student believes and experiences about the Negro that it may be rejected or soon forgotten. The fact that many blacks are in lower economic and social classes, and that they are so ultimately because of a history of white discrimination in America is not dealt with in these texts.[2]

[2] *Living as Neighbors, William, Andy and Ramos,* and *Our Working World* are exceptional in their treatment of racial material and material relevant to social class. In the first two texts, which are both in the Holt Urban Social Studies Series, blacks and whites are shown equally frequently and depicted as living in lower-middle class or even upper-lower class urban settings. These texts use photographs of blacks and whites interacting in realistic urban settings to illustrate the stories whereas other texts usually use drawings. The stories in these two texts are clearly relevant to non-middle-class children. *William, Andy and Ramos* is about an urban black child whose grandmother moves in to take care of him because both of his parents work. *Living as Neighbors* is about a white father, a grocery clerk, who

Among the five U.S. history texts used in fifth grade, only *In These United States* makes more than the most incidental references to the existence of poor people in America. It discusses urban and rural poverty, including problems of housing and unemployment, at considerable length. This text reports that in 1966, 15 percent of all American families were unable to afford food, clothing, and shelter to meet their "simplest needs" and that "millions of Americans are poor through no fault of their own" because of such difficulties as lack of skills, education, and jobs, or old age and ill health. It states:

> Poor people see the stores piled high with goods. They see the streets filled with automobiles. Everywhere advertisers call on them to buy this, buy that— and be happy like the smiling people in the pictures. Everything is around them, but somehow they cannot get it. They just haven't enough money (p. 239).

Among the five U.S. histories used in grade five, *In These United States* devotes about a page to the life of the black as slave, whereas the other texts spend only a few sentences on this topic and generally include little information other than that the slaves' work was long and hard (although all of these texts spend many pages on the life and hardships of white settlers). In contrast, *In These United States* notes that slaves were often "driven hard from dawn to dusk," lived in crude cabins, "scarcely more than huts," had food and clothing "just sufficient to enable them to live and work" and were "firmly held down" by their masters and state laws. The text says white southerners did not know how to deal with Negroes except as their masters, and

> to cover up the unpleasant truth about slavery, many southerners convinced themselves that slavery was good. . . . These white men somehow overlooked the fact that thousands of free Negroes in the U.S. and Latin America—not to mention those in Africa—were much better off than slaves were (pp. 170–71).

---

must find a new job, and a black family who must find a new home when an urban renewal project is slated for their neighborhood. *Our Working World,* an experimental economics text, realistically differentiates between the living conditions of blacks and whites in its illustrations. Mostly or all white characters are portrayed when small town, suburban, and farm scenes are shown, but when big city and run-down neighborhoods are shown, the characters are usually well-integrated or all black. Unfortunately the book offers no textual explanation as to why blacks and whites live in different conditions. This text, both pictorially and textually does make clear that people have different amounts of money, and several times discusses the problems of slums and run-down neighborhoods, where people live because "they do not have to pay much rent," such as crowded, unsanitary conditions, and lack of room to play (pp. 14–15, 110–11, 155–57). "People choose neighborhoods where they can find homes they can pay for," the book explains; it later adds, "Some people do not have enough money to get a good place to live" (pp. 19, 40). *In All Our States* also differentiates between its portrayals of blacks and whites by showing not only clearly segregated scenes but scenes which suggest segregation is the state-supported norm. This text includes sequences showing a white family visiting an all-white state legislature, a black family visiting an all-black state college, and a state folk festival in which all-white and all-black groups perform.

In their discussions of Reconstruction, all of the texts except *The Story of Our Country* explicitly or implicitly take the white southerner's position that the South was misgoverned by Congress, corrupt northerners, and ignorant southern Negroes, and their wording implies that freed Negroes were helpless without their masters and/or an unfair burden upon the South. *The Story of Our Country* notes that freed Negroes had many problems, but the stress of its discussion is on the formation of schools and organizations to help solve these problems. It omits the standard material about misgovernment of the South by corrupt northerners and ignorant, helpless blacks, and thus gives a much more positive picture of the Reconstruction-era black.

The U.S. history texts are strikingly divergent in their treatment of post-Civil War discrimination against blacks, the present status of the black, and the civil rights movement. *Your Country and Mine* ignores these topics and gives not a hint that blacks have been discriminated against since the Civil War, whereas *In These United States* is the only text not only to discuss post-Civil War discrimination against the black, but to make crystal clear the continuing inferior status of the black, to give a truly graphic description of the effects of discrimination, and to directly rather than indirectly implicate the white man. This text includes in its treatment two striking pictures of blacks living in shacks and slum areas; it points out that whereas 41 percent of non-white families are defined as poor, only 12 percent of white families are. It adds that one "very important" reason for this statistic is the "discrimination that has been practiced by the white majority against the Negro minority . . . for no good reason." This is the only text to mention the killing of civic rights workers, Martin Luther King, and Stokely Carmichael, and the black power movement and controversy (some of this material may only reflect the fact that this book was published in 1969, the others no later than 1967). This is also the only text to forthrightly state that segregation in various forms, such as housing and schools, still exists. It says that although Negroes are "no longer segregated by law," they are "segregated in fact" because the white man fears Negro cultural influences and will not sell blacks property in non-segregated areas and because black poverty keeps blacks in slum (pp. 239–44). The other three fifth grade U.S. histories all directly or indirectly discuss post-Civil War discrimination and include a cursory treatment of the civil rights movement, but their treatment of the present situation of the black man is at best vague and at worst suggests that recent civil rights laws have essentially solved the problem of discrimination. Only *In These United States* and *Our Changing Nation and Its Neighbors* include appeals for an end to prejudice and discrimination.

The five sixth grade world history and geography texts examined generally include only incidental comments relevant to race and social class in America, but *Living as World Neighbors* is the only one of the 30 textbooks examined to include any information on race. It describes the classification of man into races and states, "Scientists have made comparisons and found the people of the three races all have the same natural abilities" (p. 30).

TREATMENT OF FOREIGN COUNTRIES AND PEOPLES

The treatment of foreign countries and peoples in curricular materials —which occurs almost exclusively in the texts and curriculum guides used in grades 4–6[3]—can only be described as paradoxical. On the one hand, when discussing foreign countries and peoples in general, the curricular materials tend to include a good deal of material that seems designed to lead children to attain a feeling of solidarity and friendship with people all over the world. For example, virtually all of the guides and many of the texts stress that all people on earth have the same basic needs, are interdependent and need to cooperate, and are affected by historical, cultural, and environmental factors; and a number of the materials include truly non-ethnocentric statements which stress that people with different ways of living should not be considered odd or inferior. Yet when individual countries and areas of the world are discussed, it is clear that an implicit, and sometimes explicit, standard of industrialization and democracy—or more simply, how similar the country is to the United States—is used to measure the countries, and those that best meet these standards receive a substantially more favorable treatment. The result is that those areas most similar to the United States in color and culture, such as northwest Europe, Canada, Australia, and New Zealand, receive the most favorable treatment, along with certain other democratic-industrialized states, such as Japan, Uruguay, and Israel. The nations that fit the criteria of being democratic and industrialized, in addition to being so labelled (which in itself is likely to elicit culturally conditioned favorable responses) benefit also by: (1) being described as more similar to the United States in overall culture and as having closer political, ethnic, social, and economic ties than other areas; (2) being presented explicitly and implicitly as being more important and having made more cultural contributions to the United States and the world than other areas (this is especially true of northwestern Europe); and (3) perhaps most objectionably, being frequently praised and described with favorable evaluative characteristics such as "skilled," "energetic," and "freedom-loving," rarely applied to other peoples.

In contrast to the treatment of industrialized-democratic nations, when the unindustrialized third world is discussed (along with the relatively unindustrialized nations of southern Europe such as Spain and Greece), their peoples are pictured in terms likely to evoke largely negative reactions—they are viewed as technologically backward, poor, uneducated,

---

[3] The eight texts and 10 guides which deal extensively with foreign countries are *Regions and Social Needs, Learning to Look at Our World, Knowing Our Neighbors Around the Earth,* and the five sixth-grade texts (see References); and the guides of Chicago, Gary, Lockland, Denver, St. Louis, Mt. Lebanon, Port Arthur, Philadelphia suburban, S. Plainfield, and the Clayton. *Living in the Americas, Your Country and Mine,* and *Our Changing Nation and Its Neighbors* deal extensively with Latin America only; many of the other texts and guides deal with foreign countries to some extent.

etc. They rarely, if ever, receive praise for their personal qualities, and the warmth evident in the treatment of democratic-industrialized nations is missing. Although many of these countries are praised extensively for their ancient or medieval cultures and contributions (i.e., Egypt, India, Spain, Greece, Latin America—and in a few relatively enlightened materials the great, ancient kingdoms of Africa), and their current "progress" (by Western standards) is pointed out, the general impression transmitted is that these poor and backward nations have had little real importance in the world for the past 500 years. A typical treatment of the underdeveloped nations is the following:

> Compared to the more progressive countries, these nations lag behind. Their people are uneducated and untrained. Diseases afflict many of them. Neither the human resources nor the natural resources are used to the fullest. Poor farming methods result in poor yields of crops. . . . Many cannot read or write. . . . To overcome their many handicaps, the people of underdeveloped countries need more teachers and schools, more doctors and hospitals. They need better trained farmers and they need factories with skilled workers. They need more power plants to generate electricity for houses and industries. They need more railroads, air lines and highways to provide transportation for their products and for the goods they buy (*Living as World Neighbors*, pp. 454, 478–79).

In other words, indiscriminate westernization is the standard used to measure the underdeveloped countries and is also the prescribed solution for all their ills. The only real exceptions to this treatment among third world nations are the few democratic-industrialized states like Israel, Japan, Uruguay, and Costa Rica, which are described as democratic, prosperous, and progressive. Thus, Israelis are repeatedly praised for their skill and energy, and the Japanese are lavishly praised for such qualities as their skill, education, and receptivity to new ideas. For instance, the teacher's edition of *Exploring the Old World* spells out what the other materials imply with regard to Japan: "As a democratic, industrialized state, Japan represents what we might hope for in the many underdeveloped countries of Asia and Africa" (TE, p. 91).

Among the eight texts and 10 curriculum guides that deal extensively with foreign countries, only the fourth grade text *Regions and Social Needs* and the Denver guide show evidence of a consistent attempt to present underdeveloped nations in a positive light. Thus, *Regions and Social Needs* tells children that the nomads and oasis dwellers of the Sahara desert would find "your life strange." When the "unusual" homes, animals, and clothing of various peoples of underdeveloped nations are mentioned, children are asked to explain why these are "good" adaptations to the environment, and Mongols of the Gobi Desert and Indians of the Amazon rain forest are described as "happy with the way they live" (pp. 59, 62–63, 69, 124, 224). Aside from this text and the Denver guide, most of the other materials reflect a substantial amount of ethnocentric bias. Particularly objectionable are three of the five sixth-grade world history and geography texts examined. *World Cultures: Past and Present* spends all but a few paragraphs on Europe; the underdeveloped nations are generally mentioned only in terms of their problems and in unfavorable comparisons with Europe and the United States. *Exploring the Old World* devotes about 45 percent of its space to Europe and continually praises Europeans with such terms as "thrifty," "hard-working," "brave," "skillful," "clever," and "cheerful"; these are never applied to other peoples. *Living as World Neighbors* devotes a good deal of space to unfavorable comparisons of what it calls the "primitive" and "backwards" nations to the "modern" and "progressive" nations in such fields as education, transportation, and life expectancy (pp. 3–16, 454–59).

Despite the treatment of third world nations in the curricular materials, they are nevertheless treated more favorably then the communist nations, for their problems are treated with sympathy, whereas much of the treatment of communist countries contains definite overtones of hostility. When the communist countries are discussed, specific adverse comparisons are made with the United States on such topics as personal freedom; cold war conflicts are pointed out; distorted material is included; and distorted impressions are conveyed through omission of material. The criterion of democracy at home and abroad (i.e., aggressive foreign policy) is usually the major consideration, whereas for the underdeveloped nations the criterion of industrialization is most important (i.e., there is little material concerning personal liberties and foreign policy in the discussion of underdeveloped countries, but much material on this subject when communist countries are considered).

The general portrait drawn by the six curriculum guides and ten texts —four U.S. histories and six world histories and geographies[4]—that discuss Russia more than incidentally is not likely to create a favorable reaction. Virtually all stress the denial of personal freedom in Russia and include information on Russian expansion into Eastern Europe or other cold war material. When personal freedom is discussed, the manner of the treatment is often such as to suggest that there are no personal liberties in Russia, whereas there are virtually no limitations of or conflict over civil liberties in the United States. Cold war material is especially stressed in the U.S. histories which, along with some of the other materials, suggest that Russia or "the communists" plan to or have tried to take over the world. *Your Country and Mine* is one of several texts that assert this claim in a semihysterical manner. It says:

> Our country has stood against the spread of communism. We have spoken sternly when communist leaders have sneaked into other countries. We know how they stir up the poor and unhappy people with rosy promises. We realize how slyly they worm their way into the governments of free nations. Then they try to seize control (p. 192).

---

[4] Texts and guides which deal substantially with Russia include the five sixth-grade texts (see References), *Knowing Our Neighbors Around the Earth, Your Country and Mine, In All These States, Our Changing Nation and Its Neighbors, The Story of Our Country;* and the guides of Chicago, Gary, Lockland, St. Louis, Clayton, and Philadelphia.

Although some of the material on the cold war and personal freedoms is clearly oversimplified, it certainly is valid to include information on these topics when discussing Russia. The crucial question is to what extent the curricular materials "balance" this information by providing enough other information so that children can make an informed judgment. For example, curricular material including information on the lack of personal freedom in Russia might also be expected to include information on the denial of freedom in Russia under tsarist rule, on positive Russian achievements under communism, and on the significant voluntary support accorded the Soviet regime. Similarly, material including information on Russian expansion into Eastern Europe or other cold war information should also indicate that Russia traditionally has been expansionist, that Eastern Europe is viewed by Russia as a defensive buffer, that the cold war has declined in intensity since the days of Stalin, and that some persons feel the United States bears some, or major culpability for the cold war. Of the 16 texts and guides that include negative information about Russia, none includes all of this balancing information, and many include very little or none at all. Although about three-fourths of the materials include at least some information on tsarist repression and expansion and Russian achievements under communism in such fields as space exploration, education, and industry, virtually none includes any of the other information. Many of the materials that mention Russian achievements under communism do so grudgingly, pointing out for example that she is still behind the United States in production, that education is severely regimented, or that achievements have been gained at the cost of personal freedoms. A few materials, however, although definitely not pro-communist, express genuine appreciation for Russian achievements. Thus, *Nations of Other Lands* and *Living as World Neighbors* both include extensive "tours" of the Soviet Union in their treatment of the U.S.S.R., and their descriptions of the massive industrial might of Russia are impossible to read without gaining a sense of awe at Soviet achievements. The former text also notes that under the czars only the rich were educated, whereas the Soviets "built up a school system for all of the people" and that "today a Russian who circles the earth in a spacecraft or makes important discoveries in the scientific lab may well be the grandson of a serf" (pp. 90, 95). Taken as a whole, these two texts, plus *Knowing Our Neighbors Around the Earth* and the Chicago and suburban Philadelphia curriculum guides offer a relatively balanced view of Russia, whereas the other materials offer a very unbalanced, or in the case of the four U.S. histories, a totally unbalanced view of Russia.

Material in the texts and guides on communist countries other than Russia is often distorted. Thus, although all of the materials that discuss Communist China point out the denials of civil liberties there, when the present Nationalist government is discussed none gives even a hint that it is generally considered to be an authoritarian and corrupt government that has oppressed the native Taiwanese. Post-World War II conflicts in Indochina are generally presented as created by otherwise unidentified "communists" seeking to take over the area, rather than by indigenous forces that are composed of communists allied with nationalist and other forces. When Cuba is discussed, Castro is depicted as a communist dictator who betrayed his promises to the Cuban people, caused the rupture in relations with the United States, and failed to do anything to make life better for anyone in Cuba.

SOME CONCLUSIONS AND IMPLICATIONS

The basic findings of this study may be briefly summarized. It is clear that the highly favorable view of the country, government, and governmental officials that elementary school children hold, their increasing politicization, and their unsophisticated and uncynical view of the political process reflect in many ways the favorable treatment of the United States, the U.S. government, and citizenship in the curricular materials. The preference heirarchy for foreign countries and peoples in which elementary school children prefer northwest European cultures first, communist nations last, and underdeveloped nations in between may also be a reflection of the curricular materials. The prejudicial attitudes that elementary school children hold toward blacks and persons of low social class are not satisfactorily counteracted by the materials; the topic of social class is generally ignored altogether and although a number of the materials have made some attempt to include pictures or information on blacks that might counteract prejudicial attitudes, it is clear that they fail to include enough material or material of sufficient frankness to have much effect.

The present content of the curricular materials examined can be criticized on two grounds: that of normative desirability and that of long term effect on the political system (system stability). Through sins of both commission and omission, it is clear that the material on the United States, the U.S. government, and citizenship and on race and social class constitutes at best a sugarcoating of history and reality and at worst a rewriting of history to eliminate unpleasant facts. The material on foreign countries and peoples includes both some rewriting of history and a distinctly ethnocentric viewpoint. On normative grounds, this type of educational approach appears unworthy of a great democracy that not infrequently boasts about its passion for truth and criticizes other countries for rewriting history to suit their own purposes. Further, it seems normatively unsound not to try to counteract racial and class prejudices and to foster ethnocentrism, for all of these traits run counter to American ideals.

Yet one could make a strong defense of this type of curricular material if it could be shown that in the long run it had beneficial effects for the political system. But this seems very unlikely. The overwhelming social, psychological, economic, and moral costs of continuing racial and class tensions and discrimination in American society are obvious, and given these costs, it seems clear from the standpoint of system stability that the schools must make every effort to counteract class and race prejudices. Similarly, whereas every nation must, and inevitably will, seek to defend its own values and way of life, if Americans are to understand, get along with, and effectively aid other countries, it is clear that the present treatment of foreign countries and peoples must be substantially revised to place greater stress on encouraging feelings of solidarity, to praise the functional aspects and adaptations of other cultures, and to place less stress on American standards of industrialization and democracy in judging other countries and peoples and in prescribing for their ills. With regard to the material on the United States, U.S. government, and citizenship, the fact that material of this type is inevitable, and functional to some extent from the standpoint of system stability must be recognized. Obviously no government should be expected to nor will it allow its educational system to subvert the loyalties of its young subjects. Therefore to suggest that the curriculum take the viewpoint held by some persons that the United States and its government are fundamentally racist, imperialistic, undemocratic, and value-corrupt is to ensure that one will not be taken seriously. But a very serious argument can be made, even from the standpoint of system stability, that a much more realistic concept of the country, government, and effective democratic citizenship be included in the curricular materials. Children who are taught that their society and government are virtually infallible may well tend to reject both if, when they are growing up, events such as the Vietnam war and the urban-racial crisis occur which tend to cast the basic legitimacy of the system into question. On the other hand, children who are taught with some degree of frankness about the "warts" of their society and the body politic, *along* with material designed to gain their loyalty may be much more selective about what they reject about their society and government. This type of analysis seems to the author to best explain the current wholesale rejection of American society and government by large numbers of young people. The hypothesis advanced here is that the more childhood socialization is divorced from reality, the more likely that total rejection of that socialization will occur later under conditions of crisis. It is certainly worth noting in this regard that a major theme in the rhetoric of the "new left" is that America has betrayed its ideals—i.e., the ideals they were taught were reality when they were children.

REFERENCES

Social Studies Curriculum Guides, Grades 1–6

Chesterfield County, Va. "Man Lives in a Changing World." 1967.
Chicago, Ill. "Curriculum Guide for Social Studies," 3 vols. 1964–65.
Clayton, Mo. "Social Studies." 1964.
Denver, Colo. "The Social Studies Program of the Denver Public Schools," 6 vols. 1966.
Gary, Ind. "Social Studies in the Elementary School." 1965.
Highland Park, Tex. "Social Studies Curriculum Guidelines for Teachers." 1967.
Lockland, Ohio. "Social Studies Curriculum Guide." 1963.
Mobile, Ala. "Study Guide for Social Studies and Science." 1964.
Mt. Lebanon, Pa. "The Curriculum Guide for Social Studies." 1963.
Philadelphia, Pa., Suburban Schools (Philadelphia Suburban School Study Council, Group B, Committee on Elementary Social Studies). "Social Studies in the Ele-

mentary School" and accompanying unit volumes. 1963.
Port Arthur, Tex. "Elementary Social Studies." 1966.
St. Louis, Mo. "A Curriculum Guide for the Social Studies." 1967.
Sioux City, Iowa. "Social Studies Guide," 2 vols. 1963.
South Plainfield, N.J. "Our Social Studies World." 1967.
Springfield, N.J. "New Tentative Social Studies Guide." 1967.

Textbooks

FIRST GRADE

Buckley, P., and H. Jones. *William, Andy and Ramon.* New York: Holt, Rinehart and Winston, 1966.
Hanna, P. R., and G. A. Hoyt. *At Home* (TE). Glenview, Ill.: Scott, Foresman, 1965.
McIntire, A., and W. Hill. *Billy's Friends* (TE). Chicago: Follett, 1965.
Preston, R. C., and J. C. Bernstein. *Families Near and Far.* Lexington, Mass.: Raytheon/Heath, 1969.
Swinney, G. H., et al. *Your School and Neighborhood* (TE). Boston: Ginn, 1966.

SECOND GRADE

King, F. M., et al. *Communities and Social Needs.* River Forest, Ill.: Laidlaw Bros., 1968.
McIntire, A., and W. Hill. *Billy's Neighbors.* Chicago: Follett, 1965.
Preston, R. C., et al. *Greenfield and Far Away.* Lexington, Mass.: Raytheon/Heath, 1969.
Senesh, L. *Our Working World.* Chicago: Science Research Associates, 1965.
Thomas, E., et al. *Your Neighborhood and the World.* Boston: Ginn, 1966.

THIRD GRADE

Buckley, P., and H. Jones. *Living as Neighbors.* New York: Holt, Rinehart and Winston, 1966.
Cutright, P., et al. *Living in America Today and Yesterday* (TE). New York: Macmillan, 1966.
Hanna, P. R., et al. *In City, Town and Country* (TE). Glenview, Ill.: Scott, Foresman, 1965.
Presno, V., and C. Presno. *People and Their Action in Social Roles.* Englewood Cliffs, N.J.: Prentice-Hall, 1967.
Wann, K. D., et al. *Learning About Our Country* (TE). Boston: Allyn & Bacon, 1963.

FOURTH GRADE

Allen, J., and A. E. Howland, *The Earth and Our States* (TE). Englewood Cliffs, N.J.: Prentice-Hall, 1966.
Carols, N., et al. *Knowing Our Neighbors Around the Earth* (TE). New York: Holt, Rinehart and Winston, 1966.
Cooper, K. S., et al. *Learning to Look at Our World* (TE). Morristown, N. J.: Silver Burdett, 1964.
Hanna, P. R., et al. *In All Our States* (TE). Glenview, Ill.: Scott, Foresman, 1965.
King, F. M., et al. *Regions and Social Needs.* River Forest, Ill.: Laidlaw Bros., 1968.

FIFTH GRADE

Brown, G. S. *Your Country and Mine.* Boston: Ginn, 1965.

Cutright, P., et al. *Living in the Americas* (TE). New York: Macmillan, 1966.

Preston, R. C., and J. Tottle. *In These United States.* Lexington, Mass.: Raytheon/ Heath, 1969.

Ver Steeg, C. *The Story of Our Country.* New York: Harper & Row, 1965.

Wann, K. D., et al. *Our Changing Nation and Its Neighbors* (TE). Boston: Allyn & Bacon, 1967.

SIXTH GRADE

Allen, J., and A. E. Howland. *Nations of Other Lands.* Englewood Cliffs, N.J.: Prentice-Hall, 1966.

Cooper, K. S., et al. *The Changing Old World* (TE). Morristown, N.J.: Silver Burdett, 1964.

Cutright, P., et al. *Living as World Neighbors* (TE). New York: Macmillan, 1966.

Hagaman, A. P., and T. J. Durrell. *Word Cultures: Past and Present* (TE). New York: Harper & Row, 1964.

Hamer, E. S., et al. *Exploring the Old World* (TE). Chicago: Follett, 1966.

National Identity in U.S. and Canadian Children

3

David Statt

David Statt

GEOCENTRIC AND HELIOCENTRIC NATIONALISM

In all the voluminous theoretical writings on modern nationalism little attention has been paid to the differential factors that influence an individual to adopt a nationalist as opposed to a supranationalist ideology, i.e., an ideology that embraces more than the individual's own nation-state. This chapter is an attempt to examine the phenomenon of supranationalism from the perspective of the actor within the political system of his nation-state.

The available evidence is fragmentary and somewhat tangential, but what material there is is very significant. The now-classic Authoritarian Personality study (Adorno, 1950) provided rich material in depth for examining the association between family experiences and later political behavior. A Norwegian study by Christiansen (1959) examined the role of personality in the formation of attitudes toward foreign affairs. The psychological approach appears in the work of Piaget and Weil (1951), and of Jahoda (1962).

From these latter studies we have learned that between the ages of 5 and 11 years, the child develops the cognitive equipment to cope with the concept of nationality. Affectively, his awareness grows in a parallel way, extending outward from himself, his family, and his immediate environment to his country. His ability to understand that these experiences are universal is liable to regress under environmental pressure.

The nature of this environmental pressure raises the question of its antecedents, the differing socialization experiences that impinge upon the young child in his formation of a national identity. The relative importance of home and school environments in this respect has often been debated,

This chapter is based on the author's doctoral dissertation written at the University of Michigan. The United Nations is in no way associated with the chapter or the book in which it appears.

but as I hope to show later on, we now have enough data to resolve this debate and assess the relative salience of each influence source in the child's process of development.

Unfortunately, no direct psychological evidence exists on how the child sees his country in relation to others, and to the world as a whole. One would be interested to know, for instance, whether children retain a "geocentric" view of the political universe into their adult lives. How and when, if ever, does a "heliocentric" view emerge?

By the beginning of adolescence, all children, regardless of background, appear to possess the rudimentary psychological equipment necessary to handle the concepts of nationality and of related topics. As Adelson (1966) has shown, there is strong evidence to suppose that by the end of adolescence the political views held and the concepts comprehended are indistinguishable from those of the adult. After this period, therefore, political flesh is added to the psychological skeleton.

By way of providing some conceptual linkages between the systems level of national power role and the individual level of child development, I would like to propose the following rationale: At the systems level, there is some evidence that general attitudes toward national and international politics as transmitted by parents in child-rearing practices can change with a changing national ethos. Inkeles (1955) has demonstrated this by studying people in the Soviet Union who were socialized before, during, and after the Bolshevik Revolution. He suggests that parents, both consciously and subconsciously, may be a mediating influence between their children and processes of social and political change.

This is a very important point because we know from the literature on prejudice (Allport, 1954) and on political socialization (Hess and Torney, 1967) that the basic affective orientation to one's own nation, its values, and attitudes, is laid in pre-school childhood. Moreover, from the recent work of Hess and Torney (1967) and of Easton and Dennis (1969) there is evidence to suggest that this orientation is strongly implanted in all children regardless of socioeconomic status. These writers believe that in this respect the only difference between children is that children of very high I.Q. and social status may learn these lessons earlier, and thus they may be more deeply rooted.

However, Hess and Torney (1967) argue very strongly that the most important socializing agent is the school system that guides the process of differentiation of the ingroup from outgroups, the definition and content of the ingroup, and attitudes toward outgroups. In sum, it shapes the amorphous ingroup loyalty and transforms it into national loyalty.

As the child becomes cognitively aware of what his nation is, his parents cease to be important sources of information on international affairs, as Lambert and Klineberg (1967) have demonstrated, and television, which is an ever-present influence from the earliest years on, becomes the dominant source of such information. This source by its very nature must reflect regime norms and attitudes in its reporting of international affairs. News is made primarily by governmental action and reaction (See Figure 1, p. 36).

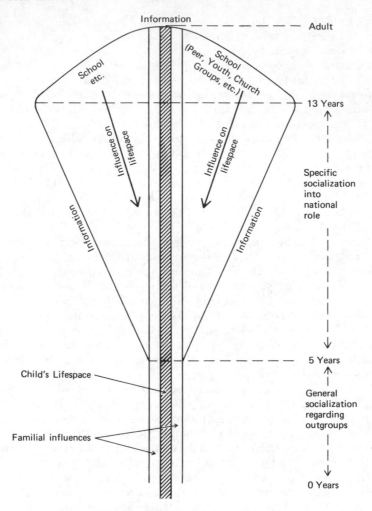

FIGURE 1. Statt Cone

The periphery represents environmental inputs of information. During the child's socialization experiences he has no mechanism for direct and independent evaluation of this information. Until he goes to school his parents mediate and interpret this information to him, whether from T.V., comic books, or personal contacts. When he goes to school his familial influences diminish sharply in relation to other sources, but the basic orientation received in the home will remain with him. By the time he goes to high school the psychological framework of his attitudes to other countries, etc., is formed, and this is filled out with increasing factual information. Finally, by the time he reaches adulthood his intellectual processes will have matured sufficiently for him perhaps to be capable of some independent assessment of environmental information, though I would argue that such information will always be largely mediated by other agencies.

Also at the systems level, there is evidence from studies of ethnocentrism (Rosenblatt, 1964) that this phenomenon and that of ingroup loyalty tend to increase in large units because of supposedly greater security, more efficient division of labor, and so on.

Allied to this is the conscious factor of perceived threat. Under threat conditions people's ethnocentrism becomes more pointed and directed at the "enemy." Nationalism and ethnocentrism are increased because of the need for defense, affiliation, and justification of loyalties. Leaders arouse ingroup loyalties and foster an increase of hostility toward the perceived sources of threat. This kind of ethos will be much more prevalent in a nation that has "enemies" sharply focused and has its national interests continually threatened in ongoing regional or global conflicts of interest.

Finally, there is a vast adult literature dealing with political efficacy, which together with the recent work on children by Easton and Dennis (1969) shows that the higher the socioeconomic level, the greater the feelings of efficacy.

A TEST CASE: AMERICAN AND CANADIAN IDENTITY

The foregoing review of the literature highlights what I consider to be the most crucial psychological process for the study of nationalism, the development of a "heliocentric" rather than "geocentric" view of the political universe. This dimension will therefore form the crux of the research to be outlined in the present chapter.

Being *heliocentric* rather than *geocentric* would imply:

1. being more inter- or supra-nationalist than nationalist;
2. being less ethnocentric;
3. having a more realistic concept about the physical attributes (including power) of one's nation;
4. being less inclined to dichotomize other nations into friends and enemies and being more aware of which countries consider themselves ideologically neutral in the cold war.

I would argue further from the foregoing review that the most important factors to study in this connection concern the development over time of the change from geocentric to heliocentric behavior and attitudes and the way in which different nations socialize their children on this dimension. There appear to be reasonable *a priori* grounds for assuming that nations involved in international power struggles, whether regional (Israel/Egypt) or global (United States/Soviet Union), would have to keep their citizens highly mobilized around the defense, honor, etc., of the nation, and one means of doing so is to use emotional appeals and traditional rhetoric.

Great emphasis would be placed on national symbols; dissent and unrest at home would be repressed or discredited; and every attempt would be made to present a united front to the rest of the world, especially, of course, to the immediate enemy. The usual relationship between citizen and state in this kind of nation would tend toward the symbolic rather than the functional (Katz, *et al.,* 1963) in that emotional and often chauvinistic attachments would be more salient than rational links.

I would argue that nations whose governments do not feel obliged to assert their military power on a daily basis can allow their citizens more freedom to dissent from official policies, while not allowing their international relations to be unduly affected by ideological or power-status considerations. The usual citizen-state relationships here will tend to be heliocentric rather than geocentric. It would be very interesting, therefore, to see how far down the educational process these attitudes and values may filter, and to surface their genesis and growth in various groups of children.

I decided to compare samples from two countries that were as similar as possible, except for their power roles, and for various reasons decided upon the United States and Canada. Few countries (certainly in the Western world) have more similar social, economic, political, and cultural systems. Sharing, as they do, a common and open 3,000 mile border, conditions are also optimum for physical contacts between the two populations.

The main physical differences between the two nations, I suggest, is that 200,000,000 people live in the United States whereas only 20,000,000 people live in Canada. Whereas the United States is a super-power, Canada has no international power aspirations, and this being the case, the United States can maintain an unchallenged hegemony over the North American region, while facing no challenge from Canada on a global basis either.

However, I would argue that because of their different power status there is some degree of political difference, both internal and external, between the two nations. (As Katz, 1965, and others have pointed out, there is a close systematic link between the domestic and foreign policy of a regime, and this in turn, I would argue, is largely dependent on that nation's power role.)

On the Canadian domestic front, as Mildred Schwartz (1967) has shown, there appears to be more sympathy with social welfare plans than in the United States. She cites evidence from public opinion data going back to the early 1940s to show that there is widespread support for government measures such as family allowances, health insurance, and old age pensions, and argues that such legislation is no longer controversial in Canada (unlike the United States) but is "part of a general consensus" (p. 100). What is perhaps even more striking, and I think symptomatic of the prevailing political climate in the two countries, is that Canada still (as of 1970) harbors United States citizens refusing the draft.

In foreign affairs, none of the five Communist regimes off-limits to United States citizens is closed to Canadians, and Canada has, for some period developed trade relations with China and in 1970 accorded diplomatic recognition to that country.

To deal with the most important developmental trends, I decided to follow the example of previous workers in this field (e.g., Jahoda, 1963; Lambert and Klineberg, 1967) and restricted the study to elementary school children. Unlike previous workers, however, I decided to sample an elite population, the children of the upper and upper-middle classes whose parents would be wealthy businessmen, government officials, prominent doctors, lawyers, etc. The samples will consist of predominantly "WASP," private-school children; my reasons for choosing elite samples were three-fold:

1. The parents of these children will "own the system." They will be able to effect changes in national policy to better their interests, and they will feel themselves to have real power and influence over their environment, to be in charge of their lives in a way that other social groups are not. Whatever their nation is and does will be more closely reflected in them than in any other groups, and in their children should possibly be found the genesis of this orientation and some clue as to how it will appear in the future.

2. Because these children are of a uniformly high I.Q., and provided with a lot of environmental stimulation, the psychological processes I would like to study will be more easily exposed than in any other group of children.

3. We don't know anything about the developmental processes of elite children because nobody ever studies them. The prevailing research ethos with its emphasis on mass society tends somewhat to discourage such endeavors, and there is also the practical consideration that public schools tend to be more accessible.

The purpose of this study is basically to explore cross-age and cross-national differences to determine what, if anything, emerges; I would predict that two main trends will be found in the data.

1. *Developmental*: Children will progress from a geocentric to a heliocentric mode of relating to their nation and its place in the world, along the criteria outlined above.

2. *Cross-National*: The Canadian children will progress farther and faster on the geocentric-heliocentric dimension than the American children. That is, the Canadian children will generally be more heliocentric than the American.

Instruments

The instruments used in this study were constructed with a view to building on previous research and obtaining the widest possible sampling of relevant behavior from the subjects in the shortest possible time. I therefore tried to devise a battery of easily administered items that would tap into both cognitive and affective developmental trends while holding the interest of the children. In the interests of methodological diversity, the test battery included both manipulative and paper and pencil items. The final list of items after pretesting was presented as follows:

1. SELF-CONCEPT. To examine the salience of nationality in the child's self-concept before any bias was introduced, he was asked the following:

1. What are you? ....
2. What else are you ....
....
9. What else are you ....

If country or nationality was not spontaneously mentioned, he was asked: What country do you live in? What nationality are you? If the child didn't understand it was explained to him.

2. PIAGET'S QUESTIONS. In his 1951 study quoted earlier, Piaget asked two questions (adapted for present purposes):

1. If you had been born without any nationality, what country would you choose and why?
2. If I asked a little Canadian (American) boy the same question, what country would he choose and why?

3. SIZE CONCEPT. The (American) child was given five black pieces of plastic, thus:

He was told that these represented five countries and that one of the large pieces was the United States. He had to find Canada. Similarly, Canadians were asked to find America. The expectation was that significantly more Canadians than Americans would choose the other large piece because of a hypothesized tendency for American children to overestimate the size of their own and underestimate the size of other countries when judging their relative sizes. Canadians are hypothesized as being more realistic in this context.

4. CONCEPT OF "FOREIGNER." Jahoda (1964) found that Piaget's investigation of this concept was hampered by the abstract and fuzzy nature of the term "nation." To help overcome this problem, nations were represented by plastic squares again, and people by matchstick men.

Thus, four squares of equal size but different colors, randomly presented, represented the United States, Canada, Russia, and China. A figure was placed beside each one.

Each figure was then placed in his square and the child asked, "This boy/girl lives in X, is he/she a foreigner in that country?"

The United States/Canadian figure was then moved to each of the other squares in turn, and the child asked, "If the American/Canadian boy went to visit X, would he be a foreigner in that country?"

4a. Social Distance Measure. The American/Canadian square was then taken, and placed on it was a quarter-circle of a different color rep-

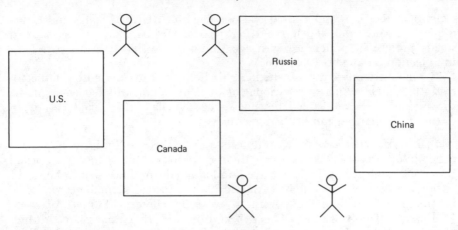

resenting the child's city, and on this a rectangle of a third color representing the child's neighborhood, thus:

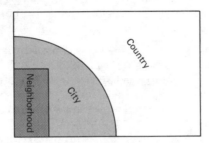

The home figure was placed in the neighborhood area, and each of the other figures was brought over one at a time. As each figure was placed in the "country" area the child was asked, "Would you have the little X boy come and live in your country?" Similarly for the "city" and "neighborhood" areas.

4b. (i) If the (little) Russian/Chinese boy was hungry, would you want to send him food? (ii) If you were hungry do you think he would want to send *you* food?

4c. (i) If your country and his country went to war, would you want to send food to the hungry (little) Russian/Chinese boy then? (ii) Would he want to send food to you?

4d. (i) If your countries were at war would you be willing to have bombs dropped on the (little) Russian/Chinese boy's home? (ii) Would he be willing to have bombs dropped on your home?

5. FLAG CHOICES. Previous studies on lower- and middle-class American and Canadian children report very similar reactions to United States,

Canadian, Russian, and United Nations flags; i.e., United States and Canadian flags were consistently rated highly, the United Nations flag showed steady growth in preference with age, and the Russian flag was persistent in rejection (Lawson, 1963, 1965).

I was interested to see whether this held true for the elite samples of this study, or whether any national or developmental differences might be shown. Subjects were asked to choose the five flags they liked best from twenty-five pictures, randomly presented.

6. CATEGORIZING NATIONS. Subjects were asked to indicate how they thought other countries regarded their own by checking the appropriate box on a table which included five "non-aligned" nations, five Communist nations which are off-limits to Americans but not to Canadians, and five members of NATO. They were given four choices "For," "Against," "Neither," "Don't Know." The expectation was that American children would be more prone to categorize "For" and "Against" than Canadian children.

7. PATRIOTISM SCALE. Adapted from Christiansen (1959) this scale includes a series of questions designed to surface patriotic emotions, e.g., "The defense of America can never justify the taking of another human life." Subjects had to rate this statement on a five-point evaluation scale ranging from (1) Strong Agreement to (5) Strong Disagreement.

8. ETHNOCENTRISM SCALE. This scale was used in a large cross-national study by Lambert and Klineberg (1967) and is used here to surface any systematic personality differences between the two samples on this dimension. Subjects responded "Yes" or "No" after each question, e.g., "Do you think there will always be war, that it is part of human nature?"

The first five of these items were administered as an individual test battery to 120 boys and girls from grades 2, 4, and 6. The last three (6, 7, and 8) of these items were administered as a separate questionnaire to entire classes at grades 4 and 6, comprising 141 children in all. A different version of this questionnaire was also administered to 77 parents and teachers. Finally, two boys and two girls in each of grades 2, 4, and 6 were given a semi-structured group interview dealing with questions of politics and nationality.

Sample

The children used were all of above average I.Q. They were drawn from two schools—both independent coeducational day schools with a Protestant background. One of these schools (where the pre-test was carried out) is in Michigan, and the other in Ontario. Both are listed in the 1969 edition of "Private Independent Schools" by Bunting and Lyon, Inc. (Connecticut), an authoritative source on leading North American private schools since 1943. The two schools have very similar tuition rates, ranging from about $500 to about $1,300, and both are proud to claim distinguished alumni on local and national levels in the fields of politics, business, the arts, and the professions.

Procedure

The American data were collected in November 1969 and the Canadian data in January 1970.

INDIVIDUAL INTERVIEW DATA. Each child was interviewed separately. The interview conditions were good, and each interview took between 5 and 10 minutes to carry out. I was aided in this phase of the study by a graduate student in developmental psychology from the University of Michigan who had a great deal of experience in child research.

QUESTIONNAIRE DATA. The questionnaires were administered by teachers in their classrooms who reported no problems in doing so. They took between 5 and 10 minutes to complete. After they had done this, the children were handed out mail questionnaires for their parents. Teacher's questionnaires were left with the school office.

GROUP INTERVIEW DATA. The six interviews were all conducted by my aforementioned colleague. Each interview lasted about 30 minutes and was tape-recorded.

THE FINDINGS AND THEIR CLASSROOM IMPLICATIONS

Cross-National Approach

The idea that the American sample would be more geocentric than the Canadian was somewhat supported by the data when the individual data were clearcut. In the questionnaire data, although the Canadians were somewhat more likely to believe that other countries were friendly toward them than did the Americans, and somewhat less likely to dichotomize other countries as being "for" or "against" them, their objective knowledge of other countries was significantly less than that of the American children.

Thus, it would appear that the American children were more sensitized to foreign affairs than were the Canadian, and more inclined to make critical judgments. Support for this argument can be adduced from two other sources of data. In the individual item 2, Piaget's questions dealing with the concept of nationality, the raw scores for understanding this concept are as follows:

TABLE 1. NUMBER OF CHILDREN WHO UNDERSTOOD THE CONCEPT OF "NATIONALITY"

Grade	United States	Canada
2	1	7
4	10	12
6	20	20
Total	31	39

If we then compare this table with that of item 4 on the concept of "foreigner" we find the following:

TABLE 2. NUMBER OF CHILDREN WHO UNDERSTOOD THE CONCEPT OF "FOREIGNER"

Grade	United States	Canada	Chi Square	P
2	19	3	22.73	.001
4	20	8	14.40	.001
6	20	16	2.5	n.s
Total	59	27		

Thus, it would appear that although the Canadian children had as much or more understanding of their nationality, they had much less understanding of what a foreigner was than did the American children. It simply was not a very relevant concept for the Canadian children. Most of them, in fact, had never even heard of the word.

It is interesting to note that Piaget (1951) considered the general understanding of the concept "foreigner" to begin at about the age of 11 (grade 6). We can see from Table 2 that this does not apply to the American children. They displayed a full understanding of the concept at grade 2 and, as the pre-test suggested, perhaps even earlier.

It seems clear that this finding is not due to any differences of cognition or understanding of nationality. The fact that Piaget's study was conducted in Switzerland is not, I would suggest, entirely without significance. I would interpret this finding as suggesting that power-oriented countries might make their citizens more aware of international relations and, hence, of concepts like "foreigner."

A final piece of evidence on this point comes from the group interview data. At both grades 4 and 6, the American children made spontaneous references to freedom and to communism. They made such remarks as "I wouldn't want to play with Russian kids because they're communists" (grade 4 boy), and "I'd choose to be born in the United States again because its a free country—not like Russia" (grade 6 girl).

In contrast to these responses, freedom to the Canadian children meant "not being in jail" (grade 2 boy), and although the grade 4 children when closely questioned thought that "communism" was a bad word rather than a good word, they knew nothing at all about the word and none of the Canadian children ever used it spontaneously.

Finally, the differences between the responses of the American and Canadian parents, on the questionnaire data (though not always statistically significant) exactly paralleled those of the children that were noted above.

Developmental Approach

Here again the basic idea that geocentrism would decrease with age was largely supported by the data. The questionnaire data were somewhat inconclusive in relation to the developmental approach. As in the individual data, there seemed to be no systematic sex differences. There were, however, no age differences either on any of the scores in the judgment of other countries.

However, an interesting trend did come to light in the patriotism scores. Not only did the older children score significantly higher than the younger children over the whole sample, but the parents scored significantly higher than the older children. In addition, each group of parents (both grades and both nationalities) scored significantly higher than the corresponding group of children.

There were no differences on patriotism between parent groups. American teachers scored on a level with the younger children, significantly lower than the grade 6 children and the parents.

The relevant means are given in the following table:

TABLE 3. PATRIOTISM SCORES BY AGE GROUP

Age Group	U.S. Mean	t	P	Canadian Mean	t	P
Grade 4	21.83			21.60		
		3.43	<.002		2.64	<.02
Grade 6	25.13			24.83		
		2.52	<.02		2.00	<.05
Parents	28.80			26.83		
U.S. teachers	22.44					

The findings of Table 3 make sense in terms of the theoretical structure outlined in the beginning of the chapter where I tried to show that the amorphous ingroup loyalty with which the child starts school is gradually molded into a national loyalty and this might be most clearly reflected in the patriotism scale which was specifically designed to measure various aspects of national loyalty.

This argument is supported by data from the self-report item which show that spontaneous expressions of nationality increase significantly with age, a finding born out by the studies of Jahoda (1963) and Lambert and Klineberg (1959) which holds good right into adulthood.

TABLE 4. CHILDREN EXPRESSING NATIONALITY
IN SELF-REPORT

		United States and Canada
	2	1
Grade	4	7
	6	10

The categorizing nations item did not yield such clearcut findings. All parent groups were significantly higher than the corresponding groups of children on nations they judged as friendly to their own, although there were no differences here between parents and teachers. Parents also dichotomized other nations as for or against their own significantly more than the corresponding group of children and more than teachers. In judging the attitudes of other countries toward their own, the general trend (which in some cases was non-significant) was for parents to be more objectively correct than children and teachers more than parents.

All of these trends, I would suggest, are in line with the increase in national awareness that occurs with age, though it should be remembered that adults are generally more suited to written items that children, and the patriotism scale was originally intended by Christiansen (1959) to be used with adults.

The lower geocentrism of teachers as compared to parents is an intriguing finding. All of our information in this area is consistent in suggesting that teachers in North America tend to belong to the middle classes and to be generally supportive of the prevailing norms of national identification. We also know from interracial school research that teacher's attitudes often conflict with those of children from lower-class homes. It may be that the upper-class home environments of the children in this study bring them into conflict with their middle-class teachers in a parallel fashion. In line with my argument that the elites will, in a sense, own the system, a higher degree of national identification than that of the middle class might well be expected from them.

I think it worth noting that the technique followed in the individual items—presenting abstract concepts to children in simple concrete terms—proved to be rather fruitful and promises well for future research in this field. The adoption of such a technique is a course that Piaget has himself suggested, though his own work in this area (1951) did not make use of it, and his research in general has often been criticized on this score. The children certainly enjoyed the experimental situation, and their enjoyment was communicated to the experimenters who never became bored or impatient with the proceedings. A good rapport between child and experimenter was thereby established, which undoubtedly increased the validity of the responses.

As an example of the benefits of using this methodology, the children, in responding to the social distance item (4a) were very clear about their feelings toward foreign children and gave consistent replies throughout, i.e., if they would allow a child to live in their neighborhood, they would also allow him to live in their country, and so on.

Comparison With Other Studies

Responses on two of the individual items can be compared with other studies, revealing differences on one item and similarities on the other thus:

ITEM 5—FLAG CHOICES. Results here were very similar to previous studies done by Lawson on American (1963) and Canadian (1965) children. The United States and Canadian flags were consistently rated highly, the United Nations flag showed steady growth in preference with age, and the Russian flag was persistently rejected, as in Lawson's studies. The children of each country rated their neighbors' flag next to their own (see Fig. 2).

ITEM 1—SELF-REPORT. Responses to this item were somewhat different from previous findings. Both Jahoda (1963) and Lambert and Klineberg

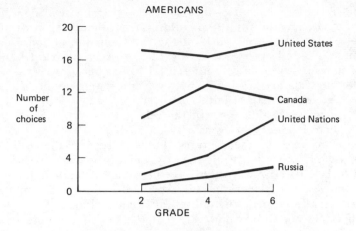

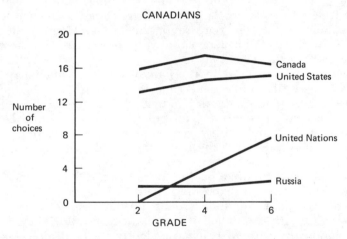

FIGURE 2. Graphs of Flag Choice Date for American
and Canadian Children

(1959) reported that 3 percent of their sample between grades 1 and 6 gave
spontaneous nationality references. In the present study the figure was 15
percent, representing 8 Canadians and 10 Americans. I would again interpret these differences in terms of different socioeconomic status levels. This
could perhaps be regarded as some evidence for the closer national idntifica-
tion exhibited by the elites as compared to the middle and lower social
status levels.

General Implications

If the premises of this study bear any relation at all to reality, the
implications for the socialization of young children are truly far-reaching

in scope. I realize, of course, that we lack critical knowledge about the effects of environmental inputs on children from the social institutions that mediate between the social world of the child and the national posture of his country. The links proposed in this study between individual and nation have, of necessity, been largely inferential in nature. However, some interesting findings about the nature of these links were found which might help to shorten the "leap of faith" involved.

If we can agree that some of the relevant social variables have been identified here for both the American and Canadian children, then in the absence of evidence to the contrary, I would suggest that differences in national power orientations might be systematically tied in with different ways of socializing citizens to think of their country and its relations with other countries. Elite American children in this study were, on the whole, somewhat more geocentric than elite Canadian children.

This does not imply, however, that the Canadians were in any way nicer or better people than the Americans. (Both groups, as a matter of fact, contained the most delightful children.) Nor does it imply that the Canadian children were uniformly more accepting of other social groups than the American children. At grade 6 there were no differences between the two samples on the ethnocentrism or patriotism scales, and on the social distance item 4a, the Canadian children were actually less accepting of other groups than the Americans.

American children were more aware of the international system than the Canadians, while at the same time less inter- or supra-nationalist in their orientations. The American children at all grade levels believed that being citizens of their country meant holding specific political beliefs that made them subject to hostility from certain other countries. They considered these political beliefs the best ones to hold, simply as a matter of course.

The Canadian children, on the other hand, did not seem to include much political content in expressing their nationality. The fact that the world is divided politically into nations did not seem to be an important datum for their attitudes about other groups of people. They were aware of their nationality without being consciously nationalistic or ideological about it.

Specific Implications

As expected, the rituals and symbols of nationalism such as the Pledge of Allegiance, the flag, the presidency, and historical figures, were much more apparent in the American school than in the Canadian. However, the significance of such things, I would argue, is that they reveal more about the people who provide them than about the people they are intended to influence. The rituals and symbols serve to strengthen and articulate the individual's links to the image he holds of his nation, but they have no effect whatsoever on the content of that image or its meaning for him.

The use of symbolism is therefore symptomatic of a particular orientation and reflects the prevailing political climate in a society. For some Americans today the highest expression of their sincere patriotism is to burn the flag and curse the president, as symbolizing a betrayal of the real American values of freedom and democracy they were taught in school. Others, of course, resolve dissonance by maintaining great respect and affection for the flag and the president while re-interpreting American ideals.

It is thus very significant, I suggest, that the Maple Leaf was just as popular with the Canadian children as Old Glory was with the Americans. The espousal of national symbols as such is a sign neither of geocentrism nor of heliocentrism in attitudes toward other countries.

I would further argue that not only are symbols irrelevant for the acquisition of a heliocentric orientation, but so too is the specific teaching of internationalist subject matter. For example, the flag studies of Lawson (1963, 1965) and the cross-national survey of Lambert and Klineberg (1967) showed clearly that the more children learn about the United Nations in school, the more positive they feel about it. There are virtually no differences between American and Canadian attitudes in any of these studies, nor in the present study either. Yet, as we have seen, these similar attitudes about the United Nations apparently have a very different meaning for the basic orientations that the American and Canadian children have toward the rest of the world.

Thus, I would argue finally, that the most important implication this study has for political socialization is the supreme importance of understanding the developmental psychological process. Children must be helped to develop their cognitive abilities, their critical faculties, and their capacity for logical reasoning, and *they must be encouraged to apply these processes to the world they live in, both physical and social*. Some interesting support for these ideas appeared in a recent article on international education by Henry Steele Commager (1970), in which he contrasts what he calls the modern and traditional approaches to education. He criticizes modern American education thus:

> The modern approach, cultivated more assiduously in the United States than elsewhere, is to expose the young to foreign cultures early and persistently . . . its aim is not so much qualitative understanding as quantitative coverage . . . [but] . . . this pervasively American method of teaching about the rest of the world has been a stunning failure. After half a century of exposure to world cultures and politics . . . we are culturally more alienated and politically more isolated than at any time in the past, and we seem totally unable to solve any of our major problems, foreign or domestic. Who can deny that the American people are today more nationalistic, chauvinistic, militaristic, parochial and intolerant in their attitudes toward other nations and cultures than at any time in the past century? (p. 233)

The remedy Commager proposes is to utilize the best points of the traditional approach to education (as exemplified by the classic British model) which tended (he claims) to foster the very capacities I mentioned earlier.

Only to the extent that this educational policy is universally adopted at all social levels can children ever escape the omnipresent nationalist straitjacket which, binding tighter in some nations, freer in others, determines how they will regard their fellow men.

As Piaget (1951) wrote, "the main problem is not to determine what must or must not be inculcated in the child; it is to discover how to develop that reciprocity in thought and action which is vital to the attainment of impartiality and affective understanding" (p. 578). It is now twenty years since Piaget suggested this course of action. It's time we got started.

REFERENCES

Adelson, J., and O'Neil, R. "The Growth of Political Ideas in Adolescence," *J. Pers. Soc. Psyc.*, 4, No. 3, (1966), 295–306.
Adorno, T. W., *et al. The Authoritarian Personality*. New York: Harper & Row, 1950.
Allport, G. W. *The Nature of Prejudice*. Reading, Mass.: Addison-Wesley, 1954.
Christiansen, B. *Attitudes Towards Foreign Affairs as a Function of Personality*. Oslo: Oslo University Press, 1959.
Commager, H. S. "Education and the International Community," *Phi Delta Kappan*, 51, No. 5, (1970), 230–234.
Easton, D., and Dennis, J. *Children in the Political System*. New York: McGraw-Hill, 1969.
Hess, R., and Torney, J. *The Development of Political Attitudes in Children*. Chicago: Aldine, 1967.
Inkeles, A. "Social Change and Social Character: The Role of Parental Mediation," *J. Soc. Issues*, 11 (1955), 12–23.
Jahoda, G. "Development of Scottish Children's Ideas and Attitudes About Other Countries," *J. Soc. Psych.*, 58 (1962), 91–108.
———. "The Development of Children's Ideas About Country and Nationality," Part I, *Br. J. Ed. Psych.*, 33, 47–60, 1963; Part 2, *Br. J. Ed. Psych.*, 33, 145–153, 1963.
———. "Children's Concepts of Nationality: A Critical Study of Piaget's Stages," *Child Dev.*, 35, 1081–1092, 1964.
Katz, D. "Nationalism and Strategies of International Conflict Resolution," in *International Behavior*, Kelman, H. C. (ed.). New York: Holt, Rinehart & Winston, 1965.
——— et al. "Some Hypotheses about the Relation of Individuals to Nation in America Today," Peace Research Society, Paper I, Chicago Conference, 1963.
Lambert, W., and Klineberg, O. "A Pilot Study of the Origins and Development of National Stereotypes," *Inter. Soc. Sci. J.*, 11 (1959), 221–238.
———. *Children's Views of Foreign Peoples*. New York: Appleton-Century-Crofts, 1967.
Lawson, E. D. "Development of Patriotism in Children—A Second Look," *J. Psych.*, 55 (1963), 279–286.
———. "Flag Preferences of Canadians: Before the Maple Leaf," *Psych. Reports*, 17 (1965), 553–554.
Piaget, J., and Weil, A. "The Development in Children of the Idea of the Homeland and of Relations with Other Countries," *Int. Soc. Sci. Bull.*, 3 (1951), 561–578.
Rosenblatt, P. "Origins and Effects of Group Ethnocentrism and Nationalism," *J. Conf. Res.*, 81 (1964), 131–146.
Schwartz, M. *Public Opinion and Canadian Identity*. Berkeley and Los Angeles: University of California, 1967.

Elementary School Children's Attitudes Toward Politics

4

Allen D. Glenn

No two children learn about politics in the same way. Each is influenced by a multitude of factors that shape and reshape his feelings and attitudes toward the political system. Some children form strong, positive attachments to the government and governmental authority. Others do not and become distrustful and cynical. A variety of factors cause these differences. Some are psychological, some physical, and some sociological in their origins. During the past decade political socialization research has provided significant insights into the development of these political attitudes. The purposes of this chapter are to acquaint the reader with some of these attitudes, to indicate some differences among various groups of children, and to raise some pertinent questions concerning research in this area. The data are from a political socialization study conducted by the author.

The study sought to examine the political attitudes of trust, efficacy, and change of children from three grade levels and three socioeconomic environments. Four hundred and twenty-two children and 16 classroom teachers responded to a questionnaire, and 36 children were interviewed. Two classes of third, fifth, and sixth grade children from a rural, a suburban, and an inner-city school took part. All three schools were from southeastern Michigan and their inclusion in the study was based on their willingness to participate. Table 1 presents a breakdown by grade and schools.

TABLE 1. NUMBER OF STUDENTS PARTICIPATING IN THE STUDY BY SCHOOL AND GRADE

Grade Level	School		
	Rural	Suburban	Inner city
Third	57	55	28
Fifth	53	57	31
Sixth	58	50	33
Total	168	162	92	422

The three major dependent variables of the study were defined in the following manner. *Political trust* was the willingness of a child to believe that the government and government officials are honest and have the individual's welfare at heart. The concept was operationalized by nine items from the questionnaire which formed a Guttman-like scale.[1]

Political change included both "traditional" and "nontraditional" methods of bringing about change in the political system. Traditional methods were activities such as voting and writing letters to government officials. Nontraditional methods referred to activities such as demonstrations, protests, and riots.[2] Five items formed a Guttman-like scale for the nontraditional change scale, and one item was used to determine attitudes toward traditional methods of change.[3]

Political efficacy was defined as a child's belief in his ability or his future ability and/or the ability of others to influence governmental action. A unidimensional scale could not be created. The reader should be aware that the lack of unidimensionality among the items greatly weakened the concept of efficacy.[4]

ATTITUDES OF POLITICAL TRUST, POLITICAL EFFICACY, AND POLITICAL CHANGE

As one might expect, children in different grade levels and schools varied in their attitudes of political trust, political efficacy, and political change. The most dramatic differences appeared between third and sixth graders, and between suburban children and inner-city children. With an upward movement across grade levels, political trust declined and political efficacy increased. Sixth graders had the lowest political trust but felt more sure that they and people like them could influence the government. The amount of increase or decrease in trust and efficacy depended on the socio-economic environment from which the children came. For suburban children the decrease in political trust was quite small and there was a steady increase in feelings of efficacy. For rural and inner-city children the decline in trust was greater and the increase in feelings of efficacy less.

Children, regardless of grade or school, were similar in one respect. All favored the more traditional methods of political change such as voting

[1] Items were first correlated using a modified eta correlation. The subsequent matrix was used in a cluster analysis computer program that formed unidimensional scales. The computer programs are contained in *OSIRIS II Computer Programs* (Ann Arbor: Institute for Social Research, University of Michigan). Some of the questions were taken from John A. Robinson, *et al., Measures of Political Attitudes* (Ann Arbor: Survey Research Center, University of Michigan, 1968).

[2] These methods are nontraditional in that they refer to activities which are not usually associated with the concept of "citizen duties" as defined by elementary school social studies curricula.

[3] These items were developed for the study. Scale formation was identical to the trust scale.

[4] With an increase in the number of statistical test there is an increase in the possibility of Type II statistical error.

and letter writing. The more nontraditional methods of protesting and demonstrating were not accepted.

In order to clarify these general comments, let us turn our attention to a more detailed discussion of the findings. From this not only will differences be placed in a clearer perspective but also opportunities will arise for a discussion of the possible reasons for these differences.

Political Trust

It was found that political trust varied across grades and schools. Two methods of analysis provide assistance: first a comparison of overall mean scores on the political trust scale, and second an examination of differences that appeared on individual items from that scale.

An analysis of variance technique was used to measure differences on the political trust scale. This statistical test resulted in significant differences between schools and grades.[5] From this analysis it was then possible to compare individual school and grade means (see Table 2). Suburban school children were found to have significantly higher scores on the political trust scale than did either rural or inner-city school children. The largest difference appeared between the suburban school mean of 5.166 and the inner-city school mean of 3.837.

TABLE 2. COMPARISON OF MEANS ON POLITICAL TRUST SCALE
WITH CORRESPONDING F-RATIOS BY SCHOOLS AND GRADES

SCHOOLS

School	N	Mean	Comparison	F-Ratio
Rural	168	4.518	Rur–Sub	8.40[a]
Suburban	162	5.166	Sub–IC	17.14[b]
Inner city	92	3.837	IC–Rur	6.57

a Significant at .05 level
b Significant beyond .01 level

GRADES

Grade	N	Mean	Comparison	F-Ratio
Third	140	5.314	Third-Fifth	8.83[a]
Fifth	141	4.588	Fifth-Sixth	6.50[a]
Sixth	141	3.957	Sixth-Third	30.33[b]

a Significant at .05 level
b Significant beyond .01 level

One can conclude from the items of the political trust scale and the statistical analysis of that scale that suburban children, more than rural and inner-city children, felt the government cared about them and their families and could be trusted to do the right thing. This difference is further exem-

[5] The F-ratio from the one-way analysis of variance by schools was 11.57 with degrees of freedom of 2,420. It was significant beyond the .01 level.

TABLE 3. CAN YOU TRUST THE GOVERNMENT TO DO THE
RIGHT THING? RESPONSE BY SCHOOL (IN PERCENTS)

		School		
Response		*Rural*	*Suburban*	*Inner city*
Yes		79	86	68
No		21	14	32
	Total	100	100	100
N		(168)	(162)	(92)
NA		(0)	(0)	(0)
	Total	(168)	(162)	(92)

Chi Square=10.213
Significant at .01 level

plified by the data in Table 3 which compares responses to an item that
asked whether or not the government could be trusted to do the right thing.
Eighty-six percent of the suburban children felt the government could be
trusted; only 68 percent of the inner-city children had similar feelings.

Throughout the remainder of the analysis suburban children were consistently more trustful of the government and government officials. They
were typical of those children characterized by the early studies of Greenstein, Easton-Dennis, and Hess-Torney.[6] They were children from white,
middle- and upper-class families whose parents most generally were well-
educated, white-collar workers. They lived in residential areas dominated
by well-kept, one-family dwellings.

Children from the rural school were not like their suburban counterparts. They came from families with lower incomes and lower adult educational attainment levels. Most parents were blue-collar workers. Although
basically trusting of the political system and political officials, these children
were not as positive as suburban children.

The inner-city children were unlike the children from either the rural
or suburban area. Many more of these children felt that the government did
not care about them, their families, and neighbors, and that no one could
trust the government to do the right thing. These children were similar to
those studied by Jaros, Hirsch, and Fleron.[7] They were less positive toward
political authority figures and more cynical in their views of the political
system than the middle- and upper-class children.

Before we discuss possible reasons for these differences, let us examine
the variation that appeared across grade levels. The lower section, of Table
2 reveals that sixth graders had lower political trust scores than did third

[6] Fred Greenstein, *Children and Politics* (New Haven: Yale University Press, 1965);
Robert Hess and Judith Torney, *The Development of Political Attitudes in Children* (Garden City, N. Y.: Anchor Books, 1968); David Easton and Jack Dennis,
Children in the Political System (New York: McGraw-Hill, 1969).
[7] Dean Jaros, Herbert Hirsch, and Frederick Fleron, Jr. "The Malevolent Leader:
Political Socialization in an American Sub-culture," *The American Political Science Review*, 62, No. 2 (June 1968), pp. 564–74.

TABLE 4. MEAN POLITICAL TRUST SCORE FOR GRADE LEVEL BY SCHOOL

| Grade | School | | | | | |
| | Rural | | Suburban | | Inner city | |
	Mean	N	Mean	N	Mean	N
Third	5.14	(57)	5.63	(55)	5.03	(28)
Fifth	4.55	(53)	5.01	(57)	3.83	(30)
Sixth	3.87	(58)	4.82	(50)	2.85	(34)
Total		(168)		(162)		(92)

or fifth graders. The sixth grade mean of 3.957 was significantly different from the third grade or fifth grade means, 5.314 and 4.588, respectively. This would indicate that third grade children view the system as being trustworthy and interested in them, but that older children view the system with more doubt.

Table 4 indicates that this occurrence was also common across all types of schools. Third graders, regardless of school, were similar in their political trust scores. Fifth graders also did not differ greatly, except for the suburban–inner-city comparison. The greatest differences appeared at the sixth grade level. Suburban sixth graders were very much like suburban fifth graders, but rural and inner-city sixth graders differed markedly from their respective fifth grades. This variation suggests that political trust decreases across grades but that the amount of the decrease may depend on factors in the socioeconomic environment.

What factors might contribute to the higher political trust among young children and suburban children? For young children, regardless of their socioeconomic environment, the political system may be viewed as benevolent and worthy of trust because: (1) they are sheltered from the "harsh" realities of politics by the family and the adult world; (2) they do not have a strong cognitive base for their feelings; (3) they feel overwhelmed by the power of the government and compensate this feeling by believing that the government is good; and (4) they have not had many experiences in the political world. As a result of these factors, young children may tend to rely on emotional or affective ties that may have little cognitive understanding behind them. Many of these feelings may simply be transferred from other experiences to the political realm.

Older children, on the other hand, may have a clearer cognitive understanding of politics and may have had more experiences with various political phenomena—authority figures, etc. As they begin to test earlier held beliefs against their increased understanding and experiences in the political world, they may find that there is either a consistency or inconsistency between these two views of the political world. As a consequence, change may or may not occur.

Factors in the socioeconomic environment may also be of crucial importance. Suburban children from upper-middle and upper-class families may be exposed to the political system through the activities of their parents and be raised in an environment that does not contradict many of the early positive attitudes. Because of this consistency their political trust attitudes remain relatively stable during the elementary years.[8]

For children from rural areas and the inner city the social matrix may not be conducive to maintaining the high level of political trust that they had as young children. Families tend to have lower incomes, lower educational attainment, and lower political interest. These children do not have the same opportunities as their suburban counterparts. It is also difficult for inner-city children to believe that the government cares about them because, as they look around, slum conditions appear to be the dominant feature. If the government cared, wouldn't something be done?

This lack of trust may also be heightened by contacts and experiences with representatives of the political system. Inner-city children's contact with the local police may lead to lower trust. The police may be viewed by many children as a repressive force whose presence is designed to keep control over them—feelings that may be justified by experience. The police, as well as other political figures, are "foreigners" to the inner-city environment. They come in for short periods of time and then leave; they are intruders and are symbols of white control. These and a multitude of other inner-city experiences work to lessen the trust of the child toward the system.

There are, of course, other important intervening factors such as peer groups, school experiences, and personality characteristics which cause changes or the lack of change in children's attitudes of trust. However, the above conclusions are given some support by the findings and suggest hypotheses for further study.

Political Efficacy

How do elementary children perceive their ability to influence the government? Similar to the earlier studies, it was found that feelings of efficacy increased as one moved upward in grade level. Table 5 presents the differences across grades and schools on the belief that one will be able to change things in the government when older.

Older children were more confident than were younger children that they, their families, and their neighbors could change things in the government. Sixty-seven percent of the sixth graders had positive feelings about being able to change the government, whereas only 30 percent of the third graders had similar feelings.

Some of the differences between grade levels may be due to cognitive development. The younger children may not have a reliable understanding of what the government is or they may see the government as too powerful to change. Older children, on the other hand, may be able to understand the meaning of government and thereby have a better concept of their relationship with it. Data collected during the interviews of the Michigan study give support to such a possibility.

Third graders either did not know what the word *government* meant

---

[8] For a discussion of various sociological factors in the socialization process, see John A. Clausen, "Perspectives on Childhood Socialization," in John A. Clausen, *Socialization and Society* (Boston: Little, Brown, 1968).

TABLE 5. WHEN I GROW UP, I WILL BE ABLE TO CHANGE
THINGS IN THE GOVERNMENT: RESPONSE BY GRADE AND SCHOOL
(IN PERCENTS)

GRADES

	Grade		
Response	Third	Fifth	Sixth
Yes	30	55	67
No	70	45	33
Total	100	100	100
N	(108)	(101)	(103)
NA	(32)	(40)	(38)
Total	(140)	(141)	(141)

Chi square=31.00
Significant beyond .01 level
Contingency coeff.=.301

SCHOOL

	School		
Response	Rural	Suburban	Inner city
Yes	51	51	47
No	49	49	53
Total	100	100	100
N	(121)	(119)	(72)
NA	(47)	(43)	(20)
Total	(168)	(162)	(92)

Chi square=.359
Significant below .10 level
Contingency coeff.=.161

or equated the president with government. Those who viewed the government as the president felt he had supreme power over people and his job entailed telling everyone what to do. With such an understanding, it would be difficult to feel a high degree of efficacy.

By the time they reached the sixth grade, however, most children felt the government was best represented by elected officials. Older children were more capable of understanding abstractions of governmental institutions and procedures. Voting, the president, and congressmen all were symbols of government. Sixth graders also knew how to influence government—they could vote.

Table 5 also indicates differences across schools. Suburban children and rural children were slightly more efficacious than inner-city children. The differences were not as great as one might expect, however. Inner-city children might be less efficacious for a number of reasons. First, they were less sophisticated in their understanding of what the government was. None of the third graders could define government and only two fifth graders responded. Most of the children in the sixth grade thought the government was represented by the president, but none mentioned Congress or elections.

They appeared to be behind the corresponding children in the suburban and rural schools.[9]

Second, inner-city children come from an environment that is not conducive to the building and maintaining of positive feelings of political efficacy. These children become aware early in life that they are from poor families in a nation of seemingly wealthy families who appear to have power and prestige. These attitudes are reinforced by experiences outside the immediate neighborhood and by exposure to the mass media.[10]

Third, the majority of inner-city children are from non-white, ethnic backgrounds. These children become aware that the "important" people in the political system are white, and to institute changes, these leaders must be dealt with. Time and experience lead inner-city children to the realization that influencing change is most difficult, if not impossible.

What can be concluded about attitudes of political efficacy among young children? From the findings discussed above and from those of earlier studies, it would appear that positive attitudes of political efficacy develop as children grow older. These feelings tend to appear toward the end of elementary school and are influenced by a variety of experiences and contacts with the political system. This may well be the case, but the reader must be cautious in reaching such conclusions. The concept of political efficacy is a highly complex one which may involve many different dimensions. The various questionnaire items used in the Michigan study, for example, did not form a unidimensional scale but broke into two or three scales. Other investigations suggest that for young children there may be an unclear line between overall patterns of personal efficacy and what social scientists call political efficacy.

Nonpolitical activities may also contribute to the development of feelings of efficacy. Almond and Verba suggest that perceived participation in classroom activities is related to efficacy,[11] and the Michigan study suggests that this might be true (see Table 6). The correlations indicate that positive feelings of classroom participation are related to a higher sense of political efficacy; however, these correlations are quite low and indicate a weak relationship. Other factors such as the content of what is discussed and the role of the teacher in providing an opportunity to take different positions on social issues might be of greater importance.

It may be best to conclude by suggesting that the reader be aware that political efficacy is not a simple concept. It is a highly complex one which includes many influential variables and one which needs much greater study and clarification.

Political Change

Children were asked how they would change things in the government if they were adults. Their responses, shown in Tables 7 and 8, overwhelm-

[9] Easton and Dennis, p. 423.

[10] Clausen, pp. 117–21.

[11] Gabriel Almond and Sidney Verba, *The Civic Culture* (Boston: Little, Brown, 1965), pp. 266–306.

TABLE 6. Pearson R Correlation Matrix: Participation-Political Efficacy

	Kids Free to Say What They Want	Help Decide Rules for Class	Talk In Class
People like me can change things in the government	.295[a]	.129[a]	.135[a]
Neighbors can change things in the government	.259[a]	.037	.163[a]
When I grow up I can change things in the government	.322[a]	.147[a]	.153[a]
The governmeut is like the weather—there's not much you can do about it	−.135[a]	−.030	−.044
Government is complicated— I can't understand it	−.016	−.034	.073

[a] Significant at .01 level

ingly endorsed voting and writing letters to either the president or congress-men. Suburban children thought letters directly to the president would be the best method of change. Voting, however, was important to 31 percent of the children. Rural and inner-city children followed a similar pattern. The major difference among the schools shown in Table 7 was the higher percentage of rural and inner-city children who fclt there would not be any-thing they could do. Twenty percent of the inner-city children believed in this manner, as contrasted with only 5 percent of the suburban children. This finding, as can be expected, is consistent with the pattern found for attitudes of political efficacy.

TABLE 7. The Best Way to Change Something in the Government: Response by School (in percents)

	School		
Response	Rural	Suburban	Inner city
Write a letter to the president	32	58	33
Take part in a demonstration or protest	7	11	8
Write a letter to your congressman	21	15	13
Vote in the next election	26	31	26
There would not be anything that you could do	14	5	20
Total	100	100	100
N	(168)	(162)	(92)
NA	(0)	(0)	(0)
Total	(168)	(162)	(92)

Chi square=17.383
Significant at .05 level
Contingency coeff.=.199

TABLE 8. BEST WAY TO CHANGE THINGS IN THE GOVERNMENT: RESPONSES BY GRADE LEVEL (IN PERCENTS)

	Grade		
Response	*Third*	*Fifth*	*Sixth*
Write a letter to the president	38	37	27
Take part in a demonstration or protest	6	9	11
Write a letter to your congressman	4	19	27
Vote in the next election	37	19	28
There would not be anything that you could do	15	14	7
Total	100	100	100
N	(140)	(141)	(141)
NA	(0)	(0)	(0)
Total	(140)	(141)	(141)

Chi Square=41.141
Contingency Coeff.=.299
Significant beyond .01 level

Only two slight differences occurred across grade levels. Third graders felt letters to the president and voting were best. Movement upward in the grades shifted the high concentration of responses in these two categories into a general dispersion across three different methods. By the sixth grade, the responses of children were about equally divided among letters to the president, to congressmen, and voting (see Table 8).

Twice as many third graders as sixth graders believed there was nothing they could do about changing the government. By the sixth grade only 17 percent of them felt powerless to bring about change. This pattern was consistent with earlier patterns of political efficacy.

Children were also asked about their acceptance of various "nontraditional" methods of change—such as demonstrations, protests, and riots. Their response was a rather emphatic "NO". Mean scores on the nontraditional change scale were quite low—the most favorable score equaled 5.00.

Table 9 presents the mean scores on the nontraditional change scale and the comparisons using Scheffe's formula.[12] No significant differences appeared across schools. Similar results were found across grade levels. The third grade mean of 1.22 was lower than the sixth grade mean of 1.43, but not significantly so (F-ratio=.94).

It can be seen that children, regardless of grade or school, rejected the nontraditional methods of change. Although many factors undoubtedly contributed to this, there is little available from the Michigan study to provide real insights into this phenomenon. However, some hypotheses might be offered.

Nontraditional methods of change may not be held up as models for children by the society and may in fact be presented in a very negative

[12] The F-ratio from the analysis of variance was 2.50. Not significant at the .10 level.

TABLE 9. COMPARISON OF SCHOOL MEANS ON NONTRADITIONAL CHANGE METHODS SCALE WITH CORRESPONDING F-RATIOS

School	N	Mean	Comparison	F-ratio
Rural	168	1.39	Rur—Sub	.58[a]
Suburban	162	1.47	Sub—IC	6.00[a]
Inner city	92	1.11	IC—Rur	1.00[a]

[a] Note significant at .10 level

manner. Children from the inner-city might also reject these methods because of the experiences they have had as a result of such activities. For example, all the inner-city children who were interviewed rejected demonstrations and riots as change mechanisms "cause people get hurt."

Teachers may also reinforce negative attitudes toward these methods. Third grade teachers in the Michigan study saw the social studies as helping children know about other people and socializing them into becoming good and loyal citizens who had respect for and obedience to authority. These teachers felt discussion about politics and political issues were not of utmost importance and that such discussion should wait until later.[13]

Sixth grade teachers on the other hand were more willing to discuss protests and demonstrations. Most felt that these topics were important because they are typical of the political world. Only one inner-city teacher said he would not discuss these topics. He felt they were too "risky" and that he would not last one day in the classroom.

Of the sixteen teachers who took part in the study it may be concluded that the third grade teachers viewed their position as one of helping children develop "correct" values and as apolitical. Sixth grade teachers were more willing to discuss politics. However, the reader must remember that there were only sixteen teachers and that this difference does not necessarily mean that sixth grade teachers did not attempt to develop obedience, respect, and "good" citizenship attitudes. The data merely suggest that sixth grade teachers were more open in their political discussions. No data were available to compare actual classroom behavior and these stated beliefs. Consequently, such findings may have little relationship to actual teacher behavior.[14]

We may conclude by noting that elementary school children favor the traditional methods of voting and writing as means of changing the government. Nontraditional methods were soundly rejected by all children in all schools. Why this strong rejection occurred is still open to investigation.

---

[13] Three indices were developed from the teacher data. They focused on student participation, delayed political discussion, and traditional citizenship values. For a discussion of these indices see: Glenn, "Elementary School Children's Attitudes of Political Trust, Political Efficacy, and Political Change" (Ph. D. dissertation, University of Michigan, 1970).

[14] Lee Ehman, "A Comparison of Three Sources of Classroom Data: Teachers, Students, and Systematic Observation" (A paper presented at the Annual Meeting of the American Educational Research Association, Minneapolis, Minn., March 4, 1970), pp. 8–9.

IMPORTANT QUESTIONS CONCERNING CHILDREN'S POLITICAL ATTITUDES

What can be concluded from this discussion of children's political attitudes? One is tempted to suggest that by the end of elementary school most political learning has taken place. It would seem that the political attitudes of trust, efficacy, and change have been developed at this stage and that any changes that might take place afterwards would be minor. Many of the early studies came to such a conclusion, and these studies lead to the belief in the primacy of the early years in the political socialization process. Since these early beginnings, additional research has suggested that such a conclusion must be considered with caution.

Other researchers in socialization do not agree that the politicization process is almost complete by the end of elementary school. Jennings and Niemi, for instance, suggest that the political learning curve may take a variety of shapes during an individual's life. They also note that attitudes such as political trust and cynicism assume irregular patterns across age groups and that major changes occur during elementary years and continue into adult life. They contend that the high school years are important transitional years to more stable adult political attitudes.[15]

Almond and Verba suggest that changes may occur after the elementary school years.[16] They conclude that despite the influence that early childhood learning may have upon political behavior, numerous other factors may intervene between early childhood and later political behavior. In fact, these other experiences may interact with family, school, and other experiences and may dampen heighten, or substitute for the effects of early socialization.

Recently some political socialization researchers have begun to question the data on young children. Questions can be raised as to whether researchers are actually investigating political attitudes or just generating random responses to various questions of a political nature. Pauline Vaillancourt analyzed the stability and reliability of elementary school children's responses to various questionnaire items and found that on many questions there was very low stability.[17] She found children to be more stable on fact items than on opinion and preference items, but older children were not a great deal more stable than younger children. Vaillancourt hypothesized that "non-attitudes" may be the cause of such low stability—children do not have political attitudes on the topics on which they are questioned but instead just give random responses.[18]

[15] M. Kent Jennings and Richard Niemi, "Patterns of Political Learning," *Harvard Education Review*, 27, No. 3 (Summer 1968), pp. 443–67; Kenneth Langton, *Political Socialization* (New York: Oxford University Press, 1969).

[16] Almond and Verba.

[17] Pauline M. Vaillancourt, "The Stability of Children's Political Orientations: A Panel Study" (Paper prepared for delivery at the Sixty-sixth Annual Meeting of the American Political Science Association, Los Angeles, Calif., September 8–12, 1970), pp. 7–10.

[18] Ibid.

These and other findings suggest that one must be very careful in generalizing about the political attitudes of young children. Research may be investigating embryonic attitudes which may or may not be of enduring quality. The questions raised by this problem also require that researchers take steps to insure that political attitudes are investigated. More studies of a longitudinal nature need to be done. Questionnaires need to incorporate means of checking children's response consistency. In-depth interviewing must be done to check on the findings from pencil-paper questionnaires. Also, better research designs and sampling techniques need to be employed to provide better controls and samples.

Political socialization research has gone through the first stage of development—educators and social scientists have gained a crude understanding of how children see the political world. What is needed is a more thorough and precise evaluation of these findings and the development of more sophisticated investigative techniques for the study of these attitudes. Until this is done we will not be able to fully understand the political world of children.

Sideline Citizens

5

THE POLITICAL EDUCATION
OF HIGH SCHOOL STUDENTS

Ellen Shantz

This study assumes that the purpose of citizenship education is to prepare students to confront problems and make decisions as citizens by helping each develop an ability for decision-making and critical thinking which can be used for clarifying attitudes and posing solutions to social problems.[1] Assessing a curriculum based on this approach means dealing with both affective attitudes associated with politicization and the cognitive skills related to inquiry and critical thinking. The questionnaire used in this study includes items related to three attitudinal variables—political interest, participation, and tolerance—and two cognitive skills—evaluation and grounding,[2] and discrimination between fact and opinion.

Although earlier studies have found few direct effects of the high school curriculum on politicization,[3] these studies used attitude change as the dependent variable. Perhaps this is not a sufficient measure of the effect of the curriculum; during adolescence already-formed attitudes are not likely to change, but the individual's grounding for his attitudes improves, along

---

[1] Shirley H. Engle, "Objectives of the Social Studies," *in* Byron G. Massialas and Frederick P. Smith, eds., *New Challenges in the Social Studies* (Belmont, Calif.: Wadsworth Publishing Co., Inc., 1965), p. 8.

[2] Defined in Benjamin Bloom, *Taxonomy of Educational Objectives: Cognitive Domain* (New York: McKay, 1961), p. 185. Evaluation is here defined as the making of judgments about the value, for some purpose, of materials, ideas, etc. Evaluation involves the use of criteria for appraising the extent of accuracy, effectiveness, etc., of the material.

[3] See, for example, Lee Ehman, "An Analysis of the Relationships of Selected Educational Variables with the Political Socialization of High School Students," *American Educational Research Journal*, 6, No. 4 (November 1969), pp. 559–79. Kenneth F. Langton and M. Kent Jennings, "Political Socialization and the High School Curriculum in the United States," *The American Political Science Review*, 62, No. 3 (September 1968), pp. 852–67. Edgar Litt, "Civic Education, Community Norms, and Political Indoctrination," *American Sociological Review*, 18 (1963), pp. 69–75.

with the ability to identify general principles and political values consistent with these attitudes. Perhaps the high school curriculum should concentrate on encouraging students to systematically examine their attitudes and values and to use cognitive skills to apply their political values to specific problems of society.

Some support for the legitimacy of this approach to the high school civics curriculum is found in Adelson and O'Neil's study of developmental trends among adolescents.[4] Evidence in social psychology also supports the idea that identification and measurement of affective attitudes and attitude change are not sufficient indicators of high school politicization, since attitude change is neither easily induced nor explained.[5]

It seems, then, that an intensive examination of the *nature* of students' attitudes might be a more valid approach to the relationship between the high school social studies curriculum and politicization. For example, on what ideological bases are attitudes grounded? Do elementary attitudes adopted unquestioningly undergo reflection and relation to general principles and values of the individual during adolescence?

Some hypotheses can be formulated which attempt to clarify existing evidence on adolescent politicization and to examine political attitudes in conjunction with student ability to use cognitive skills. Unfortunately most of these observations resulted from, rather than preceded, the questionnaire used. Hopefully later studies can further test indicators of attitude consistency, grounding, and the relation of attitudes to general principles. However, the data in this study yield some evidence which can be used to test these hypotheses:

Hypothesis 1: Students are becoming more oriented toward personal political participation than earlier studies show.

This can be predicted from two general factors. One is that activism is now sanctioned by the youth society, in contrast to the mood of the 1950s dominated by McCarthyism and the Red Scare. A second factor is anticipation of lowering the voting age to 18, giving high-school seniors political responsibility previously denied them.

This hypothesis could best be tested in a longitudinal study, with data reflecting students' orientations at the end of high school. From data in this study it is hypothesized that students will show positive attitudes on political participation questions, and will define "citizenship" in active rather than passive terms.

Hypothesis 2: Students will be positive in terms of affective attitudes related to politicization generally, but will be less positive in attitudes toward "politics" or political parties and participation through the party medium.

---

[4] Joseph Adelson and Robert O'Neil, "Growth of Political Ideas in Adolescence," *Journal of Personality and Social Psychology*, 4, No. 3 (September 1966), pp. 295–306.

[5] See, for example, William J. McGuire, "The Nature of Attitudes and Attitude Change," *in* Gardner Lindzey and Elliot Aronson, eds., *The Handbook of Social Psychology*, 3 (Reading, Mass.: Addison-Wesley, 1969).

Americans tend to regard politics and politicians as "dirty" and corrupt rather than as functional. Such a view seems to be supported by evidence showing a very low percentage of citizens who are party workers, a growing proportion of people who claim "independence" of party affiliation, and the frequently heard claim that "I vote for the man, not the party."

In spite of the fact that the party system dominates the American political system and electoral process at every level by primaries, nominating conventions, patronage, and platforms, a rather negative image persists. This may discourage active citizen participation by many who simply refuse to get involved with political parties. Contemporary political parties are rarely dealt with in the classroom, and parents explicitly and implicitly discourage such activity. Teachers themselves as a group are very inactive politically, and probably reinforce this kind of attitude.[6]

> *Hypothesis 3: Respondents in this sample will not consistently link specific examples to general ideological principles.*

Though juniors in high school, the only social studies exposure most have had is in history courses, where current political concepts and generalizations are not explicitly dealt with. Hence these students will not be aware of their consistent or inconsistent responses to questions dealing with a democratic principle. Two pairs of questions included in the section dealing with civic tolerance can be used to test this hypothesis.

> *Hypothesis 4: Students will generally perform poorly on questions dealing with cognitive skills of evaluation/grounding and fact/opinion discrimination.*

Confirmation of this hypothesis would not mean that these students have been poorly taught, but rather that they have not been explicitly or deliberately taught these cognitive skills. Such skills are not a part of traditional teaching methods, nor of most educational materials. If explicit teaching of such skills (for example, the inquiry method) is a predisposition for the ability to utilize the skills in confronting new problems and questions, then rather poor performance on this part of the questionnaire would be expected.

SAMPLE AND QUESTIONNAIRE

The data for this study were collected by using an anonymous questionnaire from 107 juniors in a suburban high school in the spring of 1970. The sample is not random, but purposive, consisting of all the students in

---

[6] Harmon Zeigler, *The Political World of the High School Teacher* (Eugene, Oregon: The Center for the Advanced Study of Educational Administration, University of Oregon, 1966), conclusions p. 156. Zeigler found teachers unpolitical especially in terms of the view of the classroom as a forum for expressing political opinions or discussing controversial issues. They often perceived such activity as improper behavior for a teacher (p. 116).

each of four intact classes, all taught by the same teacher. Since none of these classes was an ability group, and relevant demographic variables such as sex and income were randomly distributed in the sample, responses were assumed to be typical of all juniors in the school.

The questionnaire was deliberately kept short in an effort to get valid and conscientious answers from these students who, according to their teacher, had been "tested to death." One open-ended and 26 fixed-response questions were used to probe three affective attitudes regarded as goals of citizenship education: (1) to increase political interest; (2) to encourage positive attitudes toward political participation; and (3) to increase civic tolerance and acceptance of political pluralism; and two cognitive skills considered important objectives: (1) evaluation and grounding; and (2) ability to discriminate between statements of fact and opinion.

Findings

Political Interest

Table 1 shows the frequency distribution of scores on the questions designed to measure attitudes of political interest and on the summary political interest score obtained by adding scores on the individual items. It should be noted that respondents had a greater chance of falling into either the high or low categories than into the middle, so direct horizontal comparisons cannot be made.

TABLE 1. Percentage Distribution of Responses on Questions Related to Political Interest

	Interest Category			
Item*:	High	Occasional	Low	Total
Gross political interest score	51	10	39	100
I feel it is important for me to be familiar with the opinions and voting records of my senator and congressman?	67	31	2	100
How often would you say you follow what's going on in government and public affairs?	67	24	9	100
I plan to give active support to political parties and candidates who favor the same policies I do.	57	40	3	100
How frequently do you talk about public affairs and politics with your friends outside of class?	30	37	33	100
I express my own opinions about political issues and candidates to friends and acquaintances.	30	33	37	100
Not counting school assignments, how often do you read about public affairs and politics in newspapers or magazines?	21	28	51	100

For each item N=107
* Response items were appropriately worded.

The interesting observation in Table 1 is the variation in range of interest shown on each of the items. Generally students claim high political interest in terms of what they *should* do and know, but much less interest in terms of what they *do* now—discussing with friends or reading about politics and public affairs. This may be evidence of attitudes that have gone through the retention stage, but not the action stage, of attitude change.

It may also be evidence that adolescents are not highly politicized, that political questions and activities are simply not as important to them as are other interests. They seem to feel they *should* and *will* have high political interest as future citizens, but their present political interest actually is low. Then, expecting action as a result of political attitudes is an unrealistic and probably unattainable expectation, regardless of adult objectives. As Zigler and Child explain, "For most individuals adjustment to the basic demands of social living is a more pertinent issue than whether their lives resemble those of society's paragons."[7] And political demands may not be pertinent to adolescents.

Some literature on adolescence documents low politicization among high-school youth. James Coleman[8] found the peer group extremely important in setting norms for adolescents, but he did not find political issues or norms important to them. A study by Remmers and Radler[9] found that adolescents look to peers on adolescent issues—dress, leisure, and extracurricular participation—but to adults for their political opinions. Coleman suggests the use of peer influence for increasing attitudes of politicization by giving adolescents more responsibility in the school and community. This is being attempted in many schools now, and future observations of adolescent politicization will show its effect or lack of effect.

Table 2 examines the relationship between expressed interest and actual interest as indicated by actual knowledge, or the ability to name national senators and congressmen. Although many more said it was important to know the opinions and voting records of their representatives than could name those people, those who showed *high* interest were more able to

TABLE 2. ABILITY OF THOSE WITH HIGH POLITICAL INTEREST TO NAME SENATORS AND REPRESENTATIVES (IN PERCENTS)

Interest Item:	Number of Representatives Correctly Named:				
	0	1	2	3	Total
I follow what's going on in government	30	27	41	2	100 (N= 64)
It is important to be familiar with records of my national representatives	44	23	29	4	100 (N= 78)
Respondents with *high* gross political interest scores	29	23	45	3	100 (N= 56)
All respondents' gross political interest scores	47	24	27	2	100 (N=107)

[7] Edward Zigler and Irvin L. Child, "socialization," *in* Lindzey and Aronson, Vol. 3, p. 73.

[8] James S. Coleman, *The Adolescent Society* (New York: The Free Press, 1961).

[9] H. H. Remmers and D. H. Radler, *The American Teenager* (Indianapolis: Bobbs-Merrill, 1957).

name at least two of three representatives than were all respondents. Almost no one could list all three. Again these interest items may be 'future-oriented' to the student, so that he does not consider them important yet.

Political Participation

An open-ended question asking ". . . what things about a person are most important in showing that he is a good citizen?" was used to indicate how participation-oriented these students are—that is, how salient and important action or actual participation is to their conceptions of good citizenship. Responses to this question were categorized in a four-cell configuration which aimed to identify general orientations along two dimensions: participation/nonparticipation orientation, and societal/individual arena of responsibility.[10]

TABLE 3. PERCENTAGE RESPONSES TO OPEN-ENDED QUESTION CONCERNING VIEW OF CITIZENSHIP ROLE

		Orientation	
		Participatory	*Nonparticipatory*
Arena of Responsibility	individual	28	8
	societal	29	35

N=76
Nonrespondents and no opinion (not included in percentages)=31

Table 3 shows responses by these four categories. Although only 41 percent of the total sample were participation-oriented, nearly three-fifths of those responding fall into these two categories. It is not fair to assume the nonrespondents are nonparticipation-oriented, since they may not have been motivated to respond to an open-ended question or they may not have had opinions. The largest number of responses occurred in the nonparticipant/

[10] Examples of responses falling into each category are:
  (1) participatory orientation, individual responsibility:
      (a) votes
      (b) makes his opinions known
      (c) helps other people
  (2) participatory orientation, societal responsibility:
      (a) be active in community affairs
      (b) work to change laws you disagree with
      (c) support the country, whether by fighting in wars or defending principles by civil disobedience
      (d) become involved, or be active peacefully
      (e) care enough to protest when you disagree
  (3) nonparticipatory orientation, individual responsibility:
      (a) don't interfere with others
      (b) be independent
  (4) nonparticipatory orientation, societal responsibility:
      (a) keeps informed
      (b) obeys laws, obedience

societal category, consisting mainly of those who say being a good citizen means obeying the laws. A large number of students in the sample indicate that citizenship means *only* obedience. This seems a very passive conception of the citizenship role.

Table 4 shows the distribution of responses to the other three participation questions. The results here were interesting. Very few of these adolescents are interested in running for office themselves, and over half have a negative attitude on this issue; but they are more willing to take an active role in political parties. A surprising three-fifths of the students say they would take part in a protest or demonstration.

TABLE 4. PERCENTAGE DISTRIBUTION OF RESPONSES ON THREE QUESTIONS
RELATED TO POLITICAL PARTICIPATION

	Attitude Toward Political Participation[a]				
Participation Item:	*Positive*	*No opinion*	*Negative*	*No response*	*Total*
I would take part in a protest or demonstration that supported an issue I believe in.	60	25	14	1	100
I think I would make a useful contribution to good government by an active role in a political party.	36	36	27	1	100
I would like to run for political office at some level in a few years.	7	40	52	1	100

For each item N=107
[a] Positive=strongly agree or agree
Negative=strongly disagree or disagree

Hypothesis 1, which related to attitudes of political participation, states that

Students are becoming more oriented toward personal political participation than earlier studies show.

Data from this study do not permit comparison with earlier research, so the hypothesis cannot really be tested. Though students indicate generally positive attitudes toward participation of citizens, they do not yet take an active role politically, even in discussions and reading about public affairs. They indicate very low willingness to run for office themselves, but plan to work actively to support other candidates with whom they agree. Responses to the open-ended participation question show that 60 percent are participation-oriented, but even the mention of voting was coded as an active response, and very few responses mentioned political activism, community activity, or working at citizenship.

In summary, it seems these students have positive attitudes toward participation, but they do not conceive of themselves as the decision makers or political leaders. Rather they seem to see their own role as that of concerned private citizen.

Political Pluralism

Table 5 gives the general distribution of responses on the questions related to acceptance of political pluralism. These political pluralism questions have been grouped into three pairs of items relating to three different aspects of pluralism and tolerance. The first two questions probe attitudes about tolerance as it relates to freedom of speech; the middle pair, about tolerance as it relates to the electoral process; and the last pair of questions, the art of politics and the political process as a legitimate vehicle for reaching decisions in a pluralistic environment—or making pluralism work.

Table 5 shows that students are quite willing to allow freedom of speech, and aggregate responses for these two questions are nearly identical. A later table (Table 6) shows, however, that individual responses to these two questions are not consistent.

TABLE 5. PERCENTAGE DISTRIBUTION OF RESPONSES ON QUESTIONS RELATED
TO POLITICAL PLURALISM

	Acceptance of Pluralism				
Pluralism Item:	High	Un-certain	Low	No response	Total
A person should be allowed to speak against religion in this community.	81	8	10	1	100
A person should be allowed to speak against foreign policy in this community.	81	9	9	1	100
A legally elected Communist should be allowed to take office.	27	23	47	3	100
Any legally elected official should be allowed to take office.	67	25	4	4	100
Polities is a way of reaching temporary agreement within agreed-upon rules.	47	40	9	4	100
Politics is a method of bargaining among competing groups.	54	36	8	2	100

For each item N=107

Nearly half the students disagree or strongly disagree that a legally elected Communist should take office, although two-thirds boldly state that anyone legally elected, no matter what his political viewpoint, should be permitted to take office. It seems that these students either do not recognize the principle involved and are therefore unaware of their inconsistency; or they are aware, but permit the inconsistency to exist—a condition termed very unstable according to psychological theories of dissonance and balance.

The second hypothesis predicts that:

Students will be positive in terms of affective attitudes related to politicization generally, but will be less positive in their attitudes toward politics or political parties, and toward participation through the party medium.

Relevant data from this questionnaire suggest that students do not have negative attitudes toward politics or political parties, and that these attitudes are, in fact, generally positive; but that they do not see themselves as assuming "political" roles, or as actively participating as politicos themselves. Responses reported in Table 4 suggest that they are considerably more positive toward participating in a protest or demonstration than in working through political parties.

Further evidence for this hypothesis can be found in the open-ended questions on citizenship. Here *not one* student mentioned political parties or running for political office. At the very least we can say electoral political activity has low salience for these youths, if not a negative connotation. Only 7 percent showed a positive attitude toward running for office themselves, whereas over half indicated negativism on this question. Though they indicate high interest and generally high participation, politics is not seen as the vehicle by which they will be active citizens.

Hypothesis 3 can also be tested using data from questions on political pluralism. The hypothesis states:

> *Respondents in this sample will not specifically link specific examples to general ideological principles.*

This hypothesis can be tested by comparing individual responses for consistency on two pairs of questions. Testing for such variables as consistency may be regarded as a beginning effort to measure new dimensions of the nature of political attitudes. It is believed that with increased ability to utilize and apply cognitive skills would come increased consistency of attitudes, and the resolution of inconsistencies by the individual.

Consistency was defined here as qualitatively similar responses to two questions. That is, responses to two items were judged inconsistent if they were not in the same response category.

	Agreement	Strongly agree / agree
Categories:	Neutrality	Neither agree nor disagree
	Disagreement	Strongly disagree / disagree

(Responses)

Measurement of consistency/inconsistency in response was based on the first two pairs of questions related to the concept of political pluralism. Each of these pairs involves a principle fundamental to our conception of democracy —namely, freedom of speech and elective government—but each question in the pair poses a different situation in which the principle can be applied.

Therefore, if a respondent recognizes the principle involved, and what personal value is relevant to that issue, he should respond to the two questions identically, whatever his position on the scale of responses. Consistency of response is then considered an indicator of internalization of a principle and the ability to link specific examples to the principle involved. The questions which were used here are:

Question: *Principle:*

If a person wanted to make a speech in this community
against religion, he should be allowed to speak.   Freedom

If a person wanted to make a speech in this community   of
attacking U.S. foreign policy, he should be allowed to do so.   Speech

If a Communist were *legally* elected to some public office
around here, the people should allow him to take office.
                                                                            Elective
If a person, no matter what his political viewpoint, were   Process
legally elected to some public office around here, the people
should allow him to take office.

Data from the two pairs of questions are shown in Table 6. Based on these
findings this hypothesis is confirmed, since there is considerable inconsistency on both items, especially the second. Since the questions in each pair
were very similarly worded, and all appeared on the same page of the questionnaire, it seems the principle should have been obvious. This was certainly no devious or subtle attempt to identify attitudes.

TABLE 6. PERCENT CONSISTENT/INCONSISTENT RESPONSES ON QUESTIONS
INVOLVING TWO PRINCIPLES

	Nature of Response			
Principle Involved	Con-sistent	Incon-sistent	No response	Total
Freedom of speech	76	22	2	100
Elective process	45	50	5	100

N=107

Cognitive Skills

There were three questions testing student ability to evaluate generalizations and ground them in terms of evidence. Two of the four response
choices were considered "correct" in each case. The format of each question
was identical, as in the example given here:

"The Chamber of Commerce is the most powerful interest group in the
suburban community of Sunnyhill."

Which of the following statements could be used as a basis to support
this generalization?

a. In the past five years the Chamber has endorsed ten propositions in
   city elections, and eight have been passed by the voters. It has opposed
   eight propositions, and all have failed to pass.
b. Public records show that the Chamber was the largest single con-
   tributor in a recent income tax referendum campaign.
c. Three of ten city council members are also members of the Chamber
   of Commerce.
d. The editor of the only local newspaper consistently agrees with Chamber of Commerce positions.

Table 7 shows that very few students answered any of the questions in the best possible way—that is, by responding to both of the correct choices and to none of the incorrect choices—but many were apparently able to discriminate between legitimate and nonlegitimate choices to the extent that they did not mark any incorrect responses. However, for several reasons any conclusions drawn here are questionable. For instance, it is unknown how many students guessed, or how many thought there was only one correct response. Probably the best way to validly test the growth of this ability would be a longitudinal survey of students at two points in time.

TABLE 7. EVALUATION AND GROUNDING: PERCENTAGE DISTRIBUTION OF RESPONSES TO EACH OF THREE QUESTIONS

	Response					
Question	2 correct choices	1 correct choice	Mixed choices	Only incorrect choices	No response	Total
1. Voting study	4	61	5	21	9	100
2. Legislature in state Y	3	33	7	38	19	100
3. Chamber of commerce	1	48	11	19	21	100

For each item N=107

The other cognitive skill tested was the ability to discriminate between fact and opinion statements. Four of the five items contain words which are clearly value-laden and were considered opinionated statements, whereas one was considered fact. Table 8 shows the responses for each item.

TABLE 8. FACT/OPINION DISCRIMINATION: PERCENTAGE DISTRIBUTION OF RESPONSES TO EACH OF THE QUESTIONS[a]

	Response			
Item	Correct	Incorrect	No response	Total
The participation of the federal government in local affairs leads to undesirable federal controls. (op. or mostly op.)	52	44	4	100
The American form of government may not be perfect, but it's the best type of government yet devised by man. (op. or mostly op.)	46	50	4	100
The United States ought to expend more federal funds on domestic problems rather than spending so much on foreign commitments. (op.)	23	73	4	100
Underdeveloped nations of the world should attempt to enter the industrial age. (opinion)	27	69	4	100
All living things reproduce. (fact)	57	36	7	100

For each item N=107
[a] Responses given in parentheses are those which were judged 'correct'.

The fourth hypothesis was generally confirmed from these data:

Students will generally perform poorly on questions dealing with the cognitive skills of evaluation/grounding and fact/opinion discrimination.

Although no attempt was made to set any "standard" or criterion for what would be good as opposed to poor performance, these tables seem to indicate general inability to utilize the skills being tested.

SUMMARY

As other researchers have found, these students also expressed generally positive attitudes on variables associated with politicization, though commitment seems to consistently decrease as questions move from expression of feeling to admission of action. Simply put, they believe in being interested, but this apparently does not mean being active themselves.

There is some indication that these students do not yet see themselves as having responsibility as citizens or a part in the political system—that this is a role somehow reserved for adulthood. For example, one student commented on the questionnaire that he does "not have any Senator or Representative," and neither did he volunteer names of any national representatives from his district. These students have drawn for themselves what seems a very arbitrary and artificial distinction: that citizenship status as either the right or the obligation to participate politically comes only with enfranchisement or reaching the age of twenty-one. Do we mean to instill this feeling in teenagers? If not, what can schools and teachers do to make adolescents feel and act upon responsibilities as citizens?

Even the students' conception of what is important about being a citizen is rather passive. Although responses to political participation questions show the majority of these students to be participation-oriented in the sense of being concerned, making their opinions known, or even participating in a demonstration, they are negatively-oriented toward running for office themselves and do not see themselves as the citizens who actually make decisions on social policies and problems. They are more likely to see the citizenship role as one of obeying laws, which presumably have been made by others.

Attitudes relating to acceptance of political pluralism are generally positive, but the validity of these data is open to some question. Considerable amounts of individual inconsistency were found in the data concerning general principles, and the questions dealing with politics as a vehicle may be invalid. The conception of "politics" as a vehicle for maintaining and operating a pluralistic society is a difficult concept to comprehend and appreciate, and the large percentage of respondents who were uncertain about their opinions on these two questions makes it unclear to what extent students actually understand and value this idea. This view of politics is seldom dealt with in the classroom, although it seems important to politicization. More in-depth questioning of such ideas and their place in the individual's cognitive structure is needed.

Though student ability to use cognitive skills of evaluation/grounding and fact/opinion discrimination were generally low, this instrument is inadequate to draw any conclusions about the relationship of such abilities to student attitudes and to the process of politicization. A longitudinal study is probably necessary, providing evidence about change in an individual's ability as a result of a curriculum which includes such skills among its course objectives, as well as insight into the relationship between such skills and affective attitudes.

Though political attitude measurement alone is helpful, such attitude identification may not be the most important aspect of adolescent political socialization. Perhaps during these years the crucial changes or developments are the emergence of ideology, increasing ability to generalize, the grounding of opinions and values, and the acquisition of decision-making skills. If so, then political attitudes must be examined in terms of their consistency, their rational and emotional bases, and their priority within the individual's value system. In this study checks for consistency were made for two variables, revealing a significant amount of individual inconsistency. Future study should include more sophisticated ways of examining political attitudes. It also seems crucial to measure cognitive skills in studies assessing the impact of the school curriculum.

Only the simplest analysis has been utilized in these data, but some interesting findings have been observed and noted, leading to tentative conclusions and future hypotheses. It is hoped this study will lead to a more helpful, thorough, and valid study of high school students' attitudes and skills relating to citizenship in their society.

Black Activists
and
the Schools

6

Charles E. Billings

We live today in a system that is in the last stages of the protracted process of breaking up on a world-wide basis.

How many black students now attending high schools throughout this country would agree with this statement? How many of them have heard of the man who penned it? How many black youngsters, in fact, are working actively to hasten the "break-up?" These questions are important not only because they make interesting, "meaty" research problems but also because the answers are prerequisites to an understanding of today's black, high-school student whose agony threatens to engulf the educational community in never-ending crisis. Although in recent months the focus of the news media's attention has been on the nation's colleges and their struggle with the rising tide of student activism, it should not be forgotten that the country's high schools have been and are now in a state of ferment. When police officers and state militia men appear on college campuses it is a signal for massive protest. Letters, petitions, massive marches, letters to congressmen and candlelight vigils are part of the outpouring of emotion that can be summed up in short phrases—"Restore the academic community," "Welcome the police state," "Pigs off campus." But today in cities all over the country policemen are as much a fixture in high schools as are crossing guards in grade schools! Policemen protect the halls, guard the doorways, and patrol the grounds. Yet educators know that force—armed force in the public schools—creates as many problems as militia men on college campuses. The presence of armed force is merely a symptom of more deep-seated problems. It is a sign that the school has all but depleted that reservoir of diffuse administrative support upon which schools, like all compliance-oriented institutions, depend for their persistence. The use of such force should be a signal to parents, educators, and community leaders to step up efforts to communicate with young people and to jointly and cooperatively seek solutions to the problems attendant to urban adolescent education.

The first and most important step, of course, is to increase our understanding of those students who are raising questions about our society and the quality of life they anticipate after their schooling is completed. These students are asking questions and raising issues that have significance for us all. It is unfortunate that they are often regarded simply as troublemakers whose only objective is to disrupt and to confuse. In fact they are not usually found among that growing phalanx of belligerent "quasi-students" who haunt the doorways and roam the halls of urban high schools.

Toward this understanding I propose to investigate the following three questions:

1. How congruent are the concepts of black, high-school student activism to the concepts of black nationalism?
2. How congruent are the concepts of black, high-school activism to the concepts of radical political philosophy?
3. Do black activists have a different view of self from non-activists?

The data I will use to investigate these three questions were collected from a group of black, high-school students, some of whom belonged to organized high-school civil rights groups and some of whom did not. On the basis of their membership in these groups the students were tentatively separated into activists and non-activists. A number of measures were applied to determine whether the hypothesized relationship between membership in a group and some set of "militant" attitudes and behaviors would hold. The main purpose of the overall study was to *describe* the black activists' political attitudes and behaviors. The non-activists were used as a comparison group to insure that the description so devised would be specific to activists. All of the students in the study were black, all were from northern integrated high schools. All data reported here were generated from student responses on a paper and pencil questionnaire.

High-School Activism and Black Nationalism

How congruent are the concepts of black, high-school activism to the concepts of black nationalism?

Several items in the questionnaire were aimed at assessing the extent of agreement of activist students with the concepts of black nationalism. Toward this end the activists' responses to a series of statements made by spokesmen for the black nationalist position were compared with the responses of their non-activist peers. The writers' statements were arranged in the order of their militancy, and the students were not supplied with the names of the persons quoted. The following quotations were used to ascertain the strength of the two groups' militancy.

At the level of individuals, violence is a cleansing force. It frees the person from his inferiority complex and restores his self-respect (Fanon, 1963, p. 121).

We live today in a system that is in the last stages of the protracted process of breaking up on a worldwide basis (Cleaver, 1968, p. 68).

A struggle which mobilized all classes of people and which expresses their aims and their impatience, will of necessity triumph (Fanon, 1963, p. 100).

The groups were compared on these three items, and the activists were found to agree with the statements to a greater degree than did the non-activists. Table 1 displays the percentages of agreement for both groups.

TABLE 1. PERCENTAGE OF STUDENTS WHO AGREE WITH THE POSITION OF BLACK NATIONALIST SPOKESMEN

	Activists	*Non-Activists*
Violence valuable	47.8[a]	37.3
System breaking up	65.2	54.6
Popular revolution	54.4	50.0
N	(46)	(187)

[a] Only those students who reported agreement or strong agreement are included in the table.

It should be noted that the acts regarded as most militant are those acts involving violence. I might add that the least militant activities are those that are less violent or that would be expected to occur outside the boundaries of the student's immediate experience. The statements therefore are arranged in order of militancy, starting with the first statement as the most militant.

The activists are clearly inclined to agree with the more militant statements of these writers. Only on the last item, which is regarded as the least militant, do the non-activists approach the same level of agreement. The students in both groups, however, show a strong tendency to adhere to the black nationalist "line;" the difference between them is a matter of the strength of that agreement.

The question posed above refers to the concepts involved in black nationalism, and the statements quoted illustrate three of the principal concepts involved in that movement: the acceptance of violence as a viable political tool, the belief in popular revolution, and the feeling that the present political system is corrupt and in the process of passing out of existence. The data suggest that many activist and non-activist high-school students adhere to these concepts, with the students who belong to militant groups expressing a stronger adherence than those who do not belong to such groups.

What are we to make of this finding? Let us examine it more closely. First, it is a rather disquieting situation in which we find ourselves. Although I have focused our discussion so far upon the students whose overt acts clearly place them in the activist camp, at this point we cannot escape the conclusion that a fair number of *all* the black students involved in this study support the three revolutionary notions examined here.

Is it not remarkable that one-half of the students who have not elected to join the activist camp agree with one of the basic tenets of popular revolution? Of course we must remember that there exists the possibility that some students either did not understand or misinterpreted Fanon's meaning. We must remind ourselves too that this particular statement could be read only as guaranteeing that "right" will always triumph. Perhaps some students heard in the statement echoes of the Declaration of Independence. Or they may have recalled an American History teacher who impressed upon them the right of any oppressed people to reconstitute their government. Even though the principle is honored more in the breach than in the observance, our founding fathers did state that it is not only the right but the *duty* of free people to overthrow oppressive governments. Perhaps it is not as surprising as it may first appear that black youngsters both "militant" and "conservative" would hold to the view that popular revolution, popularly supported by all classes, "will of necessity triumph."

It is not so easy to reconcile the student's endorsement of the notion that the American "system" is in the process of dissolution. Here we can look to no support from the traditional social studies curriculum. I doubt seriously that many of the teachers in these schools are predicting the downfall of white-western civilization. It is perhaps possible that other agencies of politicalization, however, are doing just that. Students may get a very dim view of the health of the system from the communication media. Vietnam, from which we seem incapable of extricating ourselves; the Middle East into which we are drawn to flail about in frustration; and the domestic scene, a study in violence, confrontation, and anomie, all can give to the students an unobstructed view of the abyss that yawns before us. The disturbing factor is that these students, and we speak here of over one-half of the *non-activist* group, do not believe that we can do other than plunge headlong into the pit. They do not believe, as do many adults, that we simply face another series of crises from which we will emerge as a nation stronger and more vibrant than ever. These students have begun to lose faith not only in the American dream but in America itself!

It becomes clearer then that that which separates the activist from his non-activist peer is his sense of involvement in the process of system dissolution alluded to by Cleaver. Almost half of the activists, as opposed to about one-third of the non-activists, seem prepared to help the process of disintegration on its way. Of course it must be recalled that a reliance on violence to solve domestic and foreign disputes has a good deal of historical precedence in the United States. It should not be surprising, therefore, to find black, high-school students advocating the use of violence and embracing its psychologically therapeutic value.

It is small wonder that students develop an early appreciation for the obsequiousness of warfare in human history—smaller wonder still that they do not consider diplomacy as a serious rival to armed conflict in the arena of foreign affairs. Only recently have high-school students been exposed to more than a cursory examination of America's diplomatic history. However the practice has not yet replaced the traditional recitation of our country's prefunctory efforts in the diplomacy "game." Many high-school students are still only made cognizant of the Monroe Doctrine, Roosevelt's "Battleship Diplomacy," and Wilson's Fourteen Points, all of which could be cast as either outright failures or as examples of a growing power's naive and chauvinistic attempts at world peacekeeping.

The point of all this is simple: black youngsters, whether we classify them as militant or non-militant, are predisposed to regard the American political system as anti-black because of their own life experiences and those of their people. Furthermore, their suspicion that the system is somewhat less viable than one may at first believe is bolstered by "facts" gathered from the classroom and from the communication media and interpreted in the light of their growing black consciousness. Finally, many of them are persuaded that a violent approach is tenable because of the exaltation of the efficacy of violence by those same sources. One further point needs to be made in answer to those who would characterize the activist students' tendency to accept violence as a viable and efficacious means to achieve their liberation. Many of these students believe that whites must be *forced* to make changes in the society for the benefit of black people. We will have occasion to return to this attitude later in this chapter, but let me state here that it seems that a good proportion of the students have come to the advocacy of violence because they have witnessed the "failure" of non-violent means employed in the liberation struggle. It is significant in this regard that among the non-activists in the sample almost as many felt that changes would come through persuasion as through force, whereas among the activists fewer than one in ten felt that whites could be persuaded to "take a better attitude toward Negroes." I suspect that the events of the recent past have further reduced the number of black students who regard persuasion as a more effective means than force for the liberation of blacks.

THE BLACK ACTIVIST AS A RADICAL PHILOSOPHER

How congruent are the concepts of black, high-school activism to the concepts of radical political philosophy?

This question raises some of the same issues as the question that preceded it. We move now, however, from the area of black nationalist thought to the area of radical political philosophy. If black activists embrace the concepts of radical politics, then they should be less inclined to participate in traditional political activity and more inclined to express their political ideas in other ways. They should, in a sense, eschew the old order and "take the struggle to the streets."

It was the opinion that some difficulty was to be expected in translating the responses of black students to questions designed to test the political attitudes of white people. For this reason the investigatory instrument was augmented by questions designed to test the attitudes of the subjects along dimensions more closely related to the concerns of black people. No attempt was made to test the generalizability of these items to more than the present sample of black students. Let me at this point digress from my present discussion, lest I be guilty of moving too quickly over an area of extreme importance to any social scientist doing research among blacks. I wish to call attention particularly to those studies dealing with attitudes allegedly formulated by an interplay of psychological and environmental factors.

A case in point is the studies in political socialization that predicate the action of the family as a determining factor in the politicization process. One must ask in dealing with black children, "what are my assumptions concerning the family?" Or more simply put, what is the operational definition for the variable, "family," that I have chosen to use? If I have relied upon psychological theory to interpret the data in the light of certain family configurations (nuclear as opposed to non-nuclear, for example) have I assured myself that the theory is useful when applied to the special case of black families?

Today black scholars are concentrating their efforts on the formulation of a theory that will be more useful in the interpretation of the process of attitude formation among black Americans. While this work is going on, and until we begin to test the first fruits of their efforts, we must, as social scientists, view with extreme caution the instruments and data on black attitudes so far collected.

To illustrate, a man who harbors an *irrational* fear that everyone from the corner policeman to the president is attempting to harm him or prevent him from receiving his "just due" can quite properly be called a victim of paranoia. It follows that if those fears are justified—that is, if they are simply attitudes resulting from an objective examination of one's true status—one cannot properly be called paranoid. Too often it seems both men are "whitewashed with the same mop." The attempt to rectify this situation in the present study resulted in the formulation of three additional constructs or dimensions along which certain attitudes might cluster. The underlying dimensions involved include the following: *orientation toward revolution, sense of situational political efficacy*, and *confrontational political participation*.

Orientation toward revolution is defined as the student's willingness to subscribe to revolutionary solutions for racial problems. It includes the feeling that movements will triumph when they express the aims and impatience of all classes of people and that violence has a positive effect on the self-concept of the individual.

The difficulty with the traditional definition of political efficacy has been called to the attention of the reader. I have chosen to use the phrase, "sense of situational political efficacy" to describe the feeling among activists that they have an impact upon politics and political decisions in situations peculiar to black concerns. This new variable is defined as the feeling on the part of black students that they can, by collective action, make changes in their condition within a circumscribed area of the political realm. This definition also contains the component of collective, as opposed to individual, efficacy. I am groping here for a definition of the sense of political efficacy commensurate with the view of the black child as one who is aware that his political power in a democracy is limited because of his minority status yet realizes that under certain conditions and in certain situations his power is considerable. Perhaps we can accept the definition put forward here as a working definition in need of much refinement and hope that further reflection will lead to a more satisfactory configuration.

I defined confrontational political participation as a set of activities engaged in by students principally characterized by a crisis-negotiation-resolution pattern. Students so engaged would be presenting demands, negotiating with representatives of the educational hierarchy, and reaching some resolution of the conflict.

The extent to which the students actually participated in these activities in their own schools was taken as a measure of the strength of this variable. Table 2 compares the two groups of students on the dimension of confrontational political participation.

The table shows that activists engage in intra-school confrontational political activities much more than do non-activists. The information reported is from a series of questions asking whether the students had discussed with their principal the issues listed. The table should be read as showing that 54 percent of the activists, as opposed to 18 percent of the non-activists, had discussed problems of student unrest with their principal; 59 percent of the activists, as opposed to 28 percent of the non-activists, had complained to the principal about some aspect of school policy, etc.

TABLE 2. Confrontational Political Participation by Activist–Non-Activist (in percents)

	Activists			Non-Activists		
	Yes	*No*	*N.R.*	*Yes*	*No*	*N.R.*
Complaint with school policy	58.7	32.6	8.7	28.2	65.4	6.4
Student unrest	54.3	34.8	10.9	18.2	75.4	6.4
Student demands	45.7	43.5	10.9	22.7	70.9	6.4
Rules infraction	41.3	45.7	13.0	28.2	65.4	6.4
		(N=46)			(N=187)	

The last row in the table reveals that activists are involved in rules infractions more often than are non-activists. It follows from the kinds of confrontations that are listed here that the activists are also the students who are willing to run afoul of the rules of the school to accomplish their goals. The fact that almost 30 percent of the non-activists have also been involved in scholastic violations can be taken as a measure of the normal frequency of rules conflicts among the black, high-school students under investigation.

In the language of political behavior, the finding is that extra-legal political activities (activities that involve possible rule infractions) attract the activist students to a greater degree than the non-activists. In addition, the activists are more inclined to ignore the traditional channels of student government and take their complaints directly to the principal.

The analysis suggested here does not, of course, negate the possibility that the activists make use of both traditional and radical political structures. It is entirely feasible that the black students involved are eclectic in their political orientations. The thrust of the data, however, is that the activists are likely to view a strict adherence to the rules of democratic conduct as less effective than more radical activities. Looking next at the extent to which activists differ from non-activists in their orientation toward revolution, and recalling that the dimension also contains the feeling that violence has a positive effect upon one's self-concept, it is found that activists have a higher level of agreement than do the non-activists on the questions designed to test this factor of their political attitude.

An item in the questionnaire designed to reveal one of the dimensions involved in the students' orientation toward revolution measured the students' perception of the relative value of force versus persuasion in changing the attitudes of whites toward black problems. In this item, the students revealed their willingness to accept forceful, possibly violent, solutions, as opposed to their faith in less militant schemes. The question to which the students responded was the following:

> In the end, do you think white people will take a better attitude toward Negroes mainly because they will be forced by Negro action, or mainly because they can be persuaded that this is the only right thing to do?

Whereas the non-activists divided almost equally between those who believed that persuasion would bring about change and those who believed that "action" would be necessary, only 7 percent of the activists felt that whites could be persuaded to take a better attitude toward Afro-Americans. The majority of the activists felt that whites would have to be forced into changing things.

Although the students were not asked to characterize the kind of force they had in mind, an indication of their thinking is revealed by their responses to the following question: "Many names have been suggested for the recent violence in the ghettoes of America. Which of the following terms do you regard as most accurate?" There followed a list of five terms from which the student was to choose only one. The terms from which the students were to choose were: civil disorders, riots, race riots, insurrections, and revolts. It was anticipated that the activists would choose the most militant terms (revolts and insurrections) while the non-activists would prefer the less revolutionary terminology. The prediction was accurate. Forty-eight percent of the activists chose "revolts," whereas only 19 percent of the non-activists chose that term. At the other end of the spectrum 26 percent of the non-activists chose to characterize the ghetto violence as "civil disorders," as contrasted with 15 percent of the activists who did so. The activists, then, regard ghetto violence as essentially revolutionary in character, and as indicated by the data, do not rule out the use of force to change repressive white behaviors.

The activist students reveal a strong faith in the ability of blacks to solve this country's racial problems by their own actions. Both groups of students share the legacy of group efficacy left by the civil rights movement of the 50s. They too feel that the racial conflict now occurring can be resolved through collective action. The two groups differ, however, in the *degree* to which they trust integrationist schemes. The four items used to test this sense of group efficacy are as follow:

1. Some Afro-Americans believe that white people want to get rid of all the blacks in the country. If you, too, feel that whites want to rid themselves of blacks, how soon do you think this might occur?

   1 year—within 5 years—within 10 years—in the far future—never.

2. The concept of racial integration is based upon the belief that all men are equal. Some people doubt that all people are equal. How do you feel about this?

   _____ *Given the chance, black people can be superior to whites.*
   _____ *Given the chance, black people can be equal to whites.*
   _____ *White people are basically superior to blacks.*
   _____ *Black people are basically superior to whites.*
   _____ *All men are equal.*

3. Black people themselves can help most to solve racial problems.

   _____ *Agree*   _____ *Disagree*

4. Black people and liberal whites can help most to solve racial problems.

   _____ *Agree*   _____ *Disagree*

Unlike the traditional measures of political efficacy, the students are not being asked about their personal feelings of political power but about the chances of their group to make basic changes in their situation. The students who responded that black eradication would never come, that black people were basically superior to whites, and that black people themselves could help most to solve racial problems were regarded as having the most faith in collective black action.

For the purpose of comparing the two groups, the items were dichotomized, and the percentages of activists and non-activists who fell into the high and low ends of the dimension for each item were computed. The results of this process are shown in Table 3.

TABLE 3. GROUP EFFICACY FOR ACTIVISTS AND NON-ACTIVISTS (IN PERCENTS)

	Activists			Non-Activists		
	High	*Low*	*N.R.*	*High*	*Low*	*N.R.*
Black eradication	76.1	13.1	10.7	70.0	11.0	13.6
Racial integration	43.4	48.0	8.7	24.0	69.0	8.2
Black people alone	67.4	32.6	0.0	50.0	43.6	6.4
Black people and white	32.6	2.2	65.2	34.5	59.1	6.4
		(N=46)			(N=187)	

It is apparent from the table that the activists have much more faith in the ability of the race to change things than do the non-activists. The skewness of the distribution of percentages is consistent with the orientation of the activists throughout the table. More activists believe that blacks will never be eradicated than do non-activists. Many more activists than non-activists characterize blacks as superior or capable of achieving superiority over whites than do non-activists. Finally, the activists place more faith in the ability of black people to solve their own problems without the help of white people than do the non-activists. Again the dimension should be seen as specifically related to the situation of blacks in America; it is not intended to be indicative of the level of general political efficacy among the respondents.

The students were also asked whether they favored or opposed the position taken in the following statement: "Some black people have proposed that whites and blacks will never live together, so the only solution is to set up a separate Negro state or states in this country or in Africa." Table 4 shows that although more activists favored the statement, the difference between the two groups is small and, more importantly, more activists than non-activists chose to take no position on this item. One can only speculate as to the position held by the persons falling in the "no response" category. Traditional practice demands that the researcher accept this response as it is given: that the subjects simply have not made up their minds on the subject. This interpretation applied to high-school students is disturbing, however, since it implies that there is at least 17 percent of the activist sample that have not ruled out separation as a viable political alternative for the solution of black problems.

TABLE 4. Agreement with Racial Separation (in percents)[a]

	Favor	Oppose	N.R.	N
Activists	23.9	58.7	17.4	46
Non-activists	20.9	70.9	8.2	187

[a] The table is percentaged by rows.

The activists reflect the contemporary shift of the civil rights movement toward "black power" and away from integrationist solutions to racial problems. These students are part of the movement in the sense that they reflect its radical wing. There is, of course, a significant philosophical problem here: can we accept the evidence presented here as indicative of the activist students' adherence to radical political philosophies if we conclude that their goals, like the goals of their non-activist peers, are essentially the same? The crux of the problem is that the students may only seem to be "radical" because of the methods they choose to employ in seeking their ends. It is not clear whether these ends are in fact any different from the "housing, jobs, dignity, and justice" sought by more conservative black integrationists. We may conclude, however, that in terms of radical political thought the activists are again found to specify their political orientation in terms of the black condition. They do not seem to have any desire to formulate or embrace any political philosophy that does not relate to that specific case. The high-school activist shares the concerns of the adult activist and in many ways gives direction to the movement. The activists, it must be remembered, have not merely reported that they *would* confront their school principals with complaints and demands, but they have reported that they have actually done so.

BLACK SELF-CONCEPT AND ACTIVISM

Do black activists have a different view of self from non-activists?

One further difference between the two groups should be mentioned: the ethnic name the students prefer. This variable is, perhaps more than any other, indicative of the differences between activists and non-activists, for the racial appellation has historically indicated the relative position of blacks on the continuum of militancy. The word "Negro" has, in recent times, become a term used by black militants to describe Afro-Americans who are regarded as "behind the times."

At various times African-American, Gentleman of color, Negro, colored, black, Afro-American, Afram, Bantu, Club Member, and other terms have been used by segments of the black community to designate their political and social position. The issue of what name blacks should use in designating themselves is of such importance that *Ebony* magazine attempted to poll its readers on the subject. (It goes without saying that this issue is of much less importance in the white community.) Among blacks, however, it carries a good deal of emotional and political importance.

In the sample of students surveyed, the most popular name chosen was "black"; 76 percent of the activists and 40 percent of the non-activists opted for that designation. The next most popular appellation was Afro-American; 25 percent of the activists chose that name, and 33 percent of the non-activists agreed. Only 2 percent of the activists selected the term "Negro," whereas 10 percent of the non-activists still chose to use the term.

The importance of the difference between the two groups on this variable can only be understood by one who has experienced the devastating power of the word "black" among Afro-Americans. Formerly, to be called a black *anything* was to receive the ultimate insult! Perhaps the white reader can appreciate what is being said here if he can recall his puzzlement as a child when he heard the explanation often given by black children for some altercation: "He called me black!" The ability to voluntarily choose to call one's self black represents a conscious effort to improve one's self-concept. To the extent to which the activists have succeeded in boosting their egos by the "bootstrap," they differ from those students who prefer less militant names and who still cringe at the mention of the word "black."

This finding could be interpreted to show that only 10 percent of the "normal" black, high-school students still prefer to be called by a name that until recently was looked upon as the proper designation for one of America's minority groups. Almost 90 percent of them prefer a more militant name like "black" or "Afro-American." If I am correct in my opinion that this variable represents a profound change in the attitude of black Americans toward themselves, then it is not only the attitude of militants that has changed but the attitude of the whole group of black, high-school students involved in this study.

Conclusion

What has emerged here is a picture of activist students as those in whom racial pride and faith in the ability of black people to solve their own problems is high. These students also are more willing than are their non-associated peers to engage in political activities that bring them into conflict with the adult authority that surrounds them. They have shown an awareness and a general agreement with the statements of radical black writers and have emerged as articulate exponents of the "black power" school of thought. Their responses to open-ended questions not reported here revealed their familiarity with the issues and the rhetoric of the contemporary black movement.

It is perhaps their use of the "black power" rhetoric and their willingness to engage in confrontational political activities that bring them into conflict with adult authority. It should be remembered, however, that these students, the heirs of 400 years of repression, are angry and determined. They cannot be "put off" with empty promises. They refuse to accept things as they are. At present they make up only a small fraction of the student body, but they regularly command many times their number in specific confrontations with adult administration. It is the complicity of the many that enables the activist to persist and to be effective. Administrators and teachers cannot comfort themselves with the knowledge that "only a few of our black children are 'really' militant," for with the cooperation and sanction of the many, the few do quite well! We educators must seek ways to understand and communicate with black students and their parents, lest the rift between black and white alluded to in the Kerner Report expand to a chasm upon whose rocky bottom we all may finally come together.

Bibliography

Works Cited

Cleaver, Eldridge. *Soul on Ice*. New York: McGraw-Hill, 1968.
Fanon, Frantz. *The Wretched of the Earth*. New York: Grove Press, 1963.

Some Additional Sources

Aptheker, Herbert. *A Documentary History of the Negro People*. New York: Citadel Press, 1951.
Bardolph, Richard. *The Negro Vanguard*. New York: Holt, Rinehart and Winston, 1959.
Clark, Kenneth B. (Ed.). *The Negro Protest: James Baldwin, Malcolm X, Martin Luther King, Jr.* Boston: Beacon Press, 1963.
DuBois, W. E. B. *Black Folk, Then and Now: An Essay in the History and Sociology of the Negro Race*. New York: Holt, Rinehart and Winston, 1939.
Essien-Udom, E. U. *Black Nationalism*. Chicago: University of Chicago Press, 1963.
Frazier, E. Franklin. *Black Bourgeoisie*. New York: Free Press, 1957.

Jacobs, Paul. *Prelude to Riot.* New York: Random House, 1967.

Lincoln, E. Eric. *The Black Muslims in America.* Boston: Beacon Press, 1961.

Lomax, Louis E. *The Negro Revolt.* New York: Harper & Row, 1962.

Myrdal, Gunnar. *An American Dilemma.* New York: Harper & Row, 1944. Condensed in Arnold Rose, *The Negro in America.* New York: Harper & Row, 1948.

Powledge, Fred. *Black Power and White Resistance.* New York: World Publishing, 1967.

Redding, Jay S. *On Being Negro in America.* Indianapolis: Bobbs-Merrill, 1951.

Thompson, Daniel C. *The Negro Leadership Class.* Englewood Cliffs, N. J.: Prentice-Hall, 1963.

Political Efficacy and the High School Social Studies Curriculum

7

Lee H. Ehman

One important part of a person's political makeup is the feeling he has regarding the potential impact that his behavior will have on such political decisions as who is elected and what choices are made by political leaders. This sense of personal political effectiveness, or political efficacy, is the central concept in this chapter. We will be concerned with this attitude as it occurs among high-school students, and we will search for the answers to two main questions:

1. Does political efficacy change during the high-school years, or has it stabilized by that time?
2. Does the high-school social studies curriculum seem to have any impact on political efficacy of students?

In order to arrive at some tentative answers to these questions, we will be looking at data derived from a longitudinal study of the political attitudes of high-school students at two points in time, two years apart. Additional data concerning their social studies curriculum will be used in the analysis.

A DESCRIPTION OF THE STUDY

This study is a longitudinal investigation of the political attitudes of 103 students in an urban high school in the Detroit metropolitan area. The school was chosen because of convenience and accessibility. Questionnaire measurements were conducted at two points: in March 1967 for sophomores, and in February 1969 for the same students as seniors. For purposes of comparison, questionnaires were administered to a senior cohort in 1967 and a sophomore cohort in 1969. Live classroom observations of the social studies teachers were conducted by the investigator, using Flander's ten-category verbal interaction analysis coding system. This system involves an observer coding the verbal behavior of students and teachers in the classroom into predetermined categories. Because the coding is done in units of time spent in each category of student- and teacher-talk, the ratio of student- to teacher-talk can be computed. This is one of the variables used later in this chapter.

Description of the School

The subject high school is one of two located in an industrial city—population about 90,000—in the Detroit metropolitan area. Its enrollment is approximately 1,950, and it has grades 10 through 12. The central economic force in the city is a number of large automotive plants. Because this high school is the older of the two in town and is located in the central downtown area, its population consists of a substantial proportion of both black children—38 percent—and working-class children.

The school offers a comprehensive curriculum, with a strong cooperative training program, as well as good industrial arts facilities and staff. College preparatory students are also well-served by the academic program. Although no official tracking system is used for ability grouping, there are different course offerings—usually three—within departments for pupils of different ability levels. The primary basis for assignment to the course levels is the pupil's reading ability score. The advice of counselors and teachers is also used to make these assignments. The social studies department, staffed by 18 teachers, offers a diverse program. Two semesters of U.S. history and one of U.S. government are required for graduation; in addition, one semester of another class in social studies is usually completed.

Sampling Procedure

The population of this study is defined formally as all tenth-grade pupils who enrolled during the second semester of 1967 at the high school under study. The total number in this population is 735. Because machine processing equipment is used for pupil records, a full set of population data was available for stratifying the sample according to sex, race, and ability level. A random-number table was used to obtain a 20 percent sample of the stratified population. The initial sample comprised a group of 149 students.

The final sample for which data were obtained is somewhat smaller than the original desired number. First, not all pupils who were randomly selected in 1967 were surveyed, reducing the sample from 149 to 129. Six of these 20 pupils had dropped out of school between winter registration in February and the first questionnaire administration in March 1967. The remaining 14 were either absent during the two data collection days or could not be reached. During the two-year interval between survey points, 32 pupils from the sample left school. Two pupils from the 1967 sample who were still in school were not surveyed during the second questionnaire period. Eight of the 32 who left school after March 1967 returned mailed copies of the questionnaire and are included in the final sample. The main

TABLE 1. Population and Sample Characteristics (in percents)

Characteristics	Population 1967	Sample 1967	Sample 1969
Sex:			
Male	52.6	55.0	53.4
Female	47.4	45.0	46.6
Race:			
Black	39.7	40.3	39.8
White	60.3	59.7	60.2
Ability Level:			
Low	20.9	21.7	18.4
Medium	40.6	37.2	41.7
High	38.5	41.1	39.9
N	(735)	(129)	(103)

sample being studied, therefore, consists of a panel of 103 students from whom complete data are available from both 1967 and 1969.

Sample mortality over the two-year period requires comparisons of original population characteristics with those of the final sample. These comparisons are made on the stratification variables and are summarized in Table 1. The final sample conforms closely to the original population on these three variables. In fact, the proportions in the time-two (1969) sample categories are slightly closer in all cases to the population proportions than are those in the time-one sample (1967). The largest deviation in the comparisons is between time-one and time-two medium ability level categories, a difference of about 4.5 percent. Differences on the ability level variable were expected because the students are able to shift between English class ability groups, the criterion upon which this variable is based. Given this fact, the stability of the proportions in the three groups is high.

A comparison was also made between those in the 1967 sample who left school between administration of the two questionnaires and those who stayed in school. Substantial variations occur according to ability level and sex. More middle- than high-ability level pupils, more girls than boys, and more white than black pupils left school during this period. As far as political efficacy is concerned, however, there is no difference at all between dropouts and those who stayed in school. A previous study suggested the same conclusions. Despite the drop in sample size over the two-year period, the final sample of 103 students is considered representative of the original population from which it was randomly drawn.

Two slightly different versions of the student questionnaire were employed in the 1967 and the 1969 data collections. The initial instrument was pretested in a Detroit public high school, using 55 subjects. Some modifications were then made, and the final instrument was drawn up for use in 1967 and 1969. The Guttman scaling technique was used to produce the political efficacy scale used in this study. It has a reproducibility coefficient of 0.903.

TABLE 2. RESPONSE DISTRIBUTIONS TO POLITICAL EFFICACY ITEMS
FOR 1967 AND 1969

1. When we become adults, we won't have much influence on what the
government does.

	NR	SA	A	U	D	SD
1967	0	9	19	7	40	27
1969	0	4	13	10	44	31

2. I don't think public officials care much what people like me think.

	NR	SA	A	U	D	SD
1967	1	15	31	15	33	7
1969	3	12	30	15	36	6

3. Voting is the only way people like me will have any say about how
the government runs things.

	NR	SA	A	U	D	SD
1967	2	19	46	5	25	5
1969	0	24	39	8	20	11

4. Sometimes politics and government seem so complicated that a person
like me can't really understand what's going on.

	NR	SA	A	U	D	SD
1967	1	16	42	7	34	2
1969	0	12	37	14	33	6

FINDINGS AND INTERPRETATIONS

We will approach the data by examining the individual attitude items
used in measuring the political efficacy of the high-school students. The
items themselves were derived from the 1952 voting study *The Voter
Decides*, by Campbell, Gurin, and Miller,[1] and one item had to be reworded
slightly since the originals were used in surveying adults. The students were
asked to respond by marking one of five possible alternatives after each
item: *Strongly Agree*; *Agree*; *Uncertain*; *Disagree*; and *Strongly Disagree*.
(In the tables below these have been abbreviated as *SA, A, U, D,* and *SD*.
In the few cases in which no response was obtained, the category is labelled
NR.) The response distributions for the four items at both points of time
are given in Table 2. A careful inspection of the distributions shows that
there is very little change in the response patterns for each item. The largest
shift occurs for item one, where those either disagreeing or strongly disagreeing (indicating high efficacy) increase from 67 to 75 over the two-year
period, whereas those agreeing or strongly agreeing drop from 28 to 17. The
next most variable item is number four, where the higher efficacy responses
—*D* and *SD*—shift in number from 36 to 39, and the lower responses drop
from 58 to 49. Most of the shift in this item is apparently from those that
agree or strongly agree moving to the uncertain category, whereas there are
very few actually responding in the most highly efficacious (disagree) cate-

[1] Angus Campbell, G. Gurin, and Warren Miller, *The Voter Decides* (Evanston, Ill.:
Row, Peterson, 1954.

TABLE 3. DISTRIBUTIONS OF CHANGE SCORES FOR POLITICAL
EFFICACY BY RACE (IN PERCENTS)

	Change in Political Efficacy									
	Decrease			None			Increase			
	(1)	(2)	(3)	(4)	(5)	(6)	(7)	(8)	(9)	N
Total Sample	—	2	9	23	26	26	11	2	1	(102)
Black	—	3	7	10	30	35	10	3	3	(40)
White	—	2	10	31	23	21	12	2	0	(62)

gories. For the other two items there is no noticeable change at all. The fact that only two of the four items reflect change is most interesting when we note that the two items that show change are those that refer to that part of the attitude that is *personally* oriented, rather than the component that refers to perception of political system responsiveness. The school could be expected to influence the personal efficacy attitude, if we reason that students learning more about the political system (item four) and learning about instances in which adults have influenced political decisions (item one) will reflect that kind of knowledge in the way they react to these items. If we accept this kind of reasoning, however, we must conclude that manifest teaching concerning system responsiveness (items two and three) must have rather little impact in the high-school years.

Given the data so far we suspect that there is very little aggregate change in this attitude over the two-year period, at least if the four items used are a reasonably accurate reflection of political efficacy. Because stability of this attitude is one of the two major question areas, we might pursue the analysis in a slightly different way—by using political efficacy change scores. These are based on the total efficacy scale score, using all four items; in both years each respondent had a score of from one to five, with the higher scores indicating higher efficacy. The change scores were then derived by subtracting the 1967 score from the 1969 score and adding a constant five to the result in order to end up with positive numbers. A five, then, signifies no change at all, a three indicates a drop of two scale points, etc. Table 3 gives percentage distributions of efficacy change scores for the whole sample and by racial groups. We see that there is no clear direction for the change in political efficacy for the sample as a whole. Of those that changed, a larger proportion increased in efficacy than decreased, but the difference is a slight six percent. The fact that 75 percent of the entire sample is found in the no change or one-point change categories strongly suggests that this political attitude is quite stable by the time an adolescent reaches the tenth grade.

We must pay some heed to the rest of Table 3, however. On the whole, black students' political efficacy rose noticeably, whereas that of white students declined. In order to interpret this rather surprising finding, other data—comparisons between the main sample and groups at different grade levels for both 1967 and 1969—were needed. In 1967, when the main panel was at the sophomore level, seniors in the school were also studied for comparative purposes; similarly, sophomores were included in the data gather-

TABLE 4. COMPARISONS OF TENTH AND TWELFTH GRADE COHORTS ON MEAN POLITICAL EFFICACY SCORES, 1967 AND 1969, BY RACE[a]

Total Sample	1967		1969	
	Mean	N	Mean	N
Seniors	3.30	(96)	2.97	(103)
Sophomores	2.86	(102)	3.01	(149)

Black Sample	1967		1969	
	Mean	N	Mean	N
Seniors	3.35	(37)	3.10	(41)
Sophomores	2.62	(40)	3.04	(69)

White Sample	1967		1969	
	Mean	N	Mean	N
Seniors	3.27	(59)	2.93	(62)
Sophomores	3.00	(62)	2.95	(81)

[a] In this table, the primary data of the study are that of the 1967 sophomores (time-one sample) and the 1969 seniors (time-two sample). These two groups are made up of the same individuals, while the other two groups are used here for purposes of comparison.

ing in 1969, when the main panel was in the senior class. This allowed not only the measurement of change within the main panel—1967 sophomores to 1969 seniors—but also gave opportunity to determine whether the attitude changes result from in-school or out-of-school influence. Table 4 shows the comparisons, by mean efficacy score, between the groups. As noted before, there is a slight upward shift in efficacy for the main panel. The 1969 sophomores are just as efficacious as their senior counterparts, and thus it is not possible to attribute the slight overall change in seniors to the school experience. Furthermore, the 1967 seniors were more efficacious than the other cohorts at any point. It is difficult to tell, therefore, whether those seniors were unusually high in efficacy or the 1967 sophomores were unusually low.

For the white subsample the pattern is repeated, except that there is a slight downward shift for the 1967 sophomore–1969 senior change. For the black students, however, the change is definitely upward. Although the 1967 black seniors were not much different from the white students in efficacy (3.35 versus 3.27), the 1967 black sophomores were much lower than their white peers (2.62 versus 3.00). Yet this imbalance is actually reversed by the time these students have become seniors, with the black students' mean efficacy at 3.10, as compared to the whites' 2.93. What is more, the 1969 black sophomores are already at about the seniors' level of efficacy. This might be the strongest evidence that whatever the reason for the low 1967 black sophomore mean score, some nonschool force has shifted all the black students to a higher level of efficacy. This generational force—as contrasted with a life-cycle, or maturational influence—might well be involved with the successful political action of both students and black people generally. The great difficulty with this line of argument is that the 1967 black seniors—indeed, all of the 1967 seniors—were higher in efficacy than the subsequent cohorts sampled. There is probably a combination of factors at play here. Perhaps generational forces do shift the levels of efficacy with which adolescents enter high school, and then the school experience further modifies these levels. For the students in the sample, this would indicate a generational influence that depresses efficacy, whereas one life-cycle force—that of the school—increases efficacy for black students and depresses it slightly for whites. If more data were available—such as the sophomore levels of efficacy for the 1967 seniors, or the eighth-grade level for the present sophomores—the phenomenon might be better explained.

A methodological note is also of interest here. If one were interested in making inferences about efficacy change based on a comparison of the two 1967 grade levels, as is often done in political socialization studies, one would be led to the conclusion that there is indeed a marked shift with the passage of the two years (means of 2.86 to 3.30 for the total sample). This quasi-longitudinal inference is misleading, however, as Table 4 shows. The actual shift of the 1967 sophomores over the two-year period is very slight and does not come up to the level of the 1967 seniors, although there are interesting racial differences. Attributing the change solely to school influences is also dangerous, as shown in the black students' portion of Table 4.

Social Studies Instruction and Change in Political Efficacy

Two variables related specifically to social studies instruction will now be examined for their impact on the political efficacy of high-school students. They are (1) the number of semesters of social studies instruction received by a student and (2) the degree to which discussions of controversial political and social issues are brought into the social studies classrooms. For the first of these variables, I hypothesize that increased exposure to social studies classes in high school is related to increases in political efficacy of students. One line of reasoning supporting this hypothesis is that the good-citizen message of the social studies—that a good citizen is one who understands and involves himself in the workings of the government—has a better chance of being received and internalized if the exposure to this message is prolonged. Another reason involves the notion that as a person gains more information about the government he will feel that he better understands and is able to deal with it. The social studies curriculum is assumed to operate in the transmission of this necessary political information.

For the sample as a whole, there is support for the hypothesized relationship. The product-moment correlation between the two variables is 0.15, and the corresponding t-ratio is 2.738, which is statistically significant at the .01 level. Furthermore, after partialling out initial level of efficacy, the first-

TABLE 5. RELATIONSHIP BETWEEN NUMBER OF SOCIAL STUDIES
SEMESTERS TAKEN, AND INCREASE IN STUDENT POLITICAL EFFICACY,
OVER TWO YEARS (IN PERCENTS)

Social Studies Semesters	Change in Political Efficacy				
	Decrease	No change	Increase	Total	N
Three or Less	39	20	41	100	(44)
Four	37	41	22	100	(27)
Five or More	22	23	55	100	(31)
Total	33	27	40	100	
N	(34)	(27)	(41)		(102)

order correlation rises to 0.28, which even more strongly substantiates the hypothesis.

The nature of this relationship is examined more closely in Table 5. This table is a cross-tabulation of number of social studies courses taken, grouped for ease of analysis and change in political efficacy and trichotomized into decrease, no change, and increase categories.

When row three of the table—representing the highest number of social studies semesters—is compared with either of the other two rows, the positive relationship can be seen. Whereas only 22 percent of the high social studies group decreased in efficacy, 39 and 37 percent of the low and middle groups, respectively, decreased. Likewise, 55 percent of the high social studies exposure group increased, as compared with 41 and 22 percent of the lower exposure groups. The relationship is not monotonic, however, because of the reversal for the increased efficacy category between the two low exposure groups. The lack of a clear-cut difference between the latter two groups may stem from the fact that a senior in high school is bound to have had at least three, and possibly four, such semesters; the difference in effect between the two categories can be expected to be somewhat weak. But to have had five or more social studies semesters appears to get the student far enough from the minimum number of courses so that the marginal impact of the extra courses can be felt.

Two factors can help explain this finding. First, perhaps the course content in the elective social studies courses is more powerful in changing attitudes than the content in required courses, which are those mainly represented in the three- or four-course categories of Table 5. Second, the kind of teaching—or the teachers themselves—encountered in the electives might differ from those in required courses.

Langton and Jennings found little overall effect of the civics curriculum on political efficacy, although for black children, especially for those whose parents' education is low, exposure to the civics curriculum is quite strongly related to efficacy.[2] They reasoned that the political stimuli encoun-

---

[2] Kenneth P. Langton and M. Kent Jennings, "Formal Environment: The School," *in* Kenneth P. Langton, *Political Socialization* (New York: Oxford University Press, 1969), pp. 84–119.

TABLE 6. Zero- and First-Order Product-Moment Correlations Between Exposure to Social Studies Semesters and Increase in Political Efficacy, by Race[a]

Total Sample (N=103)	Black Students (N=41)	White Students (N=62)
.15	.13	.13
(.28)	(.27)	(.25)

[a] First-order correlations are in parentheses. Initial efficacy scores have been partialled out of these coefficients. For the subgroup correlations, the additional measures of ability level and social class have been partialled out.

tered by white students in high school are redundant; they consist of more of the same message that those youth have received in school and perhaps at home all along. But for the black students the social studies message is new and therefore not redundant. This can be referred to as the "redundancy theory." By controlling for race in these relationships, we can test the theory. If it is correct, the effects of exposure to social studies courses should be much more pronounced for the black youngsters than for the white. This difference should be reflected in the correlations between the variables for each racial subgroup.

For change in political efficacy, the redundancy theory is refuted by our data; the correlations in Table 6 are all very close to being equal. It is of interest that the marked increase in the first-order over the zero-order correlations holds equally well for both black and white students. That the theory does not hold for these data might be explained by the differences in samples. The Langton-Jennings finding is based on a national probability sample of high-school seniors, whereas the present data are representative of only one high school, or at best a limited type of school. The black seniors in this school are not representative of a national sample, in that they are probably more politically aware and have participated in politics more than their counterparts elsewhere, especially those from the South and from rural areas. This assumption is partially supported by the fact that efficacy scores of blacks and whites are similar for the present data; this is not the case for the national sample. Because the two racial groups reported here are similar on this measure, there is less reason to expect the redundancy phenomenon to hold for them than for the national sample of seniors.

The amount of controversial political and social issues discussions has been shown in other studies to be an important factor. Langton and Karns refer to this as a *politicizing* variable in their analysis of its relationship to political efficacy, implying that the more a young person is politicized by his social surroundings, the more politically efficacious he will become.[3] To explain this linkage, one might reason that increased knowledge of political reality promoted by exposure and treatment of political conflict and con-

[3] Kenneth P. Langton and David A. Karns, "Influence of Different Agencies in Political Socialization," in ibid., pp. 140–60.

TABLE 7. RELATIONSHIP BETWEEN EXPOSURE TO CONTROVERSIAL ISSUES, AND INCREASE IN STUDENT POLITICAL EFFICACY, OVER TWO YEARS (IN PERCENTS)

Exposure to Controversial Issues	Change in Political Efficacy				
	Decrease	*No change*	*Increase*	*Total*	*N*
Low	40	25	35	100	(54)
High	32	23	45	100	(37)
Total	37	24	39	100	
N	(33)	(22)	(36)		(91)

troversy, rather than by sterile accounts of the functions of government found in high-school textbooks, will make students more competent to deal with the political sphere of life. The treatment of these issues will presumably include the roles and actions of citizens and groups in the process of influencing political policy decisions. These are more believable examples of the participation and effectiveness of people in government than are generally found in social studies textbooks. In any case, I hypothesize that increased exposure to controversial issues in high-school social studies classes is related to increases in political efficacy.

Table 7 shows the hypothesized relationship. Although the relationship is weak, its direction bears out the hypothesis. There are 10 percent more in the increased efficacy category who had high rather than low controversial issues exposure; the differential is about the same for the decreased efficacy group. The product-moment correlation for this relationship, after partialling out the effects of initial efficacy, is 0.13, which is significant at the .10 level. The hypothesis is therefore tentatively supported.

It is interesting to see if the relationship holds equally well for black and white students. Table 8 summarizes this comparison. There is a difference in the effect of the independent variable between racial subgroups. For the black students, it seems that there is no effect from controversial issues on the tendency to increase in efficacy, but more exposure appears to prevent slippage into the decrease category. If one looks at only the decreased and no-change columns, the relationship that operates within these categories can be seen. For whites, on the other hand, the opposite holds. There is no difference, by exposure to controversial issues, in those that decreased in efficacy, but that exposure does appear to move students from the no-change to the increased efficacy columns. The strength of the hypothesized relationship is equivalent across the racial variable, although differences exist in what the relationships mean, or how they operate, for each group.

One way of interpreting the differential effect is that black children increase in efficacy in spite of varying exposure to controversial issues, whereas white children decrease in spite of it. Conversely, increased exposure to issues restrains black students from decreasing, while it pushes white children to increased efficacy. Perhaps black children know, from outside sources, of better examples of effective political action by blacks than they

TABLE 8. RELATIONSHIP BETWEEN EXPOSURE TO CONTROVERSIAL ISSUES, AND INCREASE IN STUDENT POLITICAL EFFICACY, BY STUDENT RACE (IN PERCENTS)

Exposure to Controversial Issues	Black Students Change in Political Efficacy				
	Decrease	No change	Increase	Total	N
Low	29	21	50	100	(17)
High	19	35	46	100	(16)
Total	24	28	48	100	
N	(8)	(9)	(16)		(33)
	White Students				
Low	44	27	29	100	(37)
High	42	14	44	100	(21)
Total	44	22	34	100	
N	(25)	(13)	(20)		(58)

find in discussions of current political topics in class. The awareness of successful political actions of black people, including student action, may account for increases in the efficacy of black adolescents today. For many of these youngsters it makes little difference that they hear of these actions in class, because the information has already been received. But for those black students whose efficacy is not going to increase, classroom exposure to controversial issues does provide enough information so that the efficacy is less likely to decrease.

Another theory explains the relationship involving whites. Increased discussion of issues gives students an opportunity to participate more and thus to feel confident about these political matters. This extra opportunity to practice vicarious political action in the classroom can be the factor within the controversial issues exposure variable that makes it effective for whites in this relationship.

The hypotheses can be tested with the data. For the measure of participation by students in controversial issues classes, the student-talk/teacher-talk (ST/TT) ratio from interaction analysis observations is used.[4] The ratios for all social studies teachers are split into two groups—high and low—and this variable is used to control the relationship between controversial issues exposure and change in efficacy. Table 9 shows this comparison of gamma correlations for each racial group.

For the total group the correlations are nearly the same, with only a slightly stronger connection between issues-exposure and efficacy-change when students are allowed to talk more in the discussions. But the com-

---

[4] Observations of controversial issues discussions being conducted by the social studies teachers makes it possible to determine, on the average, what proportion of time is taken up by teacher talk and how much by student talk in such discussions. The higher the student-talk/teacher-talk ratio, therefore, the larger the proportion of time that students participate.

TABLE 9. GAMMA CORRELATIONS BETWEEN CONTROVERSIAL ISSUES
EXPOSURE AND INCREASE IN POLITICAL EFFICACY, BY STUDENT-
TALK/TEACHER-TALK RATIO AND RACE

	Total Group	Black Students	White Students
Low ST/TT ratio	.15	.15	.06
High ST/TT ratio	.21	−.05	.40

parison across racial subgroups is different. For black students there is
actually a slight tendency toward increased efficacy with exposure to issues
where student talk is low. For the high student-talk category, there is no
relationship at all and the absolute difference between correlations is also
small. For white students, the high student-talk correlation is strong, whereas
for the low student-talk group, no relationship exists. It is not true that the
student-talk/teacher-talk ratio has an independent relationship to efficacy
change. The correlation for the white subsample is only 0.04, and 0.01 for
the whole group. Given this set of correlations, it is plausible to explain the
issues exposure-efficacy increase link for whites in terms of participation in
discussing the controversial topics; for blacks other factors must be explored.

One such factor has already been suggested—the impact of successful
black political action on the efficacy of black youngsters. This factor has
been suggested as having more force in the calculus of efficacy change for
black students than the controversial issues exposure. This hypothesis was
tested by using two items from the questionnaire that indicate how much
attention the respondent had paid to racial problems in the last two years.
One item asked, "How much attention would you say that you paid to what
went on in the Detroit riots in 1967?" The other asked about the situation
specific to their city: "Turning to _____, how much attention have you
paid to the racial problems which have continued since the time of the
Detroit riots?" Both items were followed by the following response choices:
almost none; *a little*; *quite a bit*; *a great deal*. These two items, with initial
efficacy and exposure to controversial issues, were entered into a regression
equation to predict efficacy change scores for the black subsample. The
results of this equation are given in Table 10, and indicate the independent

TABLE 10. MULTIPLE REGRESSION EQUATION TO PREDICT INCREASE IN
POLITICAL EFFICACY FOR BLACK STUDENTS[a]

Variable	Partial Beta	Standard Deviation of Beta
Controversial issues exposure	−.09	.165
Attention paid to Detroit riots	.08	.156
Attention paid to local racial problems	.30	.177

[a] Initial efficacy was also entered into the regression equation in order to
correct for regression effects. The product-moment coefficient between attention to local problems and controversial issues exposure is .03, showing that
the two variables are independent of one another.

relative strengths of these predictive variables, corrected for initial level of efficacy. Just as predicted, the independent effect of controversial issues exposure for blacks is low (beta=−.09). Betas for the two information items show that attention to the local racial situation is a stronger predictor of change in efficacy than is the classroom variable. Attention to the local situation is also stronger than attention paid to the Detroit riots. This probably stems from two facts: First, the local events are more recent than the Detroit disturbance, which took place very shortly after the initial measurement of efficacy. The local affairs, therefore, are more likely to have contributed to increase in efficacy during the two years. Second, the local situation is in closer proximity to students, and they are more apt to see the relevance of local actions for their own sense of political effectiveness.

SUMMARY

Returning to the two questions that we started with at the beginning of this chapter, we can conclude from these data that in the aggregate, students' political efficacy has pretty much stabilized by the tenth grade. School forces, nevertheless, can, and apparently do, influence efficacy to a certain extent. We have seen that prolonged exposure to the high-school social studies curriculum is related to increases of political efficacy, especially for those with five or more semesters of exposure. Likewise, exposure to discussions of political and social controversial issues appears to be related to increased political efficacy, although the nature of that relationship is different for black and white students. Overall, however, some of the modest amount of change in political efficacy throughout the high-school years can be attributed to variables operating within the school itself.

School Organization and Political Socialization

8

Simon Wittes

The school has traditionally seen itself as apolitical in nature. However, it now holds the spotlight as a context for internal political activity. Many students, angered with policies in school and society, are engaged in a common quest—a search for power. Regardless of their social, ethnic, or racial background, or their level in the school status hierarchy, they seek to control their lives—to have influence on policies which govern them—and thereby are engaging in and learning about the essence of the political process. They wish to change the bureaucratic inhibitions and prohibitions that separate them from their educators; the tracking system that sorts them out and predetermines their futures; the curriculum which they deem to be unrelated to their concerns about self and society. Although black students, in particular, often form the strongest and most organized protest group, their feelings of frustration and anger are echoed by small numbers of ideological, radical students and large numbers of "straights" or "climbers," the majority group in the schools.

As students attempt to influence decisions, implement changes, and control their own lives in school, they are *experiencing* a political system and its processes, rather than simply learning *about* it through courses in civics, government, and current events. In the past, students allowed power to rest in the hands of administrators and teachers because they trusted the image of society presented to them and the role the school played in their preparation for entrance into that society. Today most of their trust has dissipated in the realization of the glaring disparity between the ideals and the realities of the society and its institutions. They no longer believe that most educators are acting in students' best interests or providing them with relevant skills and knowledge; hence they are reacting with either the withdrawal or militant activity which stems from feelings of impotence and alienation.

Adolescent characteristics of rebelliousness, impulsiveness, defiance, or distrust interact with such school conditions as school curriculum, instruction, policies, interracial and intergenerational tensions. This interaction is reinforced by the mass media and societal forces, such as unresponsive job markets. All of these elements combine within the organizational structure of the school to create the conditions or potentials for school disruption.

The study to be reported in this chapter sought to examine this interactional basis for school crisis in the context of high schools that have experienced disruption. It examined the role played by the school's power structure in the disruption and, thus, its implications for political socialization. The study rested on the assumption that the school environment has an impact on the development of students' political attitudes and behavior. It tested the thesis that the power structure of an organization is associated with the development of personal attitudes—specifically that the power structure of a high school is associated with students' belief in internal control. *Belief in internal control* is a person's belief that rewards follow from or are contingent upon his own behavior, as opposed to the belief that rewards are controlled by forces outside himself and thus may occur independent of his own actions. This variable subsumes a sense of one's competency to influence the outcomes of situations through his own actions, plus a belief that hard work, effort, and skill are the important determinants of success in life.

The sense of internal control is an integral component of political socialization, as it is also central to academic achievement, achievement motivation, and attitudes toward teachers and learning environments. Political socialization concerns the development of attitudes, beliefs, values, and behavior of the individual toward and within the political system in which he lives. A belief that one's actions can influence the direction of that system, be it national, local, or organizational, is a function of (1) the individual's belief that he has some control over the consequences of his own action, i.e., belief in internal control; and (2) the nature of the opportunity structure within that system.

In seeking to understand the relation between school power structure and belief in internal control, I studied how this relationship differs with various groups of students. One of the features of the schools used in this study is their bi-racial character. Assuming that the perceptions and experiences of blacks and whites within an organization often differ, I examined the differential effects of school power structure and race on belief in internal control of black and white youngsters.

These, then, are some of the questions this study sought to answer: What are the relationships between differences in school power structures and student belief in internal control? Are they the same for black and white youngsters? What are the intervening variables that explain the relationships between school power structure and student belief in internal control? In the following pages I report findings that bear on these issues and present implications for school and classroom practices in organization, curriculum, and instruction that are reflected in the political socialization of today's adolescents.

PROCEDURE: SAMPLE SCHOOLS

The study's focus was a sample of ten senior high schools, located in seven states, which had been disrupted by protests or riots or where the administration had strong fears of impending disruption. The violence often took the form of fights between various groups of students, such as black and white, black and black, or white and white. At other times, it took the form of fights between educators and students. At its most extreme, the disruptions were characterized by knifings and shootings; at less extreme levels, by high tension among individuals and role groups.

Nine of the ten schools in the sample had been closed by the administration for at least a full school day as a result of disruptive events. The administration in the tenth school had a fear of impending disruption. The schools varied along dimensions of geographic location, degree of urbanization, size of the student population, and racial proportion of the student body. The sample included five urban schools, two small city schools, two suburban schools, and one small town school, and student populations ranged in size from 1,300 to 4,000. The racial proportions of the student bodies ranged from practically all black to practically all white.

INSTRUMENTS AND MEASURES

Organizational Level

The measure of power structure used in this study relies on the mean judgments by students of the amount of influence or control exercised by various groups in their school system, as reported in their responses to questionnaire items. The measure, which consists of items on student perceptions of actual distribution of influence on policies within the school, is based on those used in organization studies by Tannenbaum (1961), Tannenbaum and Kahn (1957), and Bachman et al. (1967).

The amount of power exercised by each of the hierarchical levels in a given school was computed by averaging the judgments of all respondents regarding each of these levels. *Total power* is the summation of the amounts of power perceived as being exercised by the five hierarchical levels in each school. The *distribution of power* was computed as a summation of the absolute differences between the amounts of power exercised by adjoining hiererchical levels in a given school.

Intervening Level

The respondent's perception of the amount of his own power was assessed by asking him, "How much influence do you actually have in determining educational matters?" Responses were recorded by individual on a five-point scale. A discrepancy was calculated by subtracting the respondent's rating of his own power from his rating of the power of students in general.

Individual Level

The internal versus external control dimension concerns the respondent's perception of whether one's fate is controlled by himself or by external forces. A modification of the Rotter (1966) I-E scale was used to measure this dimension.

DATA COLLECTION

The data collection utilized a random stratified sample of tenth-, eleventh-, and twelfth-grade students in each of the ten sample schools. Approximately 30 to 40 students were selected from each grade level by applying a random number procedure to an alphabetical list of students at each grade level. Students were then asked, but not required, to participate. This procedure resulted in a sample in each school at one sitting and required approximately 40 to 60 minutes for completion.

CONCEPTUAL BACKGROUND AND HYPOTHESES

Organizational Level

Just as individuals may become differently socialized because of differences in past experience, motivation, and capacity, so may they become differently socialized because of differences in the structure of the social settings in which they learn and interact. The school is an example of a people-processing organization, formally charged with the task of influencing others so that they will leave the setting with different skills, attitudes, values, or other qualities from those with which they entered.

The school is a socializing agency comparable to the family, and characteristics of its environment have effects similar to those of the family. From family socialization studies (Bronfenbrenner 1961; Elder 1965) we find that those parent-child relationships characterized by clarity of limits, consistency of rules and rule enforcement, and opportunities for adolescents in decision-making facilitate the development of autonomy. Similarly, a school environment that possesses these same characteristics will also contribute to the development of student autonomy and self-control.

Belief in internal control is dependent upon the perception that reinforcements are predictable and a function of one's own autonomous behavior. Therefore, a school environment that contributes to a student's sense of autonomy and allows opportunities for its expression facilitates the development of his belief in internal control.

Individual Level

There are few empirical guidelines available that would suggest a theory of the development of attitudes of internal versus external control. Those studies that do bear on the problem of antecedents of internal-external belief are indirect and, consequently, the derived explanatory concepts are, at best, suggestive. I believe that a characteristic of the school organization (considered a socializing agency), namely the power structure, may be one of the determining factors in the development of the students' belief in internal control. This belief may develop out of students' relationships with those socializing agencies, such as family, church, mass media, and school, with which they come in contact. Moreover, I assume that forces within these agencies have differing effects on the development of belief in internal control in various groups of students. I suspected that black youngsters and white youngsters would respond similarly to some socializing influences, and differently to others.

I therefore analyzed the differences between black and white students on the ideology of personal control,[1] sense of personal control,[2] and degree of personal power and discrepancy.

Intervening Level

The main thesis of this study was that a characteristic of the school organization, namely the power structure, is a determining factor in the development of students' belief in internal control. The following discussion presents a conceptual analysis for this potential relationship and the effect of variations in the power structure.[3] Powerlessness, or alienation from power, is used here as a concept that bridges the gap between a social situation which concentrates power in the hands of one group or person, to the exclusion from power on the organizational level, and the corresponding experience of lack of power on the individual level.

At the psychological level, powerlessness is operationalized as the expectancy or probability held by the individual that his own behavior cannot determine the occurrence of the outcomes, or reinforcements, he seeks. This concept is included in the construct of "internal versus external control of reinforcements," which was a dependent psychological variable in the study. Perception of alienation is another psychological variable associated with the condition of alienation. It was operationalized as two intervening level variables: (a) rating of students' personal power to influence policy decisions in the school, and (b) discrepancy between a student's rating of the power of students as a group and his personal power.

Therefore, the concept of alienation was utilized to link characteristics of the social organization and their consequences for personality. On the social structural level, alienation was operationalized as the patterns in the school power structure. At the personality level, alienation was operationalized as a psychological reaction to alienation, i.e., a sense of internal-external control. At the intervening level, alienation was operationalized as perception of distance from one's peers or one's ability to influence the organization.

[1] Ideology of personal control reflects a person's general beliefs about the role of internal and external forces in determining success or failure in the culture at large.

[2] Sense of personal control represents a person's belief that rewards follow from, or are contingent upon, his own behavior.

[3] We used the concept of "alienation," meaning powerlessness, to link phenomena at a social organizational level and development of personality factors.

Having influence in decisions that govern oneself is critical for the development of adolescent autonomy. The provision of opportunities for expression of one's autonomy is critical to the development of belief in personal control. However, for this relationship to have an effect, the adolescent must perceive how much power he does have in making decisions that affect him. I assumed that the perception that one has power to influence decisions in the school should evoke some sense of being able to control one's life in school. Further, I assumed that this feeling should generalize to situations outside the school and thereby result in a higher internal sense of personal control. Therefore, I analyzed the relationship between students' perceptions of personal power to control decisions in the school and their senses of personal control.

Much literature (Coleman, 1961; Douvan and Adelson, 1966) documents the importance of peer group identification for the adolescent. Alienation from one's peers was conceptualized as the second variable that intervenes between the organizational and the individual levels. A sense of personal control, which is one measure of belief in internal control, overlaps with the concept of competency. The low-discrepant student is one who feels less alienated from his peer group and therefore feels a higher sense of competency in the area of interpersonal and group relations than do his high-discrepant peers. Therefore, I predicted differences in sense of personal control between low-discrepant and high-discrepant students.

Schools allow for varying degrees of ability to influence; they may be placed on a continuum, characterized by their power structures which foster or hinder the development of a sense of competency among students. I therefore predicted that different types of school power structures would produce differences in students' belief in a sense of personal control.

RESULTS AND ANALYSIS

Organizational Level

The main source of data for the organizational level analysis derives from students' responses to the following question:

In general, how much influence do you think the following groups or persons actually have in determining educational matters (e.g., curricula, policy, etc.) in this school? For each of these groups in your school, please rate their actual influence over the way your school is run:

    (a) The school board
    (b) The superintendent
    (c) The principal
    (d) Your teachers
    (e) The students

The responses were recorded on a five-point scale: (1) little or no influence, (2) some influence, (3) moderate influence, (4) considerable influence, and (5) a great deal of influence.

From an analysis of these responses, I found that at each level of influence (i.e., school board, superintendent, principal, teacher, and student), there are statistically significant between-school differences in students' perceptions of the actual distribution of power. However, the principal's influence showed the greatest between-school differences, and the teachers' the least. Further support for the hypothesis that differences occur in students' perception of the school's actual power structure came from two other sources. One source was the difference reported within each school between levels of rank-ordering of amount of power assigned to each level. A second was the informal observations data that demonstrated ways in which power distribution reflects various situations in specific schools.

Indices of Power Structure

The three indices that were used to reflect differences in school power structure were: (1) shape of control graph, (2) amount of total power, and (3) differences in power. A control graph is one in which the horizontal base is taken to represent the hierarchical scale in an organization, and the vertical axis the amount of power possessed by the respective hierarchical echelons. The curve drawn on this graph provides a visual image of the hierarchical distribution of power. Examples of control graphs for some individual schools are presented in Figure 1.

FIGURE 1

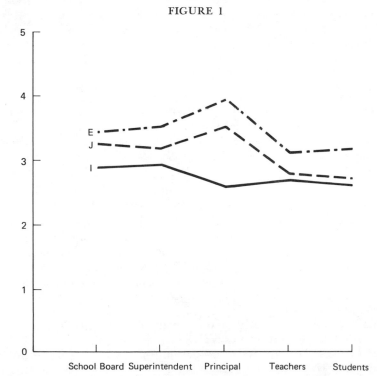

Shape of Control Graph Curve

Examination of the control graphs in Figure 1 shows that distinctions can be made among them on the basis of their shape. Classification of schools by shape of the control graph curve was made by inspection of the curves in Figure 2. Curves were classified as "Flat" (for example, school F), "Peaked Dome" (school A), "Low Negative Slope" (school B), and "Broken" (school G). For example, the graph for school I is relatively flat, with little variation in height between adjacent hierarchical echelons. This represents a school with fairly even distribution of power. On the other hand, the graph for school J is relatively uneven, with greater variation in height between adjacent hierarchical levels. This represents a school in which power is unequally distributed.

Total Amount of Power

The peaks of the control line in Figure 1 vary from school to school. For example, the peak height for any role in school I is 2.98, whereas for school E it is 3.97. A power structure with high total amount of power is reflected in a control graph curve where the entire curve is high (see school E, Figure 1). A total power index that represents the average height of the control graph was calculated for each school by computing the mean of the amount of power attributed to each echelon. The index of total amount of power, therefore, represents how much power is exercised within the school from all sources. Schools were then categorized as to high, medium, and low amounts of power.

Differences in Power

Although the total amount of power in two schools may be identical, the ways in which the power is distributed may differ. In order to measure these differences in power, we developed an index which is a summation of the absolute differences between the amounts of power seen to be possessed by adjacent hierarchical levels in a given school.

School Types

The three measures of the power structure—shape of control graph curve, amount of total power, and difference in power—were the basis for construction of a typology of schools. Classification of schools by shape of the control graph was made by inspection of the graphs in Figure 2. Amount of total power and difference in power were classified as high, medium, or low. This resulted in four types of school power structures— (1) Diffuse, (2) Local Control, (3) Centralized, and (4) Differentiated—as seen in Figure 2 and Table 1.

TYPE 1, DIFFUSE. The chief characteristics of the control graphs of this group are the flatness and lowness. The schools have a low index of power difference (flatness) and low index of amount of total power (lowness). This combination of characteristics represents a school in which students have

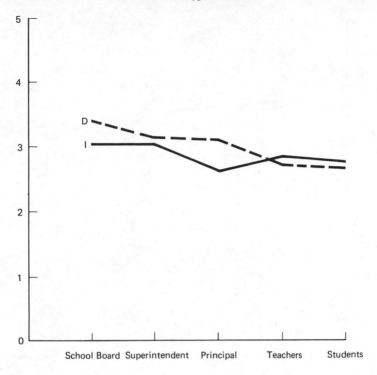

FIGURE 2. Type 1–Diffuse

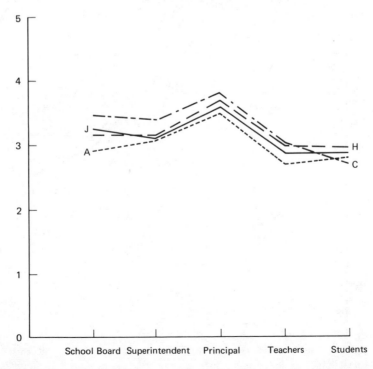

FIGURE 2 (continued). Type 2–Local Control

FIGURE 2 (continued). Type 3–Centralized

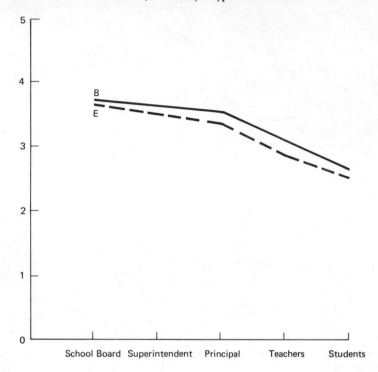

FIGURE 2 (continued). Type 4–Differentiated

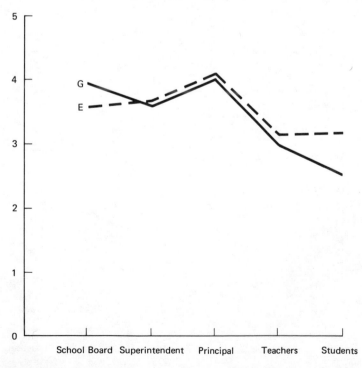

TABLE 1. TYPOLOGY OF SCHOOL POWER STRUCTURES

		Power Structure Characteristics		
		Total power index	Power difference index	Control graph shape
I Diffuse	D, I	Low	Low	Flat
II Local control	A, C, H, J	Medium	Medium	Peaked dome
III Centralized	B, F	Medium	Medium	Low negative slope
IV Differentiated	E, G	High	High	Broken

little influence and therefore are not highly subject to being influenced, where orderliness is low, and where the loci of power are unclear.

TYPE 2, LOCAL CONTROL. The peaked dome characteristic of the control graph of this category represents a school in which the principal is perceived as the possessor of a greater amount of power than the superintendent, the board of education, teachers, and students. The medium rating for index of power differences reflects a school in which the differences between amounts of power assigned to adjacent hierarchical levels are greater, and thus its power system is clearer than in the diffuse. The medium amount of total power reflects a school in which students' influence and "influenceability," as well as the degree of orderliness within it, are greater than the diffuse.

TYPE 3, CENTRALIZED. From the control graphs of this type, we see that the main sources of power are perceived to reside in offices located outside the school building—those of the superintendent and the board. The indices of amount of total power and power differences are medium, which indicates that a school in this category has students who have more influence and are more subject to being influenced; is more orderly; and has a clearer power system than a school of the diffuse type.

TYPE 4, DIFFERENTIATED. The control graph for this type shows that it is similar to the local control type, in that the principal is perceived as being the major source of power within the hierarchy. The high index of total power indicates a school in which the students have a high degree of influence and are highly subject to being influenced. The high index of power differences reflects a school in which the power system is very clear, so that the sources of power are easily identifiable.

In summary, the findings demonstrated that significant between-school differences have been found in students' perceptions of the school's actual power structure. Further, these differences, as measured by indices of amount of total power and differences in power, when coupled with distinctions in control graph shapes, provide a basis for a typology of schools based on the nature of their power structures.

Intervening Level

SCHOOL TYPE—DISCREPANCY—SENSE OF INTERNAL CONTROL. In this section, I will examine the effect of the interaction of type of school power structure and discrepancy on the development of a sense of personal control. The hypothesized nature of this relationship is diagrammed in Figure 3.

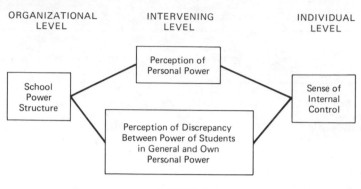

FIGURE 3

In theory, I suspected that the power structure of a differentiated school would be related differently to the low-discrepant student's sense of personal control than would that of the diffuse school, because students as a group have greater power in the former than in the latter. Therefore, the student who is more integrated with his powerful peers would have a greater feeling of his own power to influence decisions in the differentiated than in the diffuse. I further suspected that this feeling of greater personal power within the differentiated school would generalize to a higher integral sense of personal control. Therefore, I hypothesized:

> Low-discrepant students in a differentiated school will score higher on internal personal control than will low-discrepant students in a diffuse school.

The data in Table 2 support this hypothesis, in that they show that low-discrepant students in the differentiated type school score significantly higher on internal personal control than do those in the diffuse type. There are a number of factors in the nature of the school's power structure that contribute to this phenomenon. They all enable the individual to experience a sense of competence in being able to influence others. Clarification of the nature of power distribution necessitates herewith a discussion of the effects on students of differences in total power and distribution of power.

One factor is that the differentiated school has a high index of total power, which suggests that this type of school provides opportunities for students to exercise control within the school. This leads to students' involvement in and identification with the school and, hence, increases their interest in exercising influence or control and also their amenability

TABLE 2. Comparison Between Mean Personal Control Scores of Low Discrepant Students in a Diffuse and a Differentiated System

Type	N	Mean	S.D.	t	Sig.
Differentiated	38	1.707	.20	2.476	<.01
Diffuse	95	1.590	.26		

to being influenced. These students, then, as possible control agents, engage in more frequent influence attempts; as possible objects of control, they provide new opportunities for one another to exercise control. This process, which is reflected in the increased amount of total power, provides opportunities for students to gain a sense of competence from those influence attempts that the structure has made possible.

In examining the diffuse school, we turn to another concept of amount of total power. This concept suggests that since control is a means of creating order, schools that differ in their orderliness may be expected to differ in the amounts of control within them. Thus, the diffuse school, which in its extreme form would be laissez-faire or anarchic, has a lower degree of total control, and therefore a lower degree of orderliness, than the differentiated. This low degree of orderliness does not provide the student with a consistent environment that allows him to make accurate predictions about it; he finds it difficult to control that which is unpredictable. Hence, the student is likely to experience a lessened degree of confidence about his ability to control his environment in the disorderly diffuse school setting. This, in turn, would affect his sense of competence, which itself is dependent on the consequences of behavior being under one's own control. A diffuse or disorderly environment mitigates against predictable consequences, even for one's own behavior, and thus the student in such an environment is likely to feel little internal sense of personal control. In contrast to the diffuse system, the differentiated system has a high degree of order and consistency. With such an environment, a student can often predict the consequences of his behavior. Therefore, he feels that these consequences are not the result of chance or fate, and thus he may develop a higher internal sense of personal control.

Distribution of power is the second structural factor that distinguishes between the differentiated and the diffuse schools. There are greater differences between the amounts of power assigned to each echelon in the differentiated hierarchy compared to the diffuse hierarchy; this indicates that the loci of sources of power in the former school are clear, whereas in the latter they are diffuse and unclear. Where the loci of power are clear, a student can predict where he must make his influence attempts. Hence, his attempts are more likely to be successful in a differentiated rather than a diffuse system. Successful influence attempts lead to a sense of competence in that area.

I then compared the low-discrepant students in the centralized school with those in the differentiated school and found that the low-discrepant student in a differentiated school scores very significantly higher on personal control than does the low-discrepant student in a centralized school (Table 3). Here again, we see that the power structure and discrepancy interact in their effect on sense of personal control. In this case, the greater amount of total power and the clarity of its distribution within the building of a differentiated school provide greater opportunities for students to experience a sense of competence in being able to influence others than do the characteristics of the centralized school. In the latter type, where the

TABLE 3. COMPARISON BETWEEN MEAN PERSONAL CONTROL SCORES OF LOW
DISCREPANT STUDENTS IN A CENTRALIZED AND A DIFFERENTIATED SYSTEM

Type	N	Mean	S.D.	t	Sig.
Differentiated	38	1.707	.200	3.482	< .001
Centralized	110	1.555	.240		

major sources of power are located outside the building, the distribution of power is not perceived by the student with the same clarity as in the differentiated school. In addition, the student in the centralized school perceives that the main source of power is farther removed from the school and himself than does the student in the differentiated school. As a result, he may feel that his main influence target is unavailable to him. Therefore, the feelings of competency that would emerge from his ability to influence others are reduced.

We found in this comparison between the differentiated and the centralized types that the effect of power distribution differences is greater for the low- than for the high-discrepants. This supports my earlier interpretation of the powerful effect that success in interpersonal relations has upon the development of a sense of personal control. Note, then, that for differentiated schools that are characterized by high total power and a clear distribution of power, a significant relationship exists between the type of power structure and a sense of personal control when mediated through membership in a peer group.

The power structure of the differentiated school is similar to that of the local control school in that in both types the principal possesses a greater amount of power than any other group or role in the hierarchy. However, the differentiated school's power structure is clearer and has a greater amount of total power than the local control. I theorized that the differentiated power structure would provide greater opportunities for the development of a sense of personal control than would the local control school. I reasoned that the former, with its higher amount of total power, provided more opportunities for a student to influence others. For the low-discrepant student who is less alienated from his peers than is the high-discrepant, this feeling of power would be accentuated. I speculated that the feeling of greater personal power within the school would generalize to a higher internal sense of personal control. Therefore, I hypothesized:

> Low-discrepant students in a differentiated school will score higher internal personal control than will low-discrepant students in a local control school.

This hypothesis is supported by the data in Table 4. Again, the differentiated school has more total power and a higher degree of order and consistency. However, on two other power structure dimensions—clarity of loci of power and principal having the greatest amount of power of any role group in the hierarchy—the differentiated system does not differ from the local control. This suggests, then, that total amount of power and distribution of power, when mediated by discrepancy, predict more powerfully

TABLE 4. COMPARISON BETWEEN MEAN PERSONAL CONTROL SCORES OF LOW
DISCREPANT STUDENTS IN DIFFERENTIATED AND LOCAL CONTROL SCHOOLS

Type	N	Mean	S.D.	t	Sig.
Differentiated	38	1.707	.202	2.501	< .01
Local Control	160	1.587	.235		

than clarity of loci of power or locus of greatest amount of power to differences in sense of personal control.

In summary, significant differences between students' perceptions of school power structures were found. Three power structure indices were developed on which a typology of schools was built.

At the intervening level of analysis, a significant relationship was found between type of school power structure and sense of personal control when mediated through the degree of the respondent's integration with his peer group.

CONCLUSIONS

Interpretation of Findings

The findings of this study reflect three major themes. One is the relation between the nature of an individual's membership in a group and his belief in internal-external control. The second is the relation between the nature of the school power structure and the individual's belief in internal-external control, and the third is a combination of these two.

The first major theme is discussed in an interpretation of the finding that in a specific type of school (differentiated), the degree to which an individual is integrated into or alienated from a peer group is associated with his belief that he can control his own life. One possible interpretation of this association is that the individual who is integrated into a peer group is provided with a proximate and relatively constant social environment. Integration with a peer group implies fairly frequent interaction between the individual and other group members. As a result, there is more information and knowledge shared with all members about each other and the world in which they live. This would tend to reduce uncertainty about others, enable the individual to learn more about how self is perceived by others, and provide a social context in which the individual can be more accurate in his predictions about the behaviors and attitudes of other group members. The distinctive norms of the adolescent peer group provide a high degree of consistency about its demands and expectations.

The relation between the nature of the school power structure and belief in internal-external control can best be explicated by the concept of the differentiated school, which has a higher degree of orderliness and thus provides a school environment that allows the students to make predictions more accurately than in any other type of school. Students tend to feel greater confidence about their ability to control a predictable environment than an unpredictable one. Therefore, the student in an orderly school would tend to have a higher sense of personal control than one in a more disorderly one.

The findings that the interaction of the low-alienated student and the differentiated school did not predict to high internal sense of personal control suggests the following interpretation. A differentiated school has a high total amount of power, providing greater opportunities for groups of its students to be influential in the school and to be influenced by it. Therefore, the low-alienated student in the differentiated school may have a high sense of personal control as a result of more orderly and consistent environments of both his peer group and the school organization. In addition, by being integrated into a group that is more powerful, the student feels more confident in his ability to control his life than does the more alienated student in such a school, or students of varying alienation in any school type.

No evidence has been presented to indicate that there is a causal relationship between the school power structure and belief in internal control. It is possible, for example, that the differentiated power structure facilitated the development of high internality. On the other hand, the low-alienated student who ranks high on sense of personal control may perceive the school power structure in particular ways. Such findings can only be interpreted as evidence of interactive association among differentiated power structure, student alienation from peer group, and belief in internal-external control. Since the phenomenon is an active one, it is assumed that the nature of the power structure and student alienation from peers has some effect on internal-external control. Therefore, I turn now to consider the implication of this effect for schools, and the political socialization of students.

Implications for Schools

In considering the implications of our findings for political socialization of students, I suggested that an integral component of the individual's political socialization is his sense of internal control. I further noted that this sense of internal control is intimately linked to the degree of influence that the student experiences over his school environment. In the absense of this experience of control, students increasingly protest and assert their collective rights for student power or engage in vandalism and violent disruption as a response to their feelings of impotence. Evidence, too, is their increasing distrust of the holders of power.

It appears, then, to be crucial to increase student power in the school, both as a response to their feelings of impotence and for the development of internal control and political socialization. The differentiated school structure offers a model for increased student power in the school. I turn now to an examination of strategies for achieving this model and their implications for political socialization.

One way to increase the total power within a school and to more closely approximate the differentiated school is to provide more genuine shared decision-making opportunities among students, teachers, administrators, and community members. Thus a cross-role, group decision-making structure could be established in the school with responsibility in educational and personal decisions. Members of this structure would be granted legitimate authority and school time and could deliberate and make decisions on curriculum innovations, use of educational resources, and faculty competence and tenure. Another way to increase the total power of the school and facilitate development of peer group cohesion as well is to provide students with collective power in school decision-making. We recall that it was not individual power but rather integration into a powerful collective that is important in high internality of personal control. The granting of decision-making powers of a school to a congress of students and a congress of faculty could provide students with such collective power. These congresses could have complete responsibility for the initiation of school policies, while the principal's task would be to administer them. Providing this type of increased collective power to students would ensure their being seen as a clear source of power, serving to increase total power as well as the distribution of power in the school.

Our findings suggest that at the classroom level the curriculum should be designed to help students and teachers learn about the concepts of power and its uses. For example, the curriculum could include one unit on the concepts of fixed versus variable amounts of power, and another on strategies for gaining power. A greater emphasis on group process in the classroom would serve to foster group cohesion and reduce student alienation from peers, facilitating development of a higher internal sense of personal control.

These suggestions have implications for the training of administrators, teachers, students, and community people. First, it implies the necessity of training all groups in the concept of fixed and variable total power, so that all can understand that the increase of power of one group does not necessarily mean less to another. Next, it implies training in strategies for gaining power that may be alternatives to violent ones and in the effective use of power which can lead to further increases of power. Finally, it implies training in skills to understand the school structure, make decisions, and organize for collective action.

One implication of differentiated school power structure to adolescent political socialization is facilitating the student's belief in his internal control and his capacity to influence his school environment. Such experience socializes the student politically into a conviction that he can influence his political environment in the larger society as well as in his school.

Second, as the student enjoys and benefits from his political influence upon the decisions that affect his life in school, he will tend to become less anti-establishment since the established system is working *for* him and *with* his assistance and influence. This experience then affects his political socialization in favor of attitudes that support political processes, operating within the system. He is less likely to see the establishment as an enemy against which to pit his wrath or from which to retreat completely.

Third, dissent and conflict are inevitable between interest groups in society, and political socialization involves the understanding and skill to deal with conflict. Historically, citizenship training of youth in schools has stressed obedience to rules and authority and passive acceptance of establishment values and interests. Conflict has been repressed; dissent denied or buried; and the student has been denied legitimate opportunities for the political experience of working for his group's self-interest as well as the common good. In the absence of a formal apparatus for dissent and influence in the school, his political socialization has been stunted. In school, as a microcosmic society, he has not been afforded opportunities to develop critical judgment and skill as a political animal but is being trained for passive citizenship, which does not desire or seek change in response to social needs and inequities, and exists solely to support the status quo. A differentiated power structure that allows him to experience political influence in his society can do much to redress this situation. He will learn adaptive ways of handling conflict and not fear it as catastrophic. He will learn to live with divisiveness when it cannot be healed and will become creative in strategizing for collaborative relationships, as well as with negotiation processes that must occur between clashing groups. Students who like to think that political cleavages are healed when election is over and who dislike conflict within a society (Hess and Torney, 1967) will learn to recognize that cleavages are not healed merely by the vote and that conflict can be constructive. In their interaction with other interest groups in the differentiated school they will learn a norm that does not exist in most schools: that participation is desirable and that controversy is inevitable and should be dealt with, not denied.

In conclusion, through the opportunity to experience political power in a differentiated school structure, the student learns the underlying significance of the Bill of Rights and of political procedures, *affectively* as well as cognitively. This affective knowledge plays an important role in the political socialization process and should be developed through the student's opportunity for becoming an actor rather than an observer in the political arena of the school. In this manner, the political socialization potentials of the school can be optimized for the development of healthy citizens and a healthy society. By training its administrators, teachers, and students to understand the political nature of the school, by changing the characteristics of its power structure, and by dealing with political realities rather than fantasies, the school can play a major role in restoring some trust to those who are distrustful and some power to those who are powerless.

BIBLIOGRAPHY

Bachman, Jerald G. et al. *Youth in Transition.* Ann Arbor: University of Michigan, 1967, Vol. 1.
———— and Tannenbaum, Arnold J. "The Control-Satisfaction Relationship across varied Areas of Experience," *The Delta Phi Epsilon Journal,* 2 (May 1966), 16–25.

Bidwell, Charles E. "The School as a Formal Organization," *in* James G. March (ed.), *Handbook of Organization*. Skokie, Ill.: Rand McNally, 1965.

Bowerman, C. E., and Elder, G. H. Jr. "The Adolescent and his Family." Unpublished manuscript, 1962.

Brim, O. G., and Wheeler, S. *Socialization after Childhood: Two Essays*. New York: John Wiley, 1966.

Bronfenbrenner, M. "Some Familial Antecedents of Responsibility and Leadership in Adolescents," *in* L. Petrullo and B. Bass (eds.), *Leadership and Interpersonal Behavior*. New York: Holt, Rinehart and Winston, 1961.

Coleman, James. *The Adolescent Society*. New York: Free Press, 1961.

―――― et al. *Equality of Educational Opportunity*. Washington D.C.: Government Printing Office, 1966.

Crandall, Virginia C., Kathovsky, W., and Crandall, V. J. "Children's Beliefs in their own Control of Reinforcements in Intellectual-Academic Achievement Situations," *Child Development*, 36 (1965), 91–109.

Crandall, V. J. "Achievement," *Child Psychology*. Sixty-Second Yearbook of the National Society for the Study of Education. Chicago: University of Chicago Press, 1963.

Dahl, R. A. "The Concept of Power," *Behavioral Science*, 2 (1957), 201–15.

Douvan, Elizabeth, and Adelson, Joseph. *The Adolescent Experience*. New York: John Wiley, 1966.

Elder, G. H. Jr. "Structural Variations in the Child Rearing Relationship," *Sociometry*, 25 (1962), 241–62.

―――――. "Adolescent Socialization and Personality Development." Unpublished manuscript, 1965.

Erikson, E. H. "Eight Stages of Man," in *Childhood and Society*, 2nd ed. New York: Norton, 1963.

Etzioni, Amitai. *A Comparative Analysis of Complex Organizations*. New York: Free Press, 1961.

―――――. *Modern Organization*. Englewood Cliffs, N. J.: Prentice-Hall, 1964.

Gold, Martin, and Douvan, Elizabeth. "Modal Patterns in American Adolescence," *in* Lois W. Hoffman and Martin L. Hoffman (eds.), *Review of Child Development Research*. New York: Russell Sage Foundation, 1966.

Gouldner, Alvin, W. "Organizational Analysis," *in* Robert K. Merton et al. (eds.), *Sociology Today*. New York: Basic Books, 1959.

Greenstein, F. I. "The Benevolent Leader: Children's Images of Political Authority," *American Political Science Review*, 54 (1960), 934–43.

Hess, R. D. "Political Socialization in the Schools," *Harvard Educational Review*, Vol. 38, No. 3, (Summer 1968).

―――― and Easton, D. "The Child's Changing Image of the President," *Public Opinion Quarterly*, 24 (1960), 632–44.

Hess, R. D., and Torney, J. *The Development of Political Attitudes in Children*. Chicago: Aldine, 1967.

Lefcourt, Herbert W. "Internal versus External Control of Reinforcement," *Psychological Bulletin*, 65 No. 4 (1966), 206–20.

Neal, A. G., and Seeman, W. "Organization and Powerlessness: A Test of the Mediation Hypothesis," *American Sociological Review*, 24 (1964), 216–26.

Rotter, J. B. "Generalized Expectations for Internal versus External Control of Reinforcement," *Psychological Monographs*, 80 No. 1 (1966).

Seeman, Melvin. "On the Meaning of Alienation," *American Sociological Review*, 24 (1954) 783–91.

Selznick, Philip. "An Approach to a Theory of Bureaucracy," *American Sociological Review*, 8 (1943), 47–54.

Sullivan, H. S. *The Interpersonal Theory of Psychiatry.* New York: Norton, 1953.

Tannenbaum, Arnold S. "Control and Effectiveness in a Voluntary Organization," *American Journal of Sociology,* 67 (1961), 33–46.

———. *Control in Organization.* New York: McGraw-Hill, 1968.

——— and Kahn, R. L. "Organizational Control Structure," *Human Relations,* 10 (1957), 127–40.

———. *Participation in Union Locals.* New York: Harper & Row, 1955.

Tannenbaum, Arnold S., and Smith, Clagett G. "Organizational Control Structure: A Comparative Analysis," *Human Relations,* 16 (Fall 1963), 244–316.

The School's Contribution to the Learning of Participatory Responsibility

9

George B. Levenson

FOCUS: THE HIGH-SCHOOL SENIOR'S SENSE OF PARTICIPATORY RESPONSIBILITY

Recognition and acceptance of the duty to participate in political life is a widely cherished component of democratic citizenship. In this chapter, I shall examine the relevance of the American adolescent's school experiences for his awareness of the participatory responsibility of political membership. To conduct such an examination, I shall utilize data collected from interviews with a national sample of high-school seniors in public and private schools in the United States. This information was gathered in the spring of 1965 by members of the Survey Research Center at the University of Michigan under the direction of M. Kent Jennings.[1] After a number of sampling stages, 97 schools consented to participate in the study.[2] Depending on the size of the school, 15–21 seniors were designated to be interviewed in each school.[3] Ninety-nine percent of the students selected agreed to participate, and the resulting sample includes 1,669 student respondents.

In what was primarily an attempt to assess the importance of the civics curriculum in the political socialization process, data were also gathered from 317 social studies teachers in the 97 schools. Each teacher was selected according to the amount and variety of classroom contact he had with the

[1] Thanks are extended to M. Kent Jennings for making these data available. I also acknowledge the financial support of the University of Michigan's Office of Research Administration for preparation and analysis of the data.

[2] For a discussion of the experiences encountered in the course of this study, such as problems of access and the rates, nature, and sources of school cooperation, see M. Kent Jennings and Lawrence E. Fox, "The Conduct of Survey Research in Schools: Strategies and Problems of Access," *The School Review* (Fall 1968), p. 422.

[3] It should be pointed out that high-school dropouts—approximately 26 percent of this age group in 1965—were not included in the sample.

students in the sample. Less than one percent of those chosen were not interviewed.[4]

To measure the students' awareness of the obligation to participate, I shall assess the degree to which it is emphasized in conceptions of good citizenship. Seniors (as well as teachers) were asked the following open-ended question:

> People have different ideas about what being a good citizen means. We're interested in what you think. Tell me how you would describe a good citizen in this country—that is, what things about a person are most important in showing that he is a good citizen?

Up to four distinctive responses were coded for each subject's answer to the question. Together, student (and teacher) responses encompass just about all of the major qualities that civil trainers have claimed for the virtuous public man; they include everything from running for office to minding one's own business. Less than one percent of the students failed to answer the question; 8.6 percent gave only one response; 32.9 percent gave two responses; 35.3 percent gave three responses; and 22.4 percent gave four or more responses.

In delineating their private conceptions of the good citizen, students referred, in differing degrees, to various aspects of the responsibility to participate. For example, they mentioned such things as being interested in and informed about public affairs, voting, taking an active part in politics, and working to improve political institutions. In order to distinguish students according to the degree of their emphasis on the obligation to participate, I counted each respondent's participatory-oriented responses to the good citizen question, taking into account the total number of his uniquely coded answers regardless of their content. The scores on the resulting index of participatory responsibility range from 0 to 8.[5]

HYPOTHESES: THE KINDS OF SCHOOL EXPERIENCES LIKELY TO FOSTER RECOGNITION OF A PARTICIPATORY RESPONSIBILITY

A number of school-related experiences are likely to affect the saliency of the citizen's obligation to participate. In this section I shall suggest the potential importance of nine specific indicators of the student's school life,

---

[4] The size of the student and teacher samples have been "corrected" for analysis. The student sample has been adjusted or "weighted" to correct for inaccuracies in the initial estimates of twelfth-grade enrollment in 1965; schools were most often larger than they were originally believed to be. As a result, the total "raw" student sample size (N) of 1,669 respondents was upweighted to 2,063. Teacher weights were also assigned and the resulting sample size is 385.

[5] Since students differ in their verbal abilities, I constructed a measure that did not overly penalize the less articulate. I accomplished this by multiplying the proportion of participatory responses in the individual's total answer to the question by the absolute number of participatory responses. Hence, a person giving one participatory response out of *one* uniquely coded answer to the question received a higher score on the index than a person giving one participatory response out of *two* uniquely coded answers to the question.

which reflect (a) the substantive focus on his coursework; (b) the values, goals, and activities of his teachers; (c) the degree of his academic commitment; and (d) the nature of his perception of the student's role in school affairs.

Certainly the most explicit attempts to shape a person's definition of his citizen role occur within the context of his social studies. Not surprisingly, however, it has been reported that civic instruction in American public schools varies in the emphasis placed on the rights and obligations of citizenship,[6] and it is no secret that the objectives and content of the social studies curriculum have been a subject of great controversy among educators. As Jennings and Langton point out:

> While most educators can agree that the development of good citizenship is important, the "good citizen" is something of an ideal type whose attitudes and behavior vary with the values of those defining the construct.[7]

Nevertheless, formal exposure to the obligation to participate is most likely to occur in what are traditionally regarded as high-school civics courses. Hence, I expect that students who have taken such courses are more likely than those who have not to at least acknowledge an obligation to participate in political life.[8]

To be sure, placing selected social studies courses under the rubric of civics may not be as important as the student's perception that he has had a course which dealt with public affairs. In fact, over 99 percent of the students report having taken such a course, and almost half of these claim that it highly increased their interest in public affairs. When students themselves make such an assessment, they may be indirectly indicating that their coursework has increased the saliency of their citizen role and perhaps their recognition of the obligation to participate. Hence, I expect that students stating that their experience in self-designated public affairs courses increased their political interest are more likely to acknowledge the participatory dimension in good citizenship than those who see such an experience as having moderate or no impact.

The consequences of a student's coursework for his awareness of the obligation to participate may well be a function of the emphasis social studies teachers give to political participation during their civic instruction.

---

[6] Edgar Litt, "Civic Education, Community Norms, and Political Indoctrination," *American Sociological Review*, 28 (February 1963), pp. 69–75.

[7] M. Kent Jennings and Kenneth P. Langton, "Political Socialization and the High School Civics Curriculum in the United States," *American Political Science Review*, 62 (September 1968), p. 852.

[8] Civics courses are defined as those focusing on the study of citizenship and public affairs as well as political institutions and thought. The following are among the courses I shall regard as representative of this emphasis: American government, current events, senior citizenship, problems of democracy, state and local government, international relations, comparative politics, and political geography. The variable I shall use is the number of civics courses each respondent reported taking during three years of high school. Approximately one-third of the respondents never had such a course; of those who did, the great majority had not taken more than one. The variable shall be dichotomized into (a) those never taking such a course and (b) those having taken at least one civics course.

If a teacher places particular emphasis on participation in his private definition of good citizenship, then such emphasis may color his presentation of course materials and hence increase the saliency of the obligation to participate among his students. Because social studies teachers were asked the same good citizenship question as the students, and since almost all students were exposed to at least one of these teachers in a formal course setting, it is quite possible to test the hypothesis that those students exposed to teachers defining good citizenship in primarily participatory terms are more likely to place a similar emphasis on participation in their own notion of the ideal citizen role.

Moreover, since participation is widely acknowledged by social studies teachers as a component of good citizenship—albeit with varying emphasis —teachers stating that the goal of the social studies curriculum is to teach good citizenship are perhaps more likely to have the obligation to participate in mind, refer it in class, and hence transmit it to their students.[9] Perhaps more important, teachers who explicitly refer to the teaching of participatory rights and duties as among the goals of the social studies curriculum are more likely to engender awareness of the obligation to participate in their students.[10]

I also expect students to be more likely to emphasize participation as an element of good citizenship if they have had teachers who report that they frequently discuss politics with their students.[11]

Although the experiences attached to the high-school senior's formal social studies are probably his most direct encounter with the explicit teaching of the citizen role, many have argued that "citizenship is 'really learned through the whole school experience.' "[12] As Patterson rightly points out, such an argument may be posed not so that credit will be widely assigned but so that blame cannot be narrowly placed. After all, to give causal responsibility to everything may be as enlightening as assigning it to nothing.

---

[9] Teachers were asked to agree or disagree with the following statement: "The main purpose of social studies courses is to teach students to be good citizens."

[10] Teachers were asked the following open-ended question: "What would you say are the general goals of the social studies curriculum in this school?" Up to four responses were coded and those that include specific reference to participation were as follows:

1. Provide knowledge of citizen's rights and duties (rights and duties in general and specific rights and duties not covered by other code categories).
2. Teach about and encourage participation in public affairs; e.g., voting, obedience to laws, other specific citizenship acts.
3. Teach acceptance of civic responsibility; develop awareness of concern for or encourage action directed at social problems; e.g., instill in citizens a sense of social obligation; encourage participation in social action groups; provide basis for informed action.
4. Encourage students to formulate personal political positions or commitments.

[11] Teachers were specifically asked: "Would you say you talk to [students] about public affairs (a) several times a week, (b) a few times a week, (c) once or twice a year, or (d) never?"

[12] F. K. Patterson et al., *The Adolescent Citizen* (New York: The Free Press, 1960), p. 148.

Nevertheless, awareness and acceptance of the expectation to participate may be a function of the child's entire curricular experience (not to mention such informal factors as his peer culture) rather than simply his exposure to formal civic instruction. Hence, an additional school level variable is whether or not a student is enrolled in a college or vocational curriculum. I expect that the former—perhaps because of their primarily nontechnical training in the liberal arts—are more continuously exposed to the expectation that they develop an interest and become involved in public affairs.[13]

In addition, if a student's "general" school experience—both curricular and extracurricular—contributes to his awareness of the citizen's participatory responsibility, then the more committed he is to staying in school, the greater his sensitivity to the obligation to participate. One indirect measure of the student's expressive involvement in school life and his receptivity to the information conveyed in his coursework is whether he ever entertained the idea of leaving school prior to graduation. If the specific experiences attached to formal education contribute to an individual's sense of participatory responsibility, it is reasonable to hypothesize that those who considered dropping out will also be less inclined to define good citizenship in participatory terms.

Finally, the high-school senior's inclination to recognize the participatory expectation attached to citizenship may be, in part, a function of his perception of the student's role in the school environment. Like participation in the family system, seniors who view students as sharing in the running of school affairs are more likely than those who do not to develop a sense of responsibility to engage in such participation and generalize this feeling to their definition of the ideal citizen.

FINDINGS: THE IMPORTANCE OF SCHOOL EXPERIENCES IN PREDICTING EMPHASIS ON THE OBLIGATION TO PARTICIPATE

Table 1 displays the expected mean student scores on the index of participatory responsibility for each category of the nine school variables I have just discussed. These scores were derived by using multiple classification analysis (MCA).[14]

The pattern of the means for each of the nine variables in the table is an indication of the nature of its relevance for the degree of recognition of the sense of participatory responsibility. Thus, students in a college curri-

---

[13] Students were asked to specify their course program in school. Those classified in a vocational curriculum specified their course program as vocational, commercial, agricultural, or general.

[14] For a discussion of this multivariate analysis technique, see Frank Andrews, James Morgan, and John Sonquist, *Multiple Classification Analysis* (Ann Arbor, Mich.: Institute for Social Research, 1967). Briefly, MCA produces a mean score which eliminates the effects of the other variables under consideration. Hence, each table entry represents a close approximation of the *net* effect of a particular characteristic controlling for the contributions of the other variables presented in the table. Because MCA removes a case if there is missing data on at least one of the predictors or on the dependent variable, the weighted student sample size in Table 1 is 1706.

TABLE 1. "Expected"[a] Student Means on the Index of Participatory Responsibility for School Variables

Variable	Expected Mean	N
1.[b] Course program		
Vocational curriculum	4.13	(891)[c]
College curriculum	4.51	(816)
2. Degree public affairs course increased political interest		
Moderate or little	4.18	(758)
Very much	4.41	(948)
3. Goal of social studies is to teach good citizenship		
Disagree	4.38	(908)
Agree	4.22	(798)
4. Did teacher mention participation as a goal of school social studies curriculm?		
No	4.59	(175)
Yes	4.28	(1532)
5. Do students run school affairs?		
No	4.25	(898)
Somewhat	4.24	(569)
Great deal	4.37	(240)
6. Exposure to civic instruction		
None	4.22	(506)
At least one course	4.35	(1201)
7. Frequency teachers talk about politics with students		
Rarely or never	4.23	(294)
Sometimes	4.29	(576)
Very often	4.36	(837)
8. Teacher degree of participatory responsibility[d]		
(1) Low	4.33	(327)
(2)	4.28	(501)
(3)	4.32	(334)
(4) High	4.32	(544)
9. Considered dropping out of school		
Yes	4.27	(185)
No	4.32	(1522)

[a] Each mean is calculated with the effects of the other variables in the table removed.

[b] MCA generates a Beta score for each independent variable. It measures "the ability of the predictor to explain variation in the dependent variable after adjusting for the effects of all other predictors." (See Andrews, Morgan and Sonquist, *Multiple Classification Analysis, op. cit.*, p. 22.) In effect, the relative size of Beta scores across all predictors is an indication of the relative importance of each independent variable in predicting the dependent variable (in this case, the index of participatory responsibility). Variables in this table are presented according to the size of their Beta scores (i.e., the first variable has the highest Beta score). The Beta scores of these variables range from .11 to .01. The maximum possible size of a Beta is 1 and its lowest possible value is 0.

[c] Expected means are based on a reduced weighted N of 1706.

[d] While the teacher index of participatory responsibility was based on teacher responses to the good citizen question and constructed in the same manner as the student index, I have collapsed the measure into four categories to facilitate presentation of the findings.

culum have a higher mean score on the index of participatory responsibility than those in a vocational curriculum (see row 1 of Table 1). In general, many of the relationships in Table 1 are in the expected direction; that is, they support the hypotheses developed in the previous section. Hence, students are most likely to stress the citizen's participatory responsibility if they are in a college curriculum, feel their public affairs courses have increased their political interest, believe that students run school affairs, have been exposed to formal civic instruction, had teachers who frequently discussed politics in class, and never considered dropping out of school.

However, it is important to keep in mind that the relationship of each of the school variables to the index of participatory responsibility is generally quite low. By themselves, the variables examined do not make or break the student's sensitivity to the obligation to participate. Perhaps more important, the pattern of the means for two of the teacher variables is directly antithetical to my hypotheses: teachers agreeing that the aim of the social studies is to teach good citizenship and/or expressly stating that the goal of the social studies is to teach students about political participation are less inclined than their polar opposites to engender in their students a sensitivity to participatory responsibility. To be sure, the deviations of the expected scores of the categories within each of these variables from the grand mean are quite small; but in the multivariate analysis of school level variables, they are respectively the third and fourth most important school predictors of student scores on the index of participatory responsibility.

Perhaps the missing link in the unexpected relationship between the teachers' perception of the general aim of the social studies (i.e., to teach or not to teach good citizenship) and the student scores on the index of participatory responsibility is that "much of what is called citizenship training in the public schools . . . is an attempt to teach regard for the rules and standards of conduct of the school."[15] That is, teachers may be stressing discipline and obedience to school requirements (i.e., standards of dress, no smoking or chewing gum) rather than the specific responsibilities of adult citizenship and thus may give particular emphasis to the nonaggressive or nonparticipatory aspects of the citizen role. This may be even more true today than in 1965. Teachers and school administrators alike appear to be growing increasingly afraid of "student power" and may be quite reticent to openly accept and fully encourage the norm to participate. Indeed, Hess and Torney also report that

> in contrast to its emphasis on compliance, the school curriculum under-emphasizes the rights and obligations of a citizen to participate in government. The school focuses on the obligation and right to vote but does not offer the child sufficient understanding of the procedures open to individuals for legitimately influencing the government.[16]

Although Hess and Torney base their judgment on their observations of elementary school, there is some indication that these same values pre-

---

[15] R. D. Hess and J. V. Torney, *The Development of Political Attitudes in Children* (Chicago: Aldine Press, 1967), p. 218.
[16] Ibid.

vail among high-school social studies teachers. Table 2 demonstrates that teachers who view the aim of the social studies as the teaching of good citizenship tend to value obedience in children (their students?), are somewhat more reticent to publicly express their political dissatisfactions (in class?), and are more likely to erect barriers around their freedom in the classroom.

It is also true, however, that even when teachers claim that at least one goal of the civics curriculum is to teach students about political participation, their students do not manifest a special sensitivity to its normative importance. A methodological problem may have been responsible for this unexpected finding. The teacher responses that I regarded as participatory goals frequently included direct or indirect reference to other aspects of good citizenship. For example, the code category "teach about and encourage participation in public life" includes reference to voting as well as obedience to laws and other specific citizenship acts. Had I included coded responses which were only and clearly participatory, the measure of teachers' goals would have been extremely skewed; that is, very few teachers would have been regarded as mentioning participation as a goal of the social studies curriculum. The variable I constructed, however, may have seriously misrepresented the extent to which teachers view the curriculum as having such a goal. Moreover, the teaching of the opportunity and obligation to participate may very well be combined, in the teacher's mind, with the nonparticipatory expectations attached to the citizen role (e.g., loyalty, conformity to rules and regulations, being a good person). Thus, if the importance of political participation is mentioned in the classroom, it may not be emphasized over and above other and perhaps competing dimensions of good citizenship.

Conceivably, however, the finding derived from the variable I used has some substantive implications. Perhaps, for example, there is considerable interference between teachers' perceptions of the objectives of their coursework and the outcome of civic instruction. Quite likely, a crucial intervening variable is how teachers seek to accomplish their goals. As Clausen points out, "teachers obviously differ in . . . the degree to which they are aware of the various possibilities in implementing their curricular aims."[17] Perhaps even the most explicit intention to teach about the citizen's participatory responsibility may frequently yield minimal results if it is not supported by overt efforts. Clausen argues, for example, that the

> accomplishment of the teacher's goals requires recruitment of interest and the achievement of involvement and commitment on the part of the student, sustained by satisfaction or rewards for their effective participation.[18]

This appears to be consistent with the finding that only when teachers frequently talk about politics with their students are the latter more likely to include mention of participatory criteria in defining the good citizen (see row 7 in Table 1).

[17] John Clausen, "Perspectives on Childhood Socialization," *in* John Clausen, ed., *Socialization and Society* (Boston: Little, Brown, 1968), p. 158.
[18] Ibid., p. 157.

TABLE 2. FACTORS ASSOCIATED WITH TEACHERS' VIEW THAT THE SOCIAL
STUDIES ARE DESIGNED TO TEACH GOOD CITIZENSHIP

1. *Obedience and Respect for Authority are the Most Important Virtues
   Children Should Learn.*

		Agree[a]	Disagree	%	N	Gamma
Social studies should	Agree	69.1	30.9	100	348	
Teach good citizenship	Disagree	28.7	71.3	100	32[b]	+.63

2. *Do you Think a Teacher Should or Should Not Publicly Criticize Local
   Government Officials?*

		Should	Should Not	%	N	Gamma
Social studies should	Agree	65.7	34.3	100	348	
Teach good citizenship	Disagree	88.8	11.2	100	32	−.61

3. *Are There Any Particular Topics Which You Feel You Should Not
   Discuss [in class]?*

		Yes	No	%	N	Gamma
Social studies should	Agree	35.1	64.9	100	348	+.32
Teach good citizenship	Disagree	22.0	78.9	100	32	

[a] Responses were originally subdivided into degrees of agreement and disagreement.
I dichotomized them into two categories to reduce the skewness of the distributions.
[b] While the actual number of teachers disagreeing is quite small, proportion of
students exposed to these teachers is high (see Table 1).

One of the lowest of the school level relationships is that between
teacher readiness to cite participatory responsibility in their own conceptions of the good citizen and expected student scores on the same variable
(i.e., the index of participatory responsibility). This is somewhat surprising
since the pattern of the overall distribution of students and teachers on
the two indices is quite similar. Quite possibly, teachers are less agents than
reflectors and products of the values that nonacademic school experiences
might engender. Their ability and perhaps opportunity to express their
private values to their students appear minimal (see row 8 in Table 1).

Moreover, whereas enrollment in civics seems to affect student emphasis on participatory criteria, its relevance is marginal. Of all the school
predictors, it ranked among the least in importance. Indeed, only when
students report that they have had a course in public affairs which has
increased their interest in public affairs are they distinctly more likely to
mention participation as an element of good citizenship.

The most powerful of the school variables I have been examining is
the student's general curriculum level; those preparing for college are distinctly more inclined to include participation as a dimension of good citizenship. It is, however, difficult to determine precisely whether its importance is due to the range and substance of the coursework attached to a
particular curriculum or the extracurricular factors usually associated with
students' formal academic experiences. If the college curriculum exposes the

student to a less technical and more socially focused course of study, those enrolled in it are also often the members of the upper social echelons within the school. Students in the college curriculum are, by and large, "school leaders" and as such are likely to be particularly active citizens of the school society.[19] It may well be this more informal aspect of their school experiences which is most crucial in engendering an awareness of the connection between good citizenship and participation. Perhaps more important, there is a self-selective factor at work such that the more intelligent and aggressive students in general, and middle-class whites in particular, are probably most inclined to opt for the college curriculum. Indeed, it is, at this time, unclear whether particular school experiences or the opportunities and styles associated with individual social and psychological characteristics are more important in generating a readiness to acknowledge the obligation to participate. In short, whereas the nature of the student's curriculum experience is relatively highly correlated with the degree to which he recognizes his participatory responsibility, it may mask the importance of noncurricular and perhaps nonschool related experiences.

Together, the school level predictors explain only 2.6 percent of the variance in the student scores on the index of participatory responsibility. However, because not all the relationships are in the predicted direction, the specific importance of the formal curricular experiences for sensitivity to the obligation to participate remains unclear.

CONCLUSION: COMPLEX MESSAGES AND DIFFERENTIAL RECEPTIVITY

A central factor clouding the contributions of the school to the development of a sense of participatory responsibility is that the full flavor of the school-generated messages to the student is not easily disentangled. For example, although a frequently cited goal of the civics curriculum is to teach students about participatory rights and duties, civic instruction generally includes some degree of emphasis on the other expectations attached to political membership such as obedience to laws, allegiance to nation, and such personal qualities as neighborliness and a commitment to hard work. The relative stress on the different types of civic duties in the social studies curriculum probably varies both within and between schools. What is more important, the impact of the civics curriculum is undoubtedly a function of the content of the coursework as well as student receptivity to the material: courses differ in the cues offered and students differ in the cues recognized.

Thus as Table 3 demonstrates, among those enrolled in a college curriculum, the taking of civics courses is associated with a higher than average student score on the index of participatory responsibility (significant at the .01 level). Among those in a vocational curriculum, the taking

---

[19] Indeed, those in the college curriculum are more likely to have run for office in school; the relationship (gamma) between curriculum level and running for office in school is +.35. In addition, they are more likely to have held office in school clubs (gamma =+.42), helped others run for student government (gamma =+.24), and voted in school elections (gamma =+.35).

TABLE 3. THE IMPORTANCE OF CURRICULUM LEVEL FOR THE RELEVANCE OF EXPOSURE TO CIVIC INSTRUCTION

Number of Civics Courses	College Curriculum	Vocational Curriculum
None	4.30[a] (321)	4.07 (348)
At least one	4.61 (659)	4.11 (729)

[a] Table entries are the mean student score on the index of participatory responsibility.

of civics courses appears to be exceptionally minimal in importance (not significant at the .05 level). Hence, the mere fact of exposure to high-school civics does not guarantee that students will develop a special awareness of their participatory responsibility as citizens.

In addition, among blacks, the relationship between the taking of civics courses and emphasis on participatory criteria is the *reverse* of that for whites. For the blacks, those taking civics have on the average a lower score on the index of participatory responsibility than the blacks who have never had such a course. Although the difference between the means is not large (.24), it is significant at the .01 level. Among the whites, on the other hand, the difference between those taking and those not taking civics courses was in the expected direction (though the difference between the means was somewhat smaller than that among the blacks).

The difference between blacks and whites is even more dramatic when a control is introduced for curriculum level. As Table 4 demonstrates, for blacks and whites enrolled in a *vocational* curriculum, the taking of civics courses does not appear to affect intraracial scores on the index of participatory responsibility.[20]

When whites and blacks enrolled in a *college* curriculum are compared on the impact of civics courses, the pattern of means for the former is the reverse of that for the latter. Among blacks preparing for college, exposure to civic instruction is associated with a weaker inclination to emphasize participatory responsibility than lack of such exposure.[21]

TABLE 4. MEAN SCORE ON THE INDEX OF PARTICIPATORY RESPONSIBILITY FOR WHITES AND BLACKS GIVEN CURRICULUM LEVEL AND EXPOSURE TO CIVIC INSTRUCTION

Race	Curriculum Level and Exposure to Civic Instruction			
	Vocational/No civics	Vocational/Civics	College/No civics	College/Civics
White	4.22	4.22	4.26	4.67
	(287)	(643)	(307)	(613)
Black	3.30	3.24	4.97	3.76
	(58)	(87)	(15)	(38)

[20] Of course the overall differences between whites and blacks within this subsample are substantial.

[21] Although the N for college curriculum blacks who have never taken civics is quite small (15), the mean of this group is significantly different (at the .01 level) from the mean of college curriculum blacks who *have* taken civics.

A logical implication is that blacks are tuning into other components of good citizenship in their civic course experiences as a result of course material and/or their own personal value sets. This leads to a new set of questions. If blacks enrolled in a *college* curriculum and exposed to civic coursework tend to place less emphasis on the obligation to participate than those who have never taken a civics course, then what relevance, if any, does formal civic instruction have for their sensitivity to other aspects of good citizenship? Similarly, what is the relevance of civics for the emphasis blacks enrolled in a *vocational* curriculum place on the nonparticipatory dimensions of good citizenship? Parallel questions can, of course, be asked about white students.

To begin to answer these questions, I constructed indices which assessed each student's emphasis on the allegiant, obedient, and nonpolitical components of good citizenship.[22] Each index was based on responses to the good citizen question and was constructed in the same way as the index of participatory responsibility.[23] I then cross-tabulated the civics course variable with each of the four indices, controlling both for curriculum level and race.

Among college curriculum whites, the taking of civics courses proved to be most important in increasing awareness of a participatory responsibility while it seemed to make little difference for whites enrolled in a vocational curriculum. For both college and noncollege preparing blacks, exposure to civic instruction registered its most pronounced and significant impact on the student's sensitivity to *obedience* criteria.

These findings simultaneously corroborate and elaborate at least part of Jennings and Langton's findings based on only the *first* responses to the good citizen question.[24] They argue that blacks—particularly those with "higher status"—are unresponsive or less receptive to the "participation emphasis in the curriculum" because of a " 'realistic' appraisal of the institutional and social restrictions placed upon Negro participation in the United States."[25]

---

[22] Examples of responses which reflect each of these three types of citizen responsibilities are as follows:

> 1. *Allegiance*: Being patriotic, supporting the country and government; respecting and honoring symbols (i.e., the flag) and officials (i.e., the President); performing military service; fighting for the country.
> 2. *Obedience*: Obeying laws, rules, and regulations of the government; paying taxes.
> 3. *Nonpolitical:* Helping others; being a good neighbor; being honest and trustworthy; going to church; leading a moral life; being a good worker.

[23] Technically, of course, these four indices are not independent since all were developed from responses to the good citizen question. Thus a student scoring very high on one index by definition will score lower on all others. However, because the great majority of students gave a mixed response [i.e., they mentioned more than one type of criterion for good citizenship such as voting (participatory) *and* respecting the flag (allegiant)], the average score for all those exposed to formal civic instruction could be consistently higher than the mean for all those who have never had a civics course.

[24] Jennings and Langton, pp. 863–64.

[25] Ibid., p. 864.

By a similar line of reasoning, blacks may be more sensitive to the obedience dimension of good citizenship because the federal law has, in recent years, been among their most powerful allies; many of the early battles of the civil rights movement were designed to bring attention to and encourage enforcement of the guarantees of the Constitution. Blacks have much to gain if everyone feels obliged to obey and if citizens comply with the dictates of the courts. As Jennings and Langton put it, blacks (and of course whites as well) may "select out of the curriculum only those role characteristics which appear to be most congruent with [their] preconceived notion[s] of [their] political life chances."[26]

It is, of course, equally possible that blacks, by virtue of their frequently segregated school setting, are systematically discouraged (or, more neutrally, never encouraged) from developing a participatory emphasis in learning the citizen role. Litt notes, for example, that in a working class environment (which he calls *Gamma* and, incidentally, where blacks are most likely to reside), civics texts "contain only a few references to norms that encourage voting, feelings of political effectiveness and a sense of civic duty."[27] He concludes that "students in the three communities [examined] are trained to play different political roles,"[28] with those in Gamma least encouraged to adopt an obligation to participate in political life.

Whatever the major reason for racial differences in citizen role definitions, it is highly probable that the impact of civic instruction on an individual's notion of citizen expectations is both a function of what is taught and how it is interpreted by the learner.

It remains true, however, that despite apparent subcultural variation among the high-school seniors, the school level variables I have been examining are relatively weak in accounting for variation in student scores on the index of participatory responsibility even if they tend to visibly and significantly affect the degree to which students recognize participatory responsibility as a quality of good citizenship. In part this undoubtedly reflects the fact that I have isolated only a few of the variables relevant to the high-school senior's school experiences. It is also possible, as Jennings and Langton argue, "that by the time students reach high school, many of their political orientations have crystallized or have reached a temporary plateau."[29] Indeed, Hess and Torney report that by the eighth grade, students and teachers define the good adult citizen in quite similar terms.[30] For both, the most popular definition of the good adult citizen is one who is "interested in the way the country is run" and "votes and gets others to vote."[31] Perhaps as a result, formal and informal civic instruction in high school "offers little that is new [to the student]; . . . [it] simply provide[s] another layer of information which is essentially redundant."[32] Hence, the

[26] Ibid.
[27] Litt, p. 72.
[28] Ibid., p. 75.
[29] Jennings and Langton, p. 854.
[30] Hess and Torney, p. 68.
[31] Ibid., Table 7, p. 39.
[32] Jennings and Langton, p. 854.

ability of the high school and its experiential setting to account for *recognition* of the obligation to participate may be quite marginal. It remains unclear, however, if differential classroom exposures affect the individual's *behavioral commitment* to an acknowledged sense of participatory responsibility. Indeed, if the current involvement of youth in political life has any basis in a readiness to enact a well-developed sense of obligation to speak and act, we now may be witnessing the effects of a lesson well learned.

Political Socialization in
a Discontinuous Setting 10

THE EXPERIENCE OF
THREE COLOMBIAN SECONDARY SCHOOLS

Jon Parker Heggan

The growing literature on political socialization in the schools presents us with an array of seemingly conflicting results. Several studies suggest that educational institutions may exert a noticeable impact on student political attitudes and behavior. Still other findings indicate that schools are quite ineffective as agencies of political learning. One possible interpretation of these apparently contradictory findings is that they do, in fact, accurately portray some real variations in the impact of different schools on young people's political orientations, variations that are to some degree functions of differences in the internal and external environments of educational institutions. Our problem in assessing this interpretation is that present research findings can tell us little about the processes of political learning in the individual school. Available data cannot shed much light on the difficulties that confront educational institutions as socializing agencies, the efforts of school personnel to overcome these problems, and the results of such efforts.

This present paper is an attempted initial step toward correcting our research deficiencies with respect to one major area of difficulty—the tendency in nearly all countries of real political practices to diverge from formally-preferred political values. The crux of the problem from the perspective of the educator is that he must, in the face of contradictory political concepts and demands, define the "good citizen" in a socially acceptable manner and then arrive at an appropriate and effective method of instilling this concept in the young.

In Colombia, discontinuities in the political system are especially severe. Formal structural arrangements at all levels of government contrast sharply with real political practices. Despite outwardly democratic constitutional forms, the country's politics are dominated by a traditional, privileged minority of the population. Rising middle- and lower-class demands for a truly participant political system have forced some limited concessions from the bipartisan coalition of Liberal and Conservative party leaders who have ruled Colombia since 1958. But the traditionally dominant groups remain unwilling to institute the kinds of meaningful changes needed to make the nation's professed democratic ideals a reality.

An exploratory investigation that I carried out in three secondary institutions in the Colombian capital of Bogotá provided an opportunity to evaluate the efforts of a few educators to inculcate citizenship values in a highly discontinuous political setting. The schools illustrated the three main kinds of Colombian secondary training—private religious, private secular, and public. Each institution offered a six-year program of study that in content and performance resembled expectations of a low to medium quality junior-senior high-school curriculum in the United States. Students enrolled in the private religious (PR) and private secular (PS) institutions came largely from upper- and upper-middle-class families. Young people attending the public (PUB) school were mainly from lower- and lower-middle-class homes.

The reported findings deal with attempts by the three institutions to develop in their pupils deep affective attachments to domestic political leaders and to the democratic norms that supposedly regulate Colombian political behavior. Final (sixth)-year students at each school served as the principal subject populations for the study. Estimates of the political value preferences of these students during their initial year of secondary education were based on measurements of the orientations of those first-year schoolmates whose grades suggested that eventually they would earn their degrees. Comparison of the political attitudes of the beginning and final-year pupils served to indicate changes in citizenship value preferences during adolescence.

THE FIRST-YEAR YOUNG PEOPLE: POLITICAL IDEALISM AND NAIVETE

The questionnaire findings suggest that most beginning secondary pupils rated the skills of both contemporary and historical Colombian political leaders highly. A substantial portion of each first-year class agreed that recent Colombian governments generally have made good decisions (Table 1, Item 1). A small majority of each student group viewed such nineteenth-century patriots as Bolívar and Santander as possessors of almost superhuman political capabilities (Table 1, Item 2).

Other questionnaire and interview data indicate that student ratings of national political leaders were one facet of a generally favorable view of the larger society. Most first-year pupils gave religious, business, and, to a lesser degree, military elites high performance ratings. According to these young people, Colombian social structures provided numerous opportunities for upward mobility. Demonstrated ability rather than luck, influential friends, or some other ascriptive criterion was seen as the main determinant of social advancement.

Beginning secondary pupils also were favorably disposed toward various forms of political participation. All three first-year classes believed that

TABLE 1. PERCENTAGES OF FIRST-YEAR SECONDARY PUPILS WHO RATED COLOMBIAN POLITICAL LEADERS' CAPABILITIES FAVORABLY

Item	School Type		
	PR	PS	PUB
1. The Colombian government generally has made good decisions during the past seven or eight years.	88	85	72
2. A great political leader, such as Bolívar or Santander, really does not need political advisors.	52	53	53
N	(97)	(40)	(75)

For each item, agreement was considered a "favorable" response.

TABLE 2. PERCENTAGES OF FIRST-YEAR SECONDARY STUDENTS RATED AS "PARTICIPATORY" ACCORDING TO THEIR ATTITUDES TOWARD VOTING AS A CITIZEN'S DUTY

Item	School Type		
	PR	PS	PUB
1. The citizens of my country have a moral obligation to vote in elections.	88	78	81
2. I would support a law that makes the vote obligatory.	63	63	55
N	(97)	(40)	(75)

For each item, students who agreed were rated as "participatory."

Colombians have a moral obligation to vote in elections (Table 2, Item 1). Sizeable majorities of each student body even manifested a willingness to support legislation that would make the vote obligatory (Table 2, Item 2). Commitments to nonvoting types of political involvement also were widespread. Most first-year young people believed that individual citizens should study and know the programs of the country's major political parties, make known their opinions on proposed legislation, and seek the repeal of unjust laws.

Student support for Colombian political elites and institutions did not, however, have strong intellectual or behavioral foundations. First-year pupils generally demonstrated little knowledge of the ideological positions, beliefs, or policy proposals of the country's political leaders. Often, these young people could not even identify top-level governmental and party personnel other than the president. Views of the real operations of the national political process tended to be highly simplistic. According to many first-year pupils, citizens acting individually were the cornerstones of democratic politics in Colombia. The roles played by parties, interest groups, the communications media, and other key components of the political system were either downplayed or totally ignored.

Certain anti-democratic notions also were rather widespread at the first-year level. Many members of each class were intolerant of political views that differed from their own. Students who were willing to allow free expression of opposing political ideas still preferred to talk politics with individuals of like ideological persuasions. Similarly, formal commitments to political leadership responsibility tended to be somewhat shallow. Many first-year pupils were willing to follow unquestioningly the dictates of "good" political leaders. An even larger proportion of these young people held that an "intelligent" and "patriotic" president need not explain to the people his reasons for making important political decisions.

Attitudes that were consistent with democratic precepts sometimes failed to stimulate corresponding behavioral forms. Most beginning secondary pupils did not, for example, act out their "participant" political beliefs. Less than one-half of each first-year class manifested an interest in radio programs or newspaper articles dealing with politics, and only a small minority of students stated that they discussed politics with friends or relatives fairly often.

THE POLITICAL VALUES STRESSED BY SECONDARY INSTRUCTION

Citizenship training in all three institutions sought to instill in students deep and lasting affection for Colombian political leaders and institutions. To accomplish this objective, teachers and textbook authors chose to avoid domestic political realities rather than to integrate class offerings with the real political world. Course subject matter at each grade level offered students a highly idealized version of national political structures and processes. The actions of major political figures were portrayed as conforming to the most noble of the country's democratic formal political values. Political realities that might have conflicted with this idealized view of domestic politics were either ignored or shaped to fit the dominant political themes.

PR (private religious school), PS (private secular school), and PUB (public school) courses that dealt with historical events stressed the positive personality characteristics and the outstanding accomplishments of past Colombian political leaders. Professors and textbooks made considerable use of the early nineteenth-century independence struggle with Spain in developing these themes. The skill, courage, and selfless devotion of the patriotic forces to their homeland were, according to this instruction, mainly responsible for eventually evicting the "Spanish oppressors" from the national territory. The deeds and qualities of such leading patriots as Simón Bolívar and Francisco de Paula Santander were described in especially glowing terms.

The clerical authors of the three schools' Colombian history textbooks did interrupt their idealized accounts of post-independence nineteenth-century events to levy some harsh criticisms against a few political leaders of the period. Principal targets were those individuals who had most vigorously opposed the implementation of such church-supported policies as centralized government, religious control of education, and preservation of the traditional social order. *PUB* history courses were especially critical of several latter-day, nineteenth-century national political figures. The writer of the *PUB* history textbook concluded his discussion of the period's domestic politics, for instance, with a severe condemnation of leading Liberal and Conservative party politicians for allegedly fomenting the civil war that occurred at the end of the century.[1]

In his introduction to twentieth-century Colombian history, however, the same author contended that the application of lessons learned from previous political mistakes had resulted in domestic tranquility and progress during most of the country's recent past. Portrayals of national political leaders of the period 1900–1960 presented by courses in all three schools were consistent with this position. The offerings of these courses stressed, and sometimes exaggerated, the personal virtues and accomplishments of all major twentieth-century public officials. Even those liberal politicians responsible for implementing church-opposed policies were not criticized. In this connection, the author of *PUB*'s Colombian history textbook would merely state that the 1936 constitutional amendments that weakened church control over education had "caused controversy."[2]

The content of other school courses supplemented history instruction by stressing the cooperative aspects of Colombian politics. In place of analyses of underlying domestic political realities, civics professors substituted descriptions of the formal structures and the positive functions of Colombian government. Their accounts maintained that the most important governmental task is attainment of the general welfare of society and that Colombian politicians of all political persuasions work together harmoniously to achieve this objective.

Each secondary school's philosophy instruction specifically condemned all forms of human conflict as unnatural and undesirable. The few direct references made in other courses to Colombian political discord conformed to this view. History course offerings attributed nineteenth-century outbreaks of civil strife, for example, to the selfish pursuits of a few political aspirants. The disorders accordingly terminated only when altruistic leaders replaced the egoistic fomenters of violence.

The nature of the *PR, PS,* and *PUB* institutions' general approach to the social sciences probably encouraged student acceptance of the view that the Colombian political system is comprised of talented, cooperating, and selfless individuals. Teaching personnel rarely sought to stimulate the critical faculties of their pupils. Instead of adopting a problem-solving approach to the study of politics and society, instructors employed the more traditional method of requiring rote memorization of fundamental "truths." Students were rewarded according to their effectiveness in remembering such "truths," not in questioning them.

Course instruction about political institutions portrayed democracy as a decidedly superior form of government. The usual civics course pattern

[1] Hermano Justo Ramon, *Historia de Colombia* (Bogotá, Colombia: Editorial Stella, 1964), pp. 344–46.
[2] Ibid., pp. 371–72.

was first to define the term "democracy," and then to follow with a demonstration of its advantages over other types of political systems. Definitions of democratic government varied considerably, both within and between schools. Some professors subscribed to the populist notion of "government by the people"; others preferred the somewhat more realistic conception of "government by representatives of the people"; still a third group utilized variants of one or both definitions. All instructors did agree that freedom of the individual and election of political leaders are the chief features that set democracy apart from other forms of government. Lavish praise repeatedly was heaped on both characteristics by civics and related course offerings.

School efforts to develop student commitments to individual liberty and voting participation were intertwined with the attempt to instill in the young people deep affection for Colombian political personalities and institutions. History instructors extolled the virtues of national patriots who sacrificed their lives to remove foreign domination. The subject matter in civics and sociology courses portrayed modern-day Colombian leaders as dedicated enforcers of the many rights and freedoms guaranteed by the country's constitution. The voting opportunities available to most Colombian citizens allegedly offered additional testimony to the nation's democratic practices.

These exaggerated portrayals of the virtues of democracy failed, nevertheless, to provide students with meaningful concepts that could be related to everyday, real-life experiences. Discussions of individual liberty generally were rather dull and uninformative. Civics, philosophy, and sociology instruction merely listed basic freedoms found in the Colombian Constitution and in the United Nations Declaration of Human Rights and urged pupils to make the sacrifices necessary to defend them. Other course offerings simply warned that individual liberty must be kept within the limits set by God and must not infringe upon the freedom enjoyed by other members of society. Toleration of political diversity and nonconformity, a core principle in any truly free society, was not encouraged either directly or indirectly.

Classroom treatment of citizenship participation in politics was equally shallow and unimaginative. Teacher and textbook emphasis upon the cooperative aspects of politics resulted in either negative presentations or complete avoidance of most nonvoting forms of political involvement. The few references that were made to parties and interest groups argued that both types of structures had tended throughout Colombian history to exacerbate conflict in the pursuit of narrow, partisan interests. Even the discussions of voting contributed little to an understanding of participant politics. Although course offerings repeatedly urged electoral involvement and condemned absenteeism, they failed to provide satisfactory explanations of the relationship between large-scale voting and democratic government.

PR, PS, and *PUB* instruction about political authority probably encouraged a similar "nonparticipant" approach to politics. Teachers at all grade levels insisted that unquestioning obedience to public officials and the law was a prerequisite to the maintenance of an orderly society. By contending that political authority has an overriding religious foundation, several *PR* and a few *PS* and *PUB* courses reinforced this emphasis upon passive citizenship roles. The offerings of these courses alleged that the authority of the state comes directly from God. Obedience and respect for government leaders is, accordingly, merely a derivative of submission to and esteem for religious authority.

School structural patterns also tended to diverge from the participant, democratic values formally emphasized by course subject materials. Neither the *PS* nor the *PUB* institution offered students meaningful opportunities to assume active citizenship roles within the school community. The only extracurricular activities made available to pupils by *PS* were participation in weekly assembly programs and contributions to infrequent school exhibits. *PS* instructors exercised fairly tight control over the limited amount of student participation that occurred in the classroom. The *PUB* institution did encourage some pupil initiative and responsibility during school hours. The availability of only a few school-sponsored formal organizations, the absence of a student council, and teacher emphasis in most courses on the lecture method, however, kept *PUB* student participation to a rather low level.

Young people enrolled in *PR*, the private religious institution, were considerably more active during the school day than were their *PS* and *PUB* counterparts. *PR* pupils at all grade levels were eligible for membership in several types of school-sponsored formal organizations, including a few religious clubs, a charity organization, a public speaking club, and a scout organization. Students also took part in assembly programs, visits to nearby places of interest, school exhibits, and intraschool athletic events. Most *PR* teachers encouraged a similar high level of student participation in the classroom. Neither the extracurricular nor the classroom patterns were, however, designed to produce responsible, democratic citizens. *PR* administrators and teachers chose the goals and the leaders of school organizations and generally exercised detailed control over all forms of pupil involvement. School regulations specifically forbade student councils or other structures that might have given the young people a real voice in *PR* affairs.

IMPACT OF THE SCHOOLS ON STUDENT POLITICAL ORIENTATIONS

Questionnaire and interview data from the study suggest that at all three institutions' student political attitudes underwent changes during adolescence. Idealized conceptions of domestic political elites fell markedly between each school's first and sixth secondary grades, although final-year pupils continued to support most of the country's chief political figures. Conversely, student commitments to and understanding of participant, democratic values increased noticeably over the same period. The investigation produced little evidence to indicate, however, that the three secondary schools played a significant role in any of these developments.

Most final-year pupils from each institution approved of the role performances of Colombian political leaders during the recent past. The written

TABLE 3. Percentages of First- and Sixth-Year Secondary Pupils Who Rated Colombian Political Leaders' Capabilities Favorably

		School Type		
Item		PR	PS	PUB
1. The Colombian government generally has made good decisions during the past seven or eight years.	(1) 88	85	72
	(6) 75	81	79
2. A great political leader, such as Bolívar or Santander, really does not need political advisors.	(1) 52	53	53
	(6) 13	21	21
(1)ᵃ N		(97)	(40)	(75)
(6)ᵇ N		(75)	(70)	(75)

ᵃ (1)=First-year secondary school students.
ᵇ (6)=Sixth-year secondary school students.
For each item, agreement was considered a "favorable" response.

questionnaire scores suggest that the proportion of *PUB* students who rated political task accomplishments highly actually increased between the first and sixth years of secondary school. The fractions of older *PS* and *PR* students who adopted a similar positive stance were only slightly lower than the corresponding proportions of first-year schoolmates (Table 3, Item 1).

On the surface, the close correspondence between school and student ratings of the accomplishments of Colombian political leaders seems to indicate that secondary-level course offerings may have exerted a strong impact on pupil attitudes. Interview results, however, suggested otherwise. In defending their questionnaire responses, few final-year interviewees offered justifications for their positions that were consistent with the highly idealized textbook portrayals of domestic policy-making activities. The evaluations made by most students appear, instead, to have been based on more realistic and immediate concerns. Political decisions were believed good because they were viewed as having benefited not only the larger society but also relatives, friends, and the young people themselves.

A decline during adolescence in student ratings of the performance capabilities of past national heroes is additional evidence of the lack of secondary school influence on pupil evaluations of Colombian political leaders. The proportion of student respondents who believed that heroic political figures such as Bolívar and Santander were possessors of extraordinary capabilities fell to about one-fifth at *PS* and *PUB* and one-eighth at *PR* by the final secondary year (Table 3, Item 2).

The change in pupil evaluations of national political leaders evidently was part of a more general growth during adolescence in student skepticism about Colombian society. Final-year pupils at each secondary institution made decidedly more realistic appraisals of domestic social processes than had their first-year schoolmates. Most older students maintained that influential friends were more important than demonstrated ability in determining professional advancement in Colombia. Still others contended that

TABLE 4. Percentages of First- and Sixth-Year Secondary Students Rated as "Participatory" According to Their Attitudes Toward Voting as a Citizen's Duty

	School Type		
Item	PR	PS	PUB
1. The citizens of my country have a moral obligation to vote in elections.	(1) 88 (6) 96	78 96	81 95
2. I would support a law that makes the vote obligatory.	(1) 63 (6) 58	63 63	55 53
(1) ᵃ N		(97)	(40)	(75)
(6) ᵇ N		(75)	(70)	(75)

ᵃ (1)=First-year secondary school students.
ᵇ (6)=Sixth-year secondary school students.
For each item, students who agreed were rated as "participatory."

upward mobility depended mainly on luck. Sixth-year pupil evaluations of the clergy, the military, and most other domestic elites were lower than those made by the first-year young people. Only the business community appeared to escape this spirit of growing skepticism and doubt.

In contrast to pupil attitudes toward domestic political leaders, commitments to participant, democratic values became more widespread and firmer during the secondary years at each institution. The proportion of final-year students who regarded voting as a moral obligation was even larger than the substantial majority of first-year young people who had adopted this stance (Table 4, Item 1). The depth of the older students' feelings about electoral participation is suggested by the willingness of many sixth-year pupils to back compulsory voting regulations in spite of their concern for protecting individual freedom of choice (Table 4, Item 2). Support for most forms of nonvoting political involvement, interest in politics, and engagement in real political activity also increased as students got older.

Despite their stress on formal democratic values, the three schools appear to have contributed little to the strengthening of pupil attachments to participant politics. Changes in student orientations toward political involvement were greatest in those areas that were either de-emphasized or ignored by course offerings, and sixth-year young people's conceptions of real political processes often deviated sharply from the simplistic political models presented in the classroom.

Student support for party and interest group activity rose markedly during secondary school, even though civics teachers and textbooks virtually ignored nonvoting, participatory political behavior. Sixth-year pupils were far more likely than their younger colleagues to believe that the average Colombian citizen should make his services available to the party of his choice. Final-year interviewees also recognized that politics involves power and that interest groups possess more of this commodity than do individual citizens. Accordingly, they recommended that private citizens should act in concert in fulfilling their participant responsibilities.

Sixth-year student understanding of the basic principles of democracy considerably surpassed the information made available in the classroom. Unlike their first-year counterparts, most of the older respondents maintained that even intelligent and dedicated political leaders should be responsible to the citizenry. Toleration of opposing viewpoints appeared similarly widespread at the sixth-year grade level. Final-year students generally supported the basic tenets of an open society and were able to apply them to concrete political problems.

Most older pupils still did not, however, subscribe fully to participant, democratic principles. Despite the gains made during adolescence, political interest and activity levels remained relatively low at the upper grade levels. Only a bare majority of each final-year class followed newspaper articles and radio programs about politics, and less than one-third discussed political affairs fairly often. Similarly, commitments to holding public officials responsible sometimes appeared rather shaky. Some final-year students apparently derived their commitments as much from mistrust of political and other authority figures as from firm adherence to democratic standards. Still other pupils gave some evidence of being susceptible to the simplistic, emotional appeals of political demagogues.

SUMMARY AND CONCLUSION

The three secondary schools in the study probably had at least two important advantages in their efforts to shape student attitudes toward Colombian political figures and institutions. For one thing, many young people attending each institution were favorably disposed initially toward the kinds of political values stressed in the classroom. A substantial proportion of beginning secondary pupils had highly idealized conceptions of the accomplishments and the personal qualities of domestic politicians. Although this youthful idealism weakened noticeably during adolescence, most final-year students still approved of the role performances of national political leaders. Conversely, the psychological readiness of the pupils for modern democratic values actually rose somewhat during the secondary school years. Specific manifestations of this change were heightened student interest in politics, greater acceptance of political diversity, and strengthened commitments to political leadership responsibility. The intellectual growth that accompanied these developments allowed the older pupils to better understand democratic politics. They learned democratic values more easily than did their younger colleagues, and they were more likely to apply such values to a fairly wide variety of political phenomena.

Secondly, the secondary-level young people were partially sheltered from factors in the adult world that might have interfered with effective political socialization. The school as well as the family helped to shield students from some of the harsh day-to-day political realities that might have encouraged a more cynical view of domestic politicians and democracy. Both structures also protected pupils from the potentially adverse effects of economic self-interest, thereby allowing political learning to take place prior to the full emotional impact of deep concern for economic well-being. Since the insulating mechanisms were most effective at the earliest secondary grade levels, the schools seemingly had time to bring their political value preferences into harmony with the realities of the older adolescents' social and political worlds.

The three institutions were unwilling, or perhaps unable, however, to make the compromises that were necessary to capitalize on these advantages. Apparently influenced by the vast discrepancies between formal institutions and actual political processes in Colombia, teachers and administrators chose not to face the difficult task of integrating preferred values with domestic political realities. The result was presentation of a highly idealized version of politics that bore little resemblance or relationship to Colombian practices.

Gaps and inconsistencies in classroom offerings about politics probably were additional obstacles to the effective transmission of political institutional preferences. Teachers and textbooks rarely sought to utilize civics-type subject materials to develop or explore concepts that were central to the three schools' formal emphasis on democracy. Treatment of authority relationships and individual freedom often, in fact, contradicted the democratic values stressed in civics classrooms. Similarly, educators at each institution failed to encourage student councils and other forms of involvement that might have allowed pupils to act out school value preferences in some meaningful fashion.

This twofold weakness in citizenship training programs appears eventually to have contributed heavily to the undoing of all three institutions. Having become increasingly aware of the vast discrepancies between course offerings on government and domestic political realities, many upper-grade students tended to look to nonschool socializing agencies for political cues. Some school-supported values were adopted more in spite of than because of the efforts of teaching and administrative personnel. Other school preferences simply were discarded by many students sometime after the initial secondary year.

The extent of the incongruence between course instruction on politics and pupil orientations may have depended in part on the nature of vertical relationships within each institution. Data from the study suggest, for example, that *PR*'s authoritarian practices contributed to the school's ineffectiveness in instilling in students those political norms that teaching and administrative personnel deemed most important. Apparently older pupils' disenchantment with such practices eventually was generalized to school officials and then to their value preferences.[3]

Conversely, *PUB* structural patterns may have partly offset that school's failure to provide students with realistic accounts of domestic political leaders and institutions. *PUB*'s ability to combine firmness and fairness, together with its encouragement of some student initiative, seems to have

---

[3] For elaboration of this point, see my article, "The Formation of Attitudes toward Political Morality in Three Colombian Secondary Schools," *Social Science Quarterly* (September 1971), pp. 309–17.

contributed to the development of pupil trust in teaching and administrative personnel. The resulting relationship may have led the public school's students, in turn, to give greater weight to course offerings on politics than did their *PR* and *PS* counterparts.

Empirical findings from the investigation suggest that of the three institutions *PUB* was possibly the most successful in inculcating political value preferences in pupils. Despite the failure of their families to benefit from recent domestic political decision-making, the largely lower- and lower-middle-class *PUB* students rated Colombian political elites as highly as did the predominantly upper- and upper-middle-class *PS* pupils and even higher than did the well-to-do *PR* young people. The initially favorable *PUB*, *PS*, and *PR* post-primary student evaluations of Colombian political accomplishments, in fact, rose only during the secondary years of the public institution. Similarly, the *PUB* sixth-year pupils were as committed to participant, democratic politics as were their private school colleagues.

At the same time, other data from the study emphasize that even *PUB* had only a very limited impact on student political orientations. Support for the public institution's preferred values was based largely on conceptions of democracy, political achievements, and self-interest that were learned outside the school. Instead of resting on the simplistic, naive assumptions presented in the classroom, *PUB* student commitments to domestic leaders and democratic structures stemmed from fairly realistic assessments of Colombian society. Evaluations of national political heroes, as well as other school preferences that seemed inconsistent with pupils' understanding of domestic realities, simply were rejected by many *PUB* young people in the course of their secondary training.

Political Socialization and Political Participation in West Africa

11

A SURVEY OF UPPER FORM SECONDARY
SCHOOL STUDENTS IN SIERRA LEONE

Raymond J. Lewis, Jr.

POLITICAL SOCIALIZATION AND POLITICAL PARTICIPATION

The diverse forms of individual involvement in the political process have long been the subject of political inquiry. Systematic efforts to trace and define the process by which an individual social actor learns about political processes and alternative political roles are of more recent origin. As part of this effort we shall examine certain aspects of the relationship between political learning and political participation in the West African country of Sierra Leone. Measures of nonpolitical participation and political efficacy will be used in the exploration of this relationship.

The participation in decision-making measure was used in Almond and Verba's five nation survey and places primary emphasis upon the family and the school since it is in these institutions that "the child is first exposed to authority relationships."[1] In their survey, Almond and Verba found that participation in family, school, and job decision-making is related to political participation. People seem to generalize to the political realm on the basis of their decision-making experiences in nonpolitical situations.[2] If an individual's nonpolitical experiences lead him to expect that his views will be considered before decisions affecting him are made, he is more likely to get involved in the political process. The participation in decision-making measure is particularly well-suited for use in a survey of nonvoters because the items refer to nonpolitical decision-making situations.

The political efficacy scale was devised as a means of exploring an individual political actor's perception of the relationship between himself and the political system. A person's sense of political efficacy involves both his

[1] Gabriel A. Almond and Sidney Verba, *The Civic Culture* (Princeton, N.J.: Princeton University Press, 1963), p. 330.
[2] Ibid, p. 368.

149

confidence that his own individual political action will have some impact and his belief in the responsiveness of the political regime. The results of numerous surveys indicate the existence of "a strong relationship between a person's sense of political efficacy . . . and the extent of his political involvement."[3]

POTENTIAL PARTICIPANTS IN THE SIERRA LEONEAN POLITICAL SYSTEM

Sierra Leone is slightly smaller than the state of Maine and lies on the west coast of Africa. It is bounded on the north and east by Guinea, on the south by Liberia, and on the west by the Atlantic Ocean. Previously a British colony, Sierra Leone gained its independence in 1961 and with the exception of a period of military coups and governments between March 1967 and April 1968, has enjoyed a relatively peaceful history of parliamentary government under civilian control. The population of roughly 2.2 million people live primarily in rural villages and small towns where the common occupation is farming. Less than 10 percent of the entire population live in the four largest population centers.[4] The 1963 Population Census of Sierra Leone lists 18 different ethnic groups, but approximately 60 percent of the population identify themselves as either Mende or the Temne.[5] The capital city of Freetown was originally established as a settlement for freed African slaves from Europe and the New World during the latter part of the eighteenth century. These people from various tribal backgrounds and with varying exposure to Western civilization were joined by a number of liberated Africans—individuals who were rescued from slave ships enroute to the Western Hemisphere—and eventually the two groups fused into what has come to be known as the Creole community.[6] The differences between the distinct culture developed by the Creoles and the cultures of the indigenous ethnic groups of Sierra Leone are to this day very significant factors in the political, economic, and social life of the country.

The Sierra Leoneans have made few substantial alterations in the basic structure of the educational system they inherited from the British. After completing primary school, students accepted into secondary school are required to complete at least five years (forms 1–5). Following fifth form the student can continue to the sixth form, which is divided into two years and can be substituted for the preliminary year of college. In the 1967–68 academic year there were over 60 secondary schools in Sierra Leone.

Attendance at secondary school, which is so often taken for granted in industrialized Western nations, is a privilege enjoyed by only a small minor-

---

[3] Robert A. Dahl, *Modern Political Analysis* (Englewood Cliffs, N. J.: Prentice-Hall, 1963), p. 149.

[4] *1963 Population Census of Sierra Leone*, Vol. 1 (Freetown Sierra Leone: Government Printing Office, 1965), p. 16. Hereafter cited as *1963 Census*.

[5] *1963 Census*, Vol. 2, pp. 13–17.

[6] Arthur T. Porter, *Creoledom, A Study of the Development of Freetown Society* (London: Oxford University Press, 1963), pp. 5–7.

ity in sub-Sahara Africa. Writing in 1966, the distinguished antropologist Peter Lloyd made the observation that in no African state does the proportion of students attending secondary school exceed 2 percent. This figure may be higher in some areas of individual countries.[7] Of the youth old enough to attend the fifth and sixth form in Sierra Leone, approximately .5 percent were actually in school during the 1967–68 academic year. Those who successfully complete secondary school constitute an extremely small, yet potentially important, minority.

The survey of fifth- and sixth-form Sierra Leonean students upon which this study is based more closely resembles a census than a sample. Even though an accurate count was not available, by a conservative estimate, 88 percent of all the fifth- and sixth-form students were administered the same questionnaire during the first four months of the 1967–68 academic year.[8]

The 1,679 fifth- and sixth-form students attended 38 secondary schools and ranged in age from 15 to 22, with the majority falling within the 17–19 age group. In spite of the constantly increasing proportion of females in the school-going population of Sierra Leone, 73.5 percent of the respondents were male. The vast majority of students (84.3 percent) were in the fifth form, with the remainder in the sixth form. Even though the Creoles account for approximately 2 percent of the Sierra Leonean population, 23.5 percent of the students identified themselves as Creoles. The Mende and Temne account for 30.5 and 29.4 percent of the entire population, respectively. However, among the fifth- and sixth-form students, only 24.8 identified themselves as Mende and 15.5 as Temne. With one exception,[9] the Creole are the only ethnic group which is over-represented in this school-going population. The disproportionate percentage of Creole, who reside primarily in the Freetown area, and the near even representation of the Mende in this school-going population are reflections of the nineteenth- and early twentieth-century colonial practice of locating schools primarily in Freetown and in the predominately Mende areas.[10]

The urban nature of the student population is readily apparent from

---

[7] Peter C. Lloyd, ed., *The New Elites of Tropical Africa: Studies Presented and Discussed at the Sixth International African Seminar at the University of Ibaden, Nigeria, July 1964*. (London: Oxford University Press, 1966), p. 22.

[8] Only four of the 42 secondary schools which had at least a fifth-form class during the previous academic year (1966–67) were not included in the survey. One school was not included because the composition of the student body was very atypical, another school offered a substantially different curriculum than the other schools. Two others were omitted due to limits on time and financial resources. A total of 1,679 students at 38 schools were included in the survey. For a more comprehensive discussion of the school selection procedure refer to, Raymond J. Lewis, Jr., "Modernization and Political Participation: A Survey of Upper-Form Secondary School Students in Sierra Leone," (Ph.D. dissertation, Syracuse University, 1970), pp. 185–87.

[9] The Sherbro constitute 7.6 percent of the respondent population, yet this ethnic group accounts for only 3.3 percent of the national population.

[10] Martin Kilson, *Political Change in a West African State: A Study of the Modernization Process in Sierra Leone* (Cambridge: Harvard University Press, 1966), p. 26.

an examination of their geographical history. Those students who succeed to the fifth- or sixth-form level in the Sierra Leonean school system come from a more urban environment than the average Sierra Leonean. Whereas approximately 81 percent of the entire population of Sierra Leone lives in population centers of less than 2,000 people, only 30.4 percent of the students were born in such rural communities. According to the most recent census, the capital city of Freetown contains less than 8 percent of the population of the country, yet over 30 percent of all the fifth- and sixth-form students report they were born, spent their childhood, and attended secondary school in Freetown.[11]

The urban life-style that characterizes Sierra Leone's upper-form secondary school students is not exclusively a function of birthplace. Unless an individual is born in a town or village large enough to have a primary or secondary school, his pursuit of an education necessitates moving away from home. The extent of geographical mobility that characterizes so many respondents is partially due to the concentration of schools in the urban centers. Of the 45 schools in the country that had at least a fifth form in 1967–68, 17 were in Freetown and eight were in the provincial headquarters of Bo, Makeni, and Kenema. This means over half of the available schools and over two-thirds of all the spaces for fifth- and sixth-form students in the country were located in these four large urban centers which contain less than 10 percent of the entire population of the country.[12] Consequently, the availability of schools is an important factor influencing the geographic history of many students. The existence of both a primary and secondary school in a relatively small rural town would preclude the necessity for a student to move to a more urban environment where he would doubtless be exposed to a wide variety of new socializing experiences. Since this is seldom the case, the concentration of secondary schools in the large urban towns contributes directly to the high mobility of rural students and the virtual immobility of those born in large population centers.[13]

According to the 1963 census fewer than 10 percent of Sierra Leoneans who were five years of age or older had ever attended a formal educational institution.[14] In response to a question concerning the number of years their fathers had attended school, the students indicated that almost 40 percent of their fathers had never attended school. Though the possibility of exaggeration or inaccurate knowledge of paternal educational experience may justify a conservative evaluation of this figure, it is apparent the student's fathers have an educational level much higher than that found in the gen-

---

[11] A rural-urban score was obtained for each student based upon the geographical level (for purposes of analysis the country was divided into six levels of urbanism based upon population size and number of urban functions) of the locations where he was born, spent his childhood, and attended secondary school. See Lewis, pp. 67–69, 189–95.

[12] *1963 Census*, Vol. 1, p. 16.

[13] A geographical mobility score was obtained for each respondent based upon a combination of (1) the number of places he had lived, and (2) the number of geographical levels (1–6) he had passed through. See Lewis, pp. 69–72, 189–95.

[14] *1963 Census*, Vol. 2, p. 52.

eral adult male population. This corresponds to Philip Foster's findings in his 1961 study of Ghanaian fifth-form students.[15]

The student responses to the question concerning father's income are difficult to evaluate because of the dearth of economic data available on Sierra Leone. The Sierra Leone data on father's occupation support Clignet and Foster's findings in the Ivory Coast and Ghana, which indicate educational systems appear to favor selection of children of professional, administrative, and clerical workers.[16] Children of farmers, fishermen, and miners account for only 30.4 percent of the student population, although these occupations include 77.2 percent of the entire male work force in Sierra Leone.

The characteristics of the respondents vary greatly, but they can be generally described as 17 to 19 year old males whose fathers have considerably more formal education and higher incomes than most Sierra Leoneans. Their fathers tend to occupy professional, business, clerical, skilled, and semi-skilled jobs. Even though a large percentage of these upper-form students are from the more urban population centers, many do come from semi-rural and rural environments where their family may be living as subsistence farmers. However, by the time these most rural students reach the fifth form, their life-style tends to be more urban than that of the average Sierra Leonean.

The greater access to higher levels of education enjoyed by persons in the upper socioeconomic levels in every country is perpetuated in Sierra Leone by the lack of free education. The necessity to pay tuition fees, and in many cases room and board fees, in order to attend school means access to education is even more directly related to the economic position of the student's family than it might be under a system of free education.

Student Attitudes and Behavior

With the preceding description of the respondent population serving as background, we can proceed to examine the political participation measures and the student's responses to them. During the first four months of the 1967–68 academic year, the questionnaire was administered to 1,679 students at their respective secondary schools by the same American researcher and at least one of two Sierra Leonean college students. The same introduction and questionnaire was employed at each of the 38 schools included in the survey.

Participation in Decision-Making

The participation in decision-making measure is concerned with past and present behavior patterns as well as current attitudes. The questions contain references to three socializing contexts: family, school, and peer group. Each of the 13 questions was accompanied by four alternative

[15] Remi Clignet and Philip Foster, "Potential Elites in Ghana and the Ivory Coast: A Preliminary Comparison," *American Journal of Sociology*, 70 (1964), p. 356.
[16] Ibid., p. 355.

answers such as *none, very little, some,* and *much,* or *never, seldom, usually,* and *always.*[17]

The six questions concerning participation in family decision-making situations elicited affirmative responses from a substantial majority of the students. This seems to indicate that their participation experiences in the family have been generally positive. Over 65 percent of the respondents chose either of the two most positive alternatives on five of the six family decision-making questions. They indicated that they had "some" or "much" influence in family decisions affecting them; that they "usually" or "always" felt free to complain; that their influence made "some" or "much" difference in the outcome of their parent's decision; that they were "usually" or "always" satisfied with the amount of influence they had and felt people their age should have "some" or "much" voice in family decision-making. The only question receiving a majority of negative responses asked how often they complained in the family. Over 63 percent indicated they "seldom" or "never" complained. Even if one were to assume the students may exaggerate their influence and minimize the extent of their complaining in the family, it does appear that by the time they reach fifth form a substantial number of students have come to expect to participate in family decisions affecting them.

For many students, experience in secondary school seems to complement and even reinforce their positive predisposition toward participation derived from family experiences. On four of the five items concerning participation in school decision-making, over 65 percent of the 1,679 students selected one of the two most participative responses. A majority indicated that students at their school "often" or "very often" participate in decisions about school activities. Similarly, a substantial majority indicated that they felt students should have "some" or "very much" of a part in decisions affecting school activities; that they "usually" or "always" feel free to talk to teachers if they feel they have been treated unfairly or disagree with the teacher; and that if they talked to the teacher in such a situation it would make "some" or "much" difference.

The one exception to this pattern of positive responses is an item very similar to the family question that asked the student how often he complains. The percentage of positive responses dropped from more than 65 to less than 54 when the students were asked how often they themselves participate in decisions about school activities. The responses to these two items which ask the student to assess his own actual level of participation may reflect a reluctance to appear in conflict with authority figures. However, even if the student's actual participation is relatively low, the responses to the other items indicate they feel participation is possible. A feeling that they are in environments receptive to participation may be as important as actual participatory experiences in terms of its effects upon the individual's expectations concerning participation in future roles. Whether the parents or teachers are able to create an atmosphere that seems conducive to partici-

[17] A description of the weighting method and the factor analysis for the participation and political efficacy measures can be found in Lewis, pp. 32–35.

TABLE 1. MULTIPLE REGRESSION ANALYSIS OF PARTICIPATION IN
NONPOLITICAL DECISION-MAKING

Multiple R	Independent Variable	F Value	Probability of F
.3782	School level[a]	280.08	.049
.4076	Birth level[a]	164.16	.064
.4142	Father's income	15.96	.202

[a] Birth Level and School Level are measures of the urbanness of the town or village where the student was born and attended secondary school. Urbanness is defined in terms of population size and the number of urban functions in the population center.

pation may be as important as the actual level of participation they allow in their respective institutions.

The large number of Sierra Leonean secondary school students living within the school compounds during the academic year seemed to justify designing some questions to evaluate interaction within peer groups. Over 90 percent of the students expressed the feeling they had "some" or "much" influence in deciding what groups of their peers did. A slightly smaller majority (84 percent) said they were "usually" or "always" satisfied with the amount of influence they had in making peer-group decisions.

It is apparent that the experiences of most of these students in their families, schools, and peer groups have given them the feeling that they are likely to be included in any decisions affecting them and that they are also likely to have some influence upon the outcome of those decisions. However, the response patterns indicate that in decision-making situations the students have not had uniformly favorable experiences with authority figures. A demographic analysis of the data offers some insight into the reasons for these differences.

In their five nation survey, Almond and Verba found higher participation scores among the upper socioeconomic levels.[18] The same general pattern emerged from the Sierra Leone data. Students of professional people, civil servants, and businessmen scored highest on the participation measure. As might be expected, the students with the highest participation scores are from wealthier and better educated families.

The participation scores seem to correspond quite closely to the socioeconomic continuum found in the student population. However, the multiple regression analysis of the participation measure (see Table 1) indicates geography accounts for more of the variance in this measure than does socioeconomic status.

Knowledge of the urbanism of the locations in which a student was born and attended secondary school appears to tell us more about his participation experiences than knowledge of the socioeconomic status of his family. Of these two variables, school level, which measures the urbanism of the town in which the student attended secondary school, seems to account for more of the variance in the participation measure than does birth level.

[18] Almond and Verba, p. 335.

TABLE 2. MEAN SCORE PARTICIPATION IN FAMILY, SCHOOL, AND PEER
GROUP DECISION-MAKING*

		Continuous Variables			
Rural-urban	Mobility	Father's education	Father's income	Birth level	School level
Urban 1.0870	Immobile .9052	16–18 years .8745	Above 1500 LE 1.0624	1** .8964	1** .9302
Semi-urban −.0085	Highly mobile .1160	13–15 years .7379	9–1199 LE .7131	2 .2613	2 .9231
Semi-rural −.6379	Semi-mobile −.5848	10–12 years .7206	12–1499 LE .5801	4 .4330	3 −.8932
Rural −1.1350	Mobile −.6244	7–9 years .3546	6–899 LE .3727	3 −.4455	5 −1.0064
		4–6 years .1227	3–599 LE .3678	5 −.7038	4 −2.0078
		1–3 years −.3274	Below 299 LE −.6549	6 −.8835	6 −2.2190
		None −.7302			

* These mean scores are based upon the factor analysis of the participation measure.
** The birth level and school levels scores range from one (most urban) to six (most rural).

The students reporting the most favorable participation experiences are those who attend school in the large urban population centers. (See Table 2.) Among this group, the students who were born in Freetown and are, by definition, geographically immobile score highest on the participation measure. Even though the participation scores correspond closely to the rural-urban continuum, the highly mobile students constitute an important exception. They are the respondents who were born in rural villages and small towns in the districts nearest to Freetown and then moved to Freetown to attend school. These students who have moved from the rural to the urban extreme in Sierra Leone, rather than those semi-mobile individuals who have lived and attended school in various moderate sized towns, report the most favorable participation experiences of those not born in Freetown.

The family, school, and peer group portions of the participation measure were not factor-analyzed separately, so it is not possible to readily determine the extent to which experiences in secondary school alone account for the high participation scores among those attending secondary school in Freetown. Nevertheless, the data suggest that the atmosphere in the urban Freetown schools is more conducive to student participation in decision-making situations. The immobile, lifetime residents of Freetown may have encountered more consistent participation opportunities than the highly mobile students who migrate to Freetown from rural areas where both family and primary school authority patterns may well be more rigid.

The lack of congruence between the rural and urban socializing contexts may provide a partial explanation for the high participation scores of the highly mobile group. The migration from rural to urban areas in developing countries "means exposure to new and different social and political structures which result in significant discontinuities in political learning."[19] One consequence of this exposure to new socializing agents, and familiar socializing agents set in new contexts (e.g., secondary school), seems to be an increased expectation that the individual will be involved in decision-making that affects him.

Among the factors that may account for the incongruity between the rural and urban socializing contexts is the presence of numerous alternative socializing agents in the large cities of a modernizing African country like Sierra Leone. The impact of competing socializing agents in the urban environment seems to affect the role of both the family and the school. However, there are some differences between the rural and urban settings that particularly affect the socializing role of the school. At most secondary schools, at least some of the students reside on the school compound during the academic year. The percentage of resident students is generally higher in rural schools located in or near small towns where the students are less likely to have relatives with whom they can stay. Regardless of how rigid or permissive the policies of the rural school administration, the student is exposed to much the same authority pattern after, as well as during, classes. In these situations the student is exposed to few outside sources of influence other than the mass media, personal correspondence, and occasional travel on weekends and vacations.

Another factor that should be considered as part of such an assessment was suggested in the responses to one of the other items on the questionnaire. It is common for some students to transfer from one secondary school to another for either academic, financial, or personal reasons. Because of their physical proximity to alternative schools, students attending schools in or near large population centers with more than one secondary school may be more inclined to transfer than the students at rural schools. In the more urban schools many students do not reside on the school compounds. Because the student attending the urban school is likely to be exposed to many alternative socializing influences and authority patterns, he may be more liable to assert himself within the school setting. The sense of independence, whether real or fancied, that is likely to characterize the students at the more urban schools may be one of the factors accounting for the high reported participation in decision-making at these schools. The relative lack of outside influences, the physical presence of the students on the compound, and the lack of an easily accessible alternative school may account, in part, for the relatively low participation scores among the students in the rural schools.

The impact upon future behavior of favorable participation experiences in either the home, the school, or the peer group context is difficult to evaluate. Within the limits of this study it is not possible to separate the effects of socializing experiences which occur during similar periods in a

---

[19] Richard Dawson and Kenneth Prewitt, *Political Socialization* (Boston: Little, Brown, 1969), p. 94.

person's life. However, something can be said about the cumulative effect of these experiences.

> There is evidence that the impact of participation in nonpolitical decision-making—at home, school, and job—is cumulative. The individual who has consistent opportunities for nonpolitical participation—compared with someone whose ability to participate in one nonpolitical area is not matched by an ability to participate in another nonpolitical area— is more likely to generalize this to political participation.[20]

The urban, immobile students appear to have had the most consistent opportunities for such nonpolitical participation and seem most likely to generalize this to a political context.

The relationship that has been observed in modern Western societies between participation in nonpolitical decision-making situations and participation in the political system may not apply in a modernizing country like Sierra Leone. The correspondence between the Sierra Leone socio-economic data and the data reported by Almond and Verba in their five nation survey is one of the reasons it has been assumed that the tendency for individuals to generalize from nonpolitical to political participation is also present in the Sierra Leone setting. Much more research is needed to substantiate such an assumption. The age of the respondents in this survey precluded comparing reported nonpolitical participation with actual political participation as a means of testing the relationship between predispositions and behavior.

Political Efficacy

The participation in decision-making measure was concerned with nonpolitical experiences, although the items in the political efficacy scale relate to the student's indirect and direct exposure to the political system. The eight political efficacy items were adapted from the scale used by Easton and Dennis in their study of American children.[21] Students were given a choice of four alternative responses for each item: *strongly agree, agree, disagree,* or *strongly disagree.*

In response to the political efficacy items the students displayed an interesting combination of positive and negative attitudes toward government. Over 67 percent appear convinced the government is within the control of human beings, and 65 percent expressed confidence that there are many ways people like their parents can let public officials know what they are thinking. The assertion that ways do exist for citizens to communicate with government officials is not matched by a similar conviction that these channels do, in fact, have much impact upon the actual functioning of the government. On two items concerning government responsiveness, 77 percent indicated they do not feel public officials care much about what people like their families think. Responses to a third item on government respon-

---

[20] Almond and Verba, p. 366.
[21] David Easton and Jack Dennis, "The Child's Acquisition of Regime Norms: Political Efficacy," *American Political Science Review,* 56 (March 1967), p. 29. Two items were stated in a positive direction as a check for response set bias.

siveness indicate that over 68 percent of the students felt public officials were not even interested in the problems of most people.

This general lack of confidence in the responsiveness of public officials may help explain the sense of political impotency expressed by the respondents on two other items. Over 89 percent indicated most adults do not have a chance to say what they think about running the government, and 61 percent indicated they did not feel their family had any voice in what the government did. The generally weak sense of political efficacy displayed by the student population as a whole may be related to their perception of political phenomena as complicated and confusing.[22] Approximately 73 percent indicated politics and government seem so complicated that persons like themselves cannot really understand what is happening.

Unlike the participation in decision-making measure, none of the demographic variables was able to account for a significant amount of the variance in the responses to the political efficacy items. In spite of this, it is possible to proceed cautiously with an evaluation of the mean scores of some of the demographic categories. An analysis of the political efficacy mean scores reveals a geographic pattern with many similarities to the one described in the evaluation of the nonpolitical participation measure, but the socioeconomic data are sufficiently ambiguous that no easily discernible pattern emerges.

Although weak in the population as a whole, the sense of political efficacy seems to be strongest among students born in the provinces nearest the capital city. More specifically, it is the highly mobile, the semi-rural, the Temne, and those born in the Western Rural Area, Port Loko, Bombali, Kambia, and Moyamba districts who have the highest mean scores on the political efficacy measure. On the basis of these data it is difficult to ascertain whether residence in relative proximity to Freetown or migration from these areas to this large population center is the more crucial factor affecting the student's political efficacy scores.

On the basis of the nonpolitical participation and political efficacy measures, the geographically immobile residents of Freetown and the highly mobile students from districts relatively near the capital appear most positively predisposed to political participation. Just as the intensity of the influence of the capital city in African nations decreases as the distance from the source of political power increases,[23] so does the predisposition to participate in politics seem to decrease as you move further from the capital.

CONCLUSION

Without the benefit of data on actual political participation, we are limited to a discussion of predispositions. According to the responses elicited

---

[22] The mean score on six of the eight political efficacy items was less than 2.5, which is the mid-point between the extremes of one and four.

[23] Fred G. Burke, *Africa's Quest for Order* (Englewood Cliffs, N. J.: Prentice-Hall, 1964), p. 38.

by the measure of nonpolitical participation, a substantial proportion of these students appear favorably disposed to involvement in nonpolitical decision-making. If we are willing to assume people will generalize from the nonpolitical to the political realm in Sierra Leone, as they seem to in the United States and Western Europe, it appears reasonable to conclude that these students are also positively predisposed to political participation. Their indirect and direct encounters with the political system, as measured by the political efficacy scale, do not appear to reinforce their nonpolitical experiences. The confidence the students display in the responsiveness of their parents and teachers seems to be lacking in their assessment of public officials. Within the respondent population it appears to be the urban, immobile student and the highly mobile individual who migrates from the rural areas to the capital city who have the strongest sense of political efficacy and are most accustomed to participating in decisions which affect them.

Whether he resides in an urban or rural setting, the less mobile student seems to have relatively consistent socialization experiences. However, this is not the case for his highly mobile peer who migrates from a rural to a large urban population center. This student's socialization experiences are characterized by considerable discontinuity. Even though he may be exposed to inconsistent socialization patterns, the early experiences of the highly mobile student appear to be at least partially offset by his subsequent experiences in the urban school.

Since the individual, rather than the school, was the unit of analysis employed, it is not possible to determine the extent to which the nature of the urban educational institutions or their urban environment is responsible for the differences observed in the behavioral patterns of the rural and urban students. Had it been possible to include in the study an assessment of the school authority pattern and of student attitudes toward teachers and school administrators at each institution, there might have been a basis for a comparative evaluation of the effects of educational and urbanism variables upon the political socialization process.

The mere fact that we are dealing with educated individuals suggests the respondents are more likely to participate in politics than their less educated peers. The results of studies in modern Western nations, which may or may not apply in this African setting, indicate that the more educated a person is, the more likely he is to participate in politics:

> . . . education is strongly related to the probability that the citizen will be politically active. The better educated vote at a greater rate. They are also likely to engage in more demanding types of political participation such as campaigning, working for a political party, contributing money, etc.[24]

Although these young, educated Africans may be more inclined to get involved in politics than those with less education, there is considerable variation in their predispositions toward political participation.

[24] Dawson and Prewitt, p. 176.

Youth, Politics, and Education

12

ENGLAND, ITALY, SWEDEN, THE UNITED STATES, AND WEST GERMANY

Russell F. Farnen
Dan B. German

BACKGROUND OF THE FIVE-NATION STUDY

This five-nation study of the political socialization of approximately 1,800 students, ages 9–20 years of age, was conducted in 1968–69 in West Germany, the United States, England, Sweden, and Italy. The instrument used was a 22 item background questionnaire and a 22 item attitude battery, with three scales measuring sense of political legitimacy, tolerance for political dissent and opposition, and sense of political efficacy.

Typical questions in the background questionnaire dealt with age, sex, grade in school, parents' education and occupation, size of city and school, and social studies and political education course exposure. We shall focus on two of these variables below—age trends, and the effect of political and social science education on the students' response patterns.

After statistical analysis six items remained in the legitimacy scale, five in the efficacy scale, and six in the dissent/opposition scale.[1] The items are as follow:

Legitimacy Scale
If we have a great deal of trouble in making a living (like an economic depression), we should put one strong leader (a dictator) in charge of everything.

Less democracy would make our country a better place in which to live.

---

[1] Each of the scales employed in this survey was subjected to several statistical tests such as item discrimination and validity analysis. These analyses produced slightly different findings cross-nationally, but generally indicated that the items produced three distinct scales with questions which were highly intercorrelated. The dissent/opposition (Cronbach's alpha) scores ranged from .612 (Italy) to .761 (Germany); the legitimacy scale from .587 (Italy) to .712 (Germany); and the efficacy scale from .478 (Germany) to .667 (United States). All but three of the fifteen alphas in the scales were above .600. Each item was scored 1 through 5 with "Do not know" responses used as the midpoint.

Democracy is the best form of government for our nation.

The national government in our country usually makes very serious mistakes.

Our national government usually meets the important needs of the people.

A dictator (one-man ruler) might be all right if he would help our country.

Efficacy Scale

Government decisions are like the weather. There is very little people can do about them.

There are some big powerful men in the national government who are running the whole thing. They care very little about the opinions of ordinary people like my parents.

Our national government really cares about what the people think and say.

People like my family can know very little about what the government is doing because it is so big and far away.

Americans have a chance to say what they think about running the national government.

Dissent/Opposition

It would be best for our country if the political parties had the same ideas.

It would be best for our country if all the newspapers said the same thing about what was right for the government to do.

When people in our national government argue about public policy, it hurts our country.

Once the national government decides something, people should always support these decisions without question.

Citizens must always be free to criticize the national government.

We should let people make speeches against our national government.

Questions were phrased positively and negatively so as to reduce possible response bias. There were five options given: *strongly agree, agree, do not know, disagree,* and *strongly disagree.* All tests were translated by bilingual colleagues in Germany, Italy, and Sweden and were reviewed by several other academicians in England and the United States to ensure comparability. Scholars in each country involved were asked to review the questionnaires and to suggest revisions, which were then incorporated into the one common instrument administered in each of the nations.

THE SAMPLE

The size of the sample populations varied from 421 in the United States, to 336 in Germany and Sweden, and 347 in Italy and England. The age range was broken into three categories—students from 9–11, 12–14, and 15–20 (age at terminal year for high school) years of age were tested in each nation.

Students and schools were selected on the basis of what we shall call a "purposive" sample. That is, these students represented the major characteristics in which the researchers were interested with respect to age, sex, rural and suburban location, and so forth. Only the West German sample was taken from one locale in that nation—the city and suburbs of Frankfurt. In Sweden, students came from urban and suburban Stockholm and Skellefteå (in rural, northern Sweden). The American sample was taken from all sections of the country with proportionately more coming from the deep South, southern, and border states. The English sample came from Reading, Coventry, Norwich, and London. The Italian sample is widely distributed, with students coming from Agrigento, Bologna, Naples, Milan, Rome, Trieste, Padua, and Pieve di Soligo.

Overall Results

The overall results of this five-nation survey of student political orientations partially corroborate the general conclusions of the recent study conducted by Dennis et al. although this survey uses a broader range of age groups and different statistical techniques.[2] The Dennis group surveyed students in England, the United States, West Germany, and Italy. It is the only cross-national study of students in Western Europe and the United States in which children were asked questions roughly similar to those used in this five-nation survey. For this reason the Dennis et al. report will be used as a base for the overall data presentation.

Different research techniques were used in the two studies. The Dennis group, for instance, found that English students were lowest in approval of the idea that democracy is the "best" kind of government; they, however, used only one item as a measure of general support for democracy (from the legitimacy scale), i.e., "Democracy is the best form of government." The use of a single item to measure system support is obviously insufficient and leaves the results in question because the meaning of political concepts, abstract words, and so forth may vary considerably cross-nationally. Our five-nation study used a measure of system support that was based on a six-item legitimacy scale. The use of multi-item scales (even when checked by item and/or factor analysis) does not entirely eliminate the aforementioned problems of diversity of symbol and word interpretation, yet it does insure that items not measuring a given variable (e.g., legitimacy or "general support for democracy") can be weeded out.

The data in this study show that most students in the five nations support their political systems (legitimacy), often feel that the average person's political involvement would be effective at the national governmental level (efficacy), and are highly tolerant of criticism directed toward the national

---

[2] Jack Dennis, et al., "Political Socialization to Democratic Orientations in Four Western Systems," *Comparative Political Studies*, 1 (April 1968), pp. 77, 81. See also Dan B. German, "Student Political Orientations Toward Legitimacy, Efficacy, and Dissent/Opposition in the United States, England, Sweden, and West Germany," (Ph.D. dissertation, Georgetown University, 1970), pp. 166 ff., for a more extensive report on these findings. This report does not include the Italian sample or the youngest age group in England.

TABLE 1. LEGITIMACY[a]

	Low %[b]	Medium %	High %	Chi Square[c]	Significance Levels	N
United States	1	30	70	—	—	420[e]
Sweden	1	32	66	0.89	N.S.[d]	335
West Germany	1	35	64	2.55	N.S.	336
England	1	36	63	4.45	P<.05	347
Italy	6	32	62	5.17	P<.05	347

[a] The scoring scheme used for legitimacy was 1–8 low, 9–17 medium, and 18–25 high.

[b] Because of rounding, some percentages do not equal 100.

[c] Chi square computed for each nation in relation to the nation ranked highest. In each case the low and medium scale score categories were collapsed to form a four celled matrix. The number of respondents, not the percent as shown in the table, falling into each cell was used to compute chi square, e.g. the matrix for the United States and Sweden was as follows:

U.S.	127	293
Sweden	112	223

[d] N.S.=Not significant at the $p<.05$ level or above.

[e] The number of respondents (N) varies slightly due to the failure of some respondents to answer several items.

government (dissent/opposition). Furthermore, the students' overall response patterns were not appreciably different from one nation to another, although some significant differences did appear. In other words, although the Italian students in the total sample scored lower on the legitimacy scale than students from the other four nations, their performance was not so low as to indicate a crisis in support for the Italian political system when compared with the other nations in the survey (see Table 1).

The same generalization applies to performance on the dissent/opposition measure for students in the five nations. That is, student performance varies by less than 14 percent on the high category across nations in terms of tolerance of political conflict or disagreement (see Table 2). We see that differences between the United States, Sweden, and Germany are not significant but comparisons between the United States, Italy, and England do rise to levels of significance.

With respect to efficacy scale performance, there are a larger dispersion of results (a range of 28 percentage points) and appreciably higher significant differences between nations (see Table 3). United States students feel by far the most efficacious, followed by those of West Germany; then, with larger percentage and highly significant differences, come students in Sweden, Italy, and England.

It should be understood, however, that those nations where students did not score very high on legitimacy, dissent/opposition, or efficacy scales, in turn, had few students who fell into the low category. That is, no nation rose above 6 percent in the low category on any measure. Thus, those students who did not fall into the high category on any of the three measures

TABLE 2. Dissent/Opposition[a]

	Low %[b]	Medium %	High %	Chi Square[c]	Significance Level	N
United States	0	24	76	—	—	420[e]
Sweden	1	27	71	1.60	N.S.[d]	335
West Germany	2	28	69	3.59	N.S.	335
Italy	6	29	65	9.80	$p < .01$	347
England	1	36	63	15.00	$p < .001$	347

[a] The scoring scheme used for dissent/opposition was 1–10 low, 11–20 medium, and 21–30 high.

[b] Because of rounding, some percentages do not equal 100.

[c] Chi square computed for each nation in relation to the nation ranked highest. In each case the low and medium scale score categories were collapsed to form a four celled matrix. The number of respondents, not the percent as shown in the table, falling into each cell was used to compute chi square, e.g. the matrix for the United States and Sweden was as follows:

U.S.	102	318
Sweden	95	240

[d] N.S.=Not significant at the $p < .05$ level or above.

[e] The number of respondents (N) varies slightly due to the failure of some respondents to answer several items.

TABLE 3. Efficacy[a]

	Low %[b]	Medium %	High %	Chi Square[c]	Significance Level	N
United States	1	48	51	—	—	421[e]
West Germany	1	57	41	6.03	$p < .02$	334
Sweden	3	59	38	12.13	$p < .001$	335
Italy	6	56	38	13.03	$p < .001$	346
England	6	72	22	63.89	$p < .001$	347

[a] The scoring scheme used for efficacy was 1–10 low, 11–12 medium, and 21–30 high.

[b] Because of rounding, some percentages do not equal 100.

[c] Chi square computed for each nation in relation to the nation ranked highest. In each case the low and medium scale score categories were collapsed to form a four celled matrix. The number of respondents, not the percent as shown in the table, falling into each cell was used to compute chi square, e.g. the matrix for the United States and West Germany was as follows:

U.S.	208	213
W. Germany	195	139

[d] The number of respondents (N) varies slightly due to the failure of some respondents to answer several items.

usually fell into the medium category, indicating an absence of extreme polarization in any nation.[3]

[3] An analysis of variance run on these data showed a lack of significant differences for Sweden and West Germany on the legitimacy scale (as was the case with chi

The total samples in each nation indicate some cross-national similarities and variations with respect to scores on the three scales. For instance, in all five nations the intercorrelations[4] among student performance on the three measures are quite high, so that a student who is politically efficacious is likely to accord legitimacy to the political system at the same time that he is tolerant of political dissent and opposition. However, this consistency of results does not appear on other measures.

A number of variables, such as level of parental education, type of occupation, and size of community, seem to have some effect on scale performance cross-nationally. These effects do not appear to be large, however, and are mixed, in contrast to the neutral influence of sex, which does not appear to be an important explanatory variable in this research. Consequently, let us turn our attention to age trends.

Age Trends

The data show a somewhat mixed relationship between increase in age and a higher performance on the scales. The study by Dennis et al. similarly disclosed inconsistent findings. For instance, on the statement "There are some big, powerful men in the government who are running the whole thing, and they do not really care about the rest of us," the percentage of "democratic" responses (i.e., disagreement with the item) increased with age in only one nation—West Germany. Furthermore, the percentage of uncommitted responses increased with age in the United States; this contradicts the usual decrease in "don't know" responses found in most studies, a phenomenon usually attributed to cognitive development.

In comparing 9–11 year olds, 12–14 year olds, and 15–20 year olds who scored high on the three scales, we find that the older the English student the more likely he is to be efficacious and to support the political system and the concept of political dissent (see Figures 1, 2, and 3). This is generally the case for American students, although change in level of scale

---

square), an absence of a significant difference for Sweden on the dissent/opposition scale, and West Germany differing at the $p<.01$ level from the United States. The chi square levels of statistical difference shown here were somewhat magnified when the results were measured by an analysis of variance. However, we do not feel that these results alter our conclusions about these data, nor should these observed statistical differences be interpreted as illustrating any appreciable or substantial differences among the five nations. The low numbers of respondents from all five nations in the low scale score categories indicate that none of the nations appears to be threatened by a sizable lack of system support or democratic orientations.

[4] The measure of association used in this study was Pearson product moment correlation (r). This statistic has the property of indicating the direction and strength of the effect of an independent variable upon a dependent variable. The range is from -1.00 (perfect negative) to 0.00 (neutral) to $+1.00$ (perfect positive) and significance is determined by the r factor which depends upon sample size. We have used the .05 level $= p < .05$ as our significance baseline indicating that the probability (p) of the results found occurring by chance is less than 1 in 20, or 5 in 100.

performance appears to stabilize when the student reaches the medium age grouping. Consistent trends emerge for Sweden, West Germany, and Italy in terms of increased scale performance level and age increase on the dissent/ opposition and legitimacy scales. Here, the upward trend continues through all age groups in contrast to the United States where negligible shifts are seen between the medium and high age categories. The trends are more

FIGURE 1. Efficacy Age Trend Analysis: High Scale Score Category

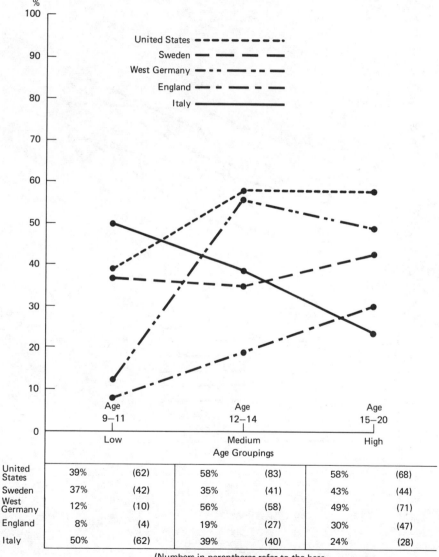

	Age 9–11 Low		Age 12–14 Medium		Age 15–20 High	
United States	39%	(62)	58%	(83)	58%	(68)
Sweden	37%	(42)	35%	(41)	43%	(44)
West Germany	12%	(10)	56%	(58)	49%	(71)
England	8%	(4)	19%	(27)	30%	(47)
Italy	50%	(62)	39%	(40)	24%	(28)

(Numbers in parentheses refer to the base
upon which percentage is calculated)

mixed on the efficacy scale, with Swedish students dropping from the low to the medium age category and then rising between the medium and high age categories. The performance of German students increases considerably between the low and medium age categories, but decreases between the medium and high age categories. The Italian students exhibit consistent decreases in scale performance on the efficacy measure across age groupings.

FIGURE 2. Dissent/Opposition Age Trend Analysis: High Scale Score Category

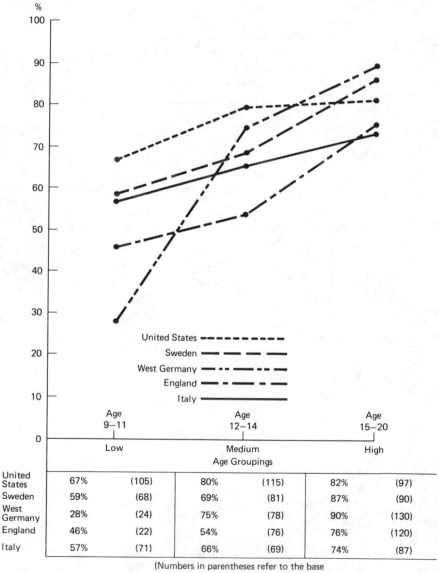

	Low		Medium		High	
United States	67%	(105)	80%	(115)	82%	(97)
Sweden	59%	(68)	69%	(81)	87%	(90)
West Germany	28%	(24)	75%	(78)	90%	(130)
England	46%	(22)	54%	(76)	76%	(120)
Italy	57%	(71)	66%	(69)	74%	(87)

(Numbers in parentheses refer to the base
upon which percentage is calculated)

However, these figures do not tell the whole story, since in absolute percentages the largest changes in all five countries were registered in Germany and the smallest in Sweden. All five ranged from 67 to 89 percent in the high category on legitimacy and dissent/opposition at the terminal age of secondary school, but only from 23 to 58 percent on efficacy. Both England and Italy had *lower* percentages of students in the terminal year

FIGURE 3. Legitimacy Age Trend Analysis: High Scale Score Category

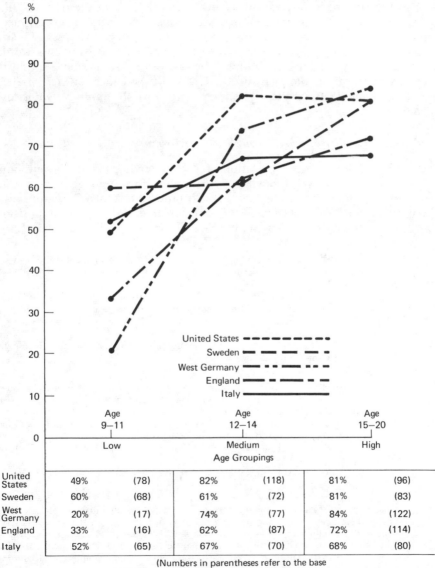

	Age 9–11 Low		Age 12–14 Medium		Age 15–20 High	
United States	49%	(78)	82%	(118)	81%	(96)
Sweden	60%	(68)	61%	(72)	81%	(83)
West Germany	20%	(17)	74%	(77)	84%	(122)
England	33%	(16)	62%	(87)	72%	(114)
Italy	52%	(65)	67%	(70)	68%	(80)

(Numbers in parentheses refer to the base
upon which percentage is calculated)

scoring of the high category than the youngest age groups in the United States and Sweden. These results indicate that considerable research must occur in the future if we are to chart the development of political attitudes cross-nationally.

POLITICAL EDUCATION

The students were asked to indicate if they were studying or had studied political science—political science being defined in the item as "like civics, problems courses, international relations, constitutions, government courses, etc."[5] The students were separated into two age groups, 9–11 and 12–20, the latter being the more likely years in which the students would take a formal political science course. The exception to this rule is found in Italy where the time allotment devoted to political education *decreases* as the student moves from the *elementary school* to the *middle school* and beyond.

Past Study of Political Science and Scale Performance

Examination of the correlations between having taken one or more political science courses and scale performance for the 12–20 age group shows that in only one instance is the association substantively significant.[6] Having had political science is positively correlated with dissent/opposition scale performance ($r=+.257$) in the English sample. The absence of sig-

---

[5] The wording of the "now studying" question was: Which of the following courses or subjects dealing with government and politics *are you now studying?* (Check one or more than one as needed.)
_____ Political science courses (like civics, problems courses, international relations, constitutions, government courses, etc.)
_____ Other specific social studies courses (such as economics, sociology, geography, etc.)
_____ Other such courses (Please describe them on the line below by name, content, etc.)
_____ I do not know

The exact wording of the "previously studied" question was: Which of the following courses or subjects dealing with government and politics *have you studied before?* (Check one or more than one as needed.)
_____ Political science courses (like civics, problems courses, international relations, constitutions, government courses, etc.)
_____ Other specific social studies courses (such as economics, sociology, geography, etc.)
_____ Other such courses (Please describe them on the line below by name, content, etc.)
_____ I do not know

[6] Since the samples used in this survey are not national probability samples we have not used statistical significance tests in this part of our analysis. It may not be possible to draw valid samples for comparison since too many unknown, uncontrolled, and/or significant variables in the particular culture of each nation may affect the results. Even if the sampling frame was a random national sample and accounted

nificant course impact in all other instances suggests that the formal political education curriculum *per se* does not appreciably affect student responses in the other four nations on the three attitude scales used in this study.

Present Study of Political Science Courses and Scale Performance

Our measures of efficacy scale performance using the criterion of the student *now* taking courses with political science content yielded no significant results. The highest correlation was in Italy ($r=+.139$ on the efficacy scale), but zero level r's were found in all other nations on all three scales—except in Germany, which showed an r of $+.101$ between dissent/opposition and taking political science now. The results did indicate that nearly all Swedish students were presently studying a civic education course as contrasted with about one-half of the Americans and West Germans and very few of the Italians and English.

Some Observations on Political Education and Scale Performance

In interpreting these results the reader must keep in mind that many more Swedish students across age groups take formal political education than is the case for the other four nations; yet their overall scale performance is *not* higher than that of students in the remaining nations. If formal political, Western democratic-oriented education had an impact on students' efficacy, legitimacy, and dissent/opposition attitudes, Sweden would be the obvious choice for a prediction of highest scale performance. This hypothesis was not confirmed in the study.

The results presented above measure only the general absence of significant impact of formal political education in terms of having taken no courses or one or more courses. Under other conditions (such as a sufficient number of students who have not received any political education in the 12–20 age groups, type of course, classroom atmosphere, extent to which the teacher actually is able to teach the materials to be covered in a specified course, and so forth), the lack of such relationships may change. Further-

---

for a sufficient number of these influential variables, statistical significance should not be accepted without question. The statistical significance level is only one element in a possible array of empirical evidence that could or could not demonstrate that observed differences are significant. The corroboratory studies presented in this report are supportive (but by no means definitive) evidence of the accuracy of the results as herein presented. The magnitude of the correlation, instead of a statistical significance test, is the dominant criterion used to analyze this data. However, it should be clear that statistical significance tests can be useful aids in determining whether or not high magnitude correlations are meaningful, especially if the sample is small (i.e., with a sample of 100, .19 is statistically significant at the .05 level and with a sample of 22, .42 is statistically significant at the same level). For elucidation of the problems of significance tests use, see Hannan C. Selvin, "A Critique of Tests of Significance in Survey Research," *American Sociological Review*, 22 (October 1957), pp. 519–27.

more, we are dealing here with affective measures. The courses may have an impact on the cognitive development of the students that in turn may or may not have a latent effect on attitudes and behavior and which simply does not manifest itself until later in the life cycle.

We do not know whether or not the formal political education courses are having the effect of reinforcing attitude profiles developed earlier in life or whether, without the civic education course or courses, these profiles would be subject to greater change later in the life-cycle. We might hypothesize that the effect of the courses is not one of changing attitudes, but one of attitude profile support and maintenance. If this is actually the case, the research design used in this study did not account for it.

The data presented here find support in several within-nation surveys. They essentially corroborate the Langton-Jennings findings related to American students and the high-school formal political education curriculum. The Langton-Jennings survey is based on the results of a national probability sample of high-school seniors and is the most extensive study conducted in the United States comparing the effects of political education on those with *and* without this special training. It shows that aside from some meager differences, students taking civics, American government, problems of democracy, and other political education courses are virtually indistinguishable in terms of their political orientations from those not taking these courses. Differences did appear however for the black subpopulation.[7]

These findings indicate that formal political education courses do not have meaningful influence on the political information and attitudes held by a majority of American students. It is possible that the material presented in these courses is a repeat of the elementary school curriculum—in more depth, yet not enough to have a significantly demonstrable impact.

An analysis of Frankfurt University students in West Germany concerning their secondary school social studies courses disclosed a situation similar to that found in this cross-national student survey—students completing these courses do not differ noticeably from those students who have not taken formal social science.[8] In this survey the social science students were more interested in politics; however, neither in their political knowledge, their attitudes toward the political system, nor in their propensity to become involved in politics could any fundamental differences be found when they were compared with students without formal political education in the schools.

Current studies also indicate difficulties for political instruction in Sweden. A number of investigations made in Sweden show that political education is a popular subject among students aged 10 to 11 years but that

[7] Kenneth P. Langton and M. Kent Jennings, "Political Socialization and the High School Civics Curriculum in the United States," *American Political Science Review*, 62 (September 1968), pp. 852–67.

[8] Jürgen Habermas, *Student und Politik: Eine Soziologische Untersuchung zum Politischen Bewusstsein Frankfurter Studenten* (Neuwied: Hermann Luchterhand Verlag, 1961), pp. 267–77.

the subject is the least popular among students aged 14 to 16.[9] One such study involved a random probability sample of 1,958 students in elementary school and junior secondary school. The data disclosed that these students' formal school training fostered a lowered interest in the political education courses to which they were exposed. Further analysis disclosed that the subject matter covered "a little about everything" and that the time spent on individual subject matter items was too short to allow a high level of pupil interest. The conclusion that low student interest may be caused by the course itself was substantiated by comparing the students' interest in politics with the results of a similar survey of working adults' attitudes. Politics was a subject to which the adults showed a positive attitude and about which they tried to increase their knowledge.[10]

A cross-national survey of "civic" education in Europe[11] (which included Italy, England, West Germany, and Sweden) arrived at the following results:

1. The problems encountered by civic education have two basic sources: the lack of appeal of the civics course and the lack of preparation of the teachers.

2. The two are closely related, and often seem to form a vicious circle: if teachers were better able to awaken the pupils' interest, the latter would no longer regard the subject as a useless addition to their intellectual baggage.

3. Why does civics lack appeal for the students? Because, as now taught, it is too theoretical, bookish and therefore boring. At all costs, even where the course is an accepted part of the curriculum, this subject must be overhauled and regenerated; new techniques are absolutely essential.

Existing studies of the English educational system have not probed the role that formal political education plays in the transmission of political attitudes. There seems to be little doubt that the particular school that a student attends has an impact on the amount of political education he receives.[12] Although separate and formal political education courses exist in very few English schools, politics is taught in a wide variety of courses, particularly history and geography. The offerings of separate social science and political education courses are steadily increasing in England and might presage a change in impact as demonstrated by the small but positive effect found in the study between course exposure and support for the democratic concepts of dissent/opposition and legitimacy. Nevertheless, little or no

[9] Sixten Marklund, *Civic Education: Sweden* (unpublished report, Stockholm: University of Stockholm, July 1967), p. 11.

[10] Birger Bromsjö *Samhällskunskap som skolämne* (Stockholm: Scandinavia University Books, 1965), pp. 269–76.

[11] Council for Cultural Co-operation, *Education in Europe: Civics and European Education at the Secondary and Primary Level* (Strasbourg: Council of Europe, 1963), p. 149.

[12] Paul Abramson, "The Differential Political Socialization of English Secondary School Students," *Sociology of Education,* (Summer 1967), p. 254.

impact is likely to occur unless these new courses differ in content from traditional courses such as history.

In England we have found some positive and significant associations between having had political science and the dissent/opposition scale (mentioned above). In addition, social science courses previously taken correlated significantly with scale performance on dissent/opposition and legitimacy ($r=+.312$ on the dissent/opposition scale and $+.197$ on the legitimacy scale), but not with efficacy. Positive correlations between taking social science now and scale performance were found for the English students, although the associations did not reach levels of meaningful significance.

Since this is the sole example of significant findings with respect to course exposure, it requires some explanation. At the present time England is undergoing "steady growth," rather than "radical change" in its social studies curricula. Traditional history still dominates the curriculum, especially for university-bound students. However, there are many straws in the wind. Since the early 1960s, interdisciplinary studies, world affairs, contemporary and modern studies, and inquiry-based courses in sociology, anthropology, and psychology have been field tested. New programs in the humanities deal with conflict resolution, decision-making, and other concepts such as "just war." Many of these projects operate outside the restrictive examinations system and deal with nonhistorical topics such as "freedom and control," "conscientious objection," "dissent, resistance, and revolution," and similar provocative topics that would be supportive of dissent/ opposition.

There are many organizations involved in this new English social science movement; among these are the Humanities Curriculum Project at Philippa Fawcett College, London; The Schools Council Project for the integration of the Humanities at the University of Keele; and the general studies project at the University of York. The Interdisciplinary Enquiry (IDE) Project located at Goldsmith's College Curriculum Laboratory, University of London, has developed pilot courses in the social and behavioral sciences and for several years has been engaged in a publications and in-service seminar program to bring change into the schools. Some of the students in our London area sample have taken these courses. In sum, it may be that these new social science courses partially account for the positive results found in the English sample.[13]

SUMMARY

In our examination of political socialization we have given an overview of the more important agents affecting the development of political orientations, in the hope that this discussion will sensitize the reader to the innumerable variables that influence the political socialization process. In

---

[13] William A. Nesbitt, "World Order Education in England," *World Law Fund Progress Report*, 2 (Fall 1970), p. 4. See also the numerous publications of the University of London Goldsmiths' College Curriculum Laboratory, such as Leslie

addition, we have attempted to delineate the need for future research in this area of social scientific inquiry. We then considered the results of a five-nation survey of student orientations toward legitimacy, efficacy, and dissent/opposition. Generally speaking, appreciable differences did not occur across the five nations on the legitimacy and dissent/opposition scales; however, the English and Italian students' performance on these measures was statistically and significantly different from that of United States, Swedish, and West German students.

A greater dispersion of results occurred on the efficacy scale, with the English students scoring much lower on the high category of scale performance than students in the other four nations. However, few students in any nation fell into the low category of scale performance, thus suggesting the absence of a democratic support crisis in the five nations.

The age trend results of the five-nation study show a mixed pattern and suggest that the complex political learning process assumes a variety of shapes that can be measured only partially with the research techniques now in use.[14]

The next variables considered were the effects that formal political education and social sciences had on students' attitude profiles. Considering the multiplicity of factors affecting the political socialization process, it is perhaps not too surprising that we failed to discover high-order correlations between formal political education and social science course exposure, and student performance on these scales. Since so many factors are at play in shaping children's political personalities, no single one will normally show an appreciable effect on the individual's political orientations. However, the negligible impact shown by political education and social science courses (except for the positive association between previous political and social science course exposure and legitimacy and dissent/opposition in England) suggests that these courses as presently constituted are in serious need of revision.

It appears that the fundamental problem of much of the normal political education curriculum is replete with redundant materials that the student has been exposed to in a variety of ways from grade one on, such as saluting the flag, singing patriotic songs, learning the structure and function of the three branches of government, memorizing the Constitution, learning the names of government officials, developing respect for the political authorities and the society, and so forth. Specifically, the courses are mostly non-reality oriented. Conflict, systemic difficulties, difficulties of institutional adaptation, and so forth are virtually ignored in the curricula of all nations surveyed.

A. Smith, ed., *Ideas*, Series 1 and 2; the magazine of the Curriculum Laboratory; and the "Reports of Pilot Courses For Experienced Teachers," six booklets on such topics as the role of the school in a changing society, new roles for the learner, curriculum and resources, and education of children under social handicap.

[14] M. Kent Jennings and Richard G. Niemi, "Patterns of Political Learning," *Harvard Educational Review,* 38 (Summer 1968), pp. 443-67.

SUGGESTED REFORMS FOR POLITICAL EDUCATION: A CROSS-NATIONAL LIST

A list of needed reforms in the school system of all five nations here under consideration would include the following:

1. Accept an integrated set of curricula in the social sciences, arts, and humanities which will expose youth from the early grades through college to the major concepts and generalizations about political man in different settings.

2. Provide for individual differences with respect to sex, personality, ethnic group, region, reading ability, and other crucial variables in the implementation of the new, integrated political curriculum.

3. Balance out cognitive with emotional and behavioral components in the new civic education curriculum so that the large affective part of the human being is involved. Understanding political behavior now and later must become the major goal of civic education rather than the mere teaching and testing of recall knowledge or the abilities to abstract, comprehend, synthesize, or create. Now that the vote for students under the age of twenty-one has become a reality in Europe and the United States, society can begin to put the student's ideas and emotions into action, rather than promising him eventual gratification for his labor at a later age when he will achieve political "maturity."

4. Make certain in the new curriculum that the realities of the political system, not the constitutional or "rule book" maxims, are brought home to students. The students of today and tomorrow must know how the political elites in these nations function, how they got to be elites, and how any new group or individual who wants to influence the system must operate.

5. Lay bare the real conflicts, hates, and frustrations of groups and individuals in the society as well as what can and cannot be done in the short and long run toward conflict resolution and active pursuit of peacekeeping operations.

6. Humanize the political and social system on an individual basis in classroom instruction in and out of class experiences. The venality as well as the noble elements of technological, political, and social man must be treated from the perspective of the individual. The new curriculum must deal with bureaucracies that influence a person's life; with conflicts, such as the draft; and with public or private problems related to the students' socio-economic class, such as university reform, restrictive housing practices, or urban renewal. In other words writing letters to one's representatives in the local, state or regional, or national legislature may really be less relevant now and later than knowing how to file a claim for unemployment insurance, how to deal with hospital bureaucrats, or how to obtain redress for a grievance delivered at the hand of a teacher or policeman.

7. The new curriculum must focus on social adaptation and its mechanisms as well as on other basic concepts mentioned above. The devices for social

change are many, ranging from personal influence to civil disobedience, strikes, subversion, or revolution; focusing the power of individuals and groups to effect such change has to be a primary goal of a new curriculum for the political socialization of youth.

8. The new curriculum also must be worldwide in its dimensions and founded on those social sciences and humanities that contribute to greater understanding and empathy toward other peoples in our "global village." We are constantly touching one another's environments and lives. The arms race, military intervention in the Middle East, overpopulation, mass communications, ecology, and a host of other common problems are worldwide and transcend all national barriers. Any new curriculum for the future can use the modern techniques and findings of the social sciences and humanities to build the know-how for a common alliance and frontal assault on such problems.

Kenneth Boulding has asked, "Dare we take the social sciences seriously?"[15] He says:

> . . . the social sciences are creating a world in which national loyalty and the national state can no longer be taken for granted as sacred institutions, in which religion has to change profoundly its views on the nature of man and of sin, in which family loyalty and affection becomes a much more self-conscious and less simple-minded affair, and in which, indeed, all ethical systems are profoundly desacralized.

The natural sciences have driven off our ghosts and witches, debunked our views of racial purity and superiority, and destroyed our simple notions of why we exist as men. But they, like the social sciences, have brought other problems in new bags labeled fission, fusion, behavior modification, and thought control. Yet it may be left to the social sciences and humanities to clean up some of these problems (including some of their own creation), since the natural sciences still seem to be at the level of the folk or conventional wisdom in social problem solving The goal of social science must be to apply its findings for the good of the world and its communities. Perhaps then it will make some difference if one studies a new curriculum with science, man, and society as its basic themes.*

[15] Kenneth Boulding, "Dare We Take the Social Sciences Seriously?" *American Behavioral Scientist,* 10 (June 1967), pp. 15–16.

* The authors would like to acknowledge the professional advice and assistance in this research received from Siegfried George, Justus Liebig—Universität, Abt. für Erziehungswissenschaften, Giessen, West Germany, Sixten Marklund, Director, Bureau of Research and Development, National Board of Education, Stockholm, Sweden, Leslie A. Smith, Director of the Consultative Service, University of London Goldsmiths' College Curriculum Laboratory, London, England, Ray Whittaker, College of Education, Norwich, Norfolk, England, and Maria Laura Martini, Johns Hopkins University Bologna Center, Bologna, Italy.

Student and Faculty Socialization into the Academic Political Process

13

Robert T. Blackburn
John D. Lindquist

The shifting thrust of student pressure from administrators to faculty dramatically accelerates the importance of understanding how faculty approach the legislative process. If actual behavior and professed principle proceed in disparate directions, the most cogent arguments for or against student preticipation may be written on the wind. Although there has not been previous evidence that such may be the case, a recent course of events in the School of Education of a major midwestern university afforded a natural exploratory laboratory for testing the congruence of faculty beliefs versus faculty actions. A remarkable sequence of recorded faculty decisions and response to an opinion versus action questionnaire provide sufficient data for drawing inferences about expected and actual professorial behavior toward student participation in the guild. By this means, assertions by and about faculty attitudes toward student involvement in decision-making can be judged on the basis of performance rather than on guarded responses to an attitude survey or to public pronouncements not necessarily accompanied by subsequent deeds.

Several studies (Lazarsfeld and Thielens, 1958; Yee, 1963; Schuman and Laumann, 1967; Spaulding and Turner, 1968; Freedman, Kanset, and Carr, n.d.; Ladd, 1969) inform us in a general way about conservative versus liberal stances that faculty assume on external social issues. None, however, focuses on the political process within the academy. Others (Deutsch, 1949; Bennis, Berkowitz, and Affinito, 1958; Raven and French, 1958; Kelman, 1961; Cartwright, 1965) provide conceptual frameworks for studying—and experimental findings on—the voting behavior of people in organizations. None, however, tested theory on or applied outcomes to faculty or the college or university setting. Dykes (1968) speculates on faculty desires to

A modified version of this article appeared in *Sociology of Education*, 44 (Fall 1971), 398–421.

participate in governance and Parsons and Platt (1968) report faculty response to power. Although they too do not address themselves to the student-faculty interface, they (with the other sources just cited) collectively reinforce notions that academic discipline and career stage (professorial rank) are variables on which faculty differ in their behavior.[1] Thus this inquiry was also designed to test faculty behavior as it relates to rank and discipline, as well as to faculty knowledge about and behavior in the political process.

Intended to be merely a pilot, exploratory investigation, this study's strong response and statistically significant patterns lead the authors to offer it as food for reflection for those concerned with an issue as crucial to institutional health as student participation in academic governance.

THE SETTING

Regental by-laws regarding the School of Education under study call for periodic self-review. A faculty-elected Appraisal Committee fulfilled this task by conducting an exhaustive analysis of the School during 1967–68. Lengthy questionnaires, extended data collection, periodic reports, a faculty retreat, special hearings, and the like extended over that period. The examination was prompted by several factors—pockets of faculty discontent and reported low morale, a new president of the University, the impending retirement of the Dean, and a faculty group with low productivity, among others. A Dean's Search Committee was also operative, as was an External Review Committee of prominent national figures. Concurrently, for it was the season, a handful of students had organized, called themselves Students for Educational Innovation (SEI), recruited a membership, circulated literature for "change" and "relevance," and received recognition as a "legal body." In their efforts to attain memberships on decision-making bodies, they promptly began having members attend faculty meetings, a not uncommon innovation in higher educational governance. Though not Weatherman types, SEI members were genuine activists in their approach to political influence.

March 11, 1969: Proposal for a Joint Student-Faculty Assembly— Preliminary Acceptance

A high-priority recommendation stemming from the Appraisal Committee's deliberations was the creation of a faculty Assembly, not an operational body (such as the Executive Committee) but a forum to be concerned with School-wide problems and to "advise the Faculty, Dean and Executive Committee and other By-Law Committees." It was introduced as a motion

---

[1] Gamson (1967) found discipline differences in faculty relationships with students, but her setting did not involve response to student pressure nor to faculty in the legislative process. Wilson and Gaff (1969) relate faculty expressed liberalism to expressed openness to student participation, but their findings are not reported by rank or by discipline nor are they verified by behavioral observations in actual situations.

at the School's governing faculty meeting on March 11, 1969. Originally proposed as a ten-member Assembly, it was suggested in that meeting to enlarge the group to twenty faculty members. At that point, the president of SEI advanced the notion of a joint student-faculty Assembly, on a 5:15 ratio. Apparently without prior deliberation, and after brief discussion, the 5:15 proposal was passed by a *show of hands*: Aye, 42; Nay, 15. The majority was impressive, and the faculty hands were quite visible to colleagues and students.

March 18: Faculty Representation in Student Government

Because the motion constituted a By-Law change, a three-member faculty committee was appointed to phrase the motion in the required formal language and present it for final approval at the next regular meeting. One week later, however, at a special faculty meeting originally called to discuss other Appraisal Committee recommendations, the tentatively approved student-faculty Assembly was vigorously debated. One action which spoke to the growing controversy was a droll motion to place faculty members on the boards of all student organizations. SEI was receptive to the idea, but, then, it was too early to face the questions of voting rights or parity.

April 1: The Second Vote Defeats the Assembly

Two weeks later, just three weeks after the first resounding victory for student participation, the formal By-Law motion (requiring a two-thirds majority) was defeated: Aye, 23; Nay, 29. Before this formal vote, a substitute motion calling for *separate* student and faculty Assemblies and a joint Forum was in introduced. All debate centered on this motion, which was also defeated: Aye, 20; Nay, 24. Both April 1 votes were conducted by *secret ballot*.

Autumn 1969: The Questionnaire and a Third Vote on the Assembly

Are faculty politically fickle toward student participation? Were there serious issues of principle neglected on March 11 but made manifest by April 1? Did political maneuvering or ambiguity take its toll? Many were the interpretations, but the evidence was scant. To find answers to these and other questions, the authors probed this sequence of events with a questionnaire in the fall of 1969. Shortly thereafter, following a student-faculty retreat, the Executive Committee and the new dean (a prominent national figure) presented at a highly attended faculty meeting their strong endorsement of four proposals for action. One of these was an *ad hoc* student-faculty Assembly, twelve students and twelve faculty (parity rather than 5:15). Without a word of debate and by a "closed" ballot (seldom marked more than a seat away from a student), the motion carried: Aye, 72; Nay, 14.

Winter 1969: The Coupe de Grace

The circle had gone full turn, apparently, but a final counter-reversal abraded progress. A few weeks later, a secret, mail ballot by faculty for their representatives to the new Assembly elected a controlling majority from the department of the champion of the substitute motion—the anti-student participation motion—and nearly every familiar spokesman of student participation was defeated.

For both the pro- and anti-student participation cynic, interpretations are abundant. To the more detached observer, such perplexing reversals challenge analysis and interpretation.

METHODOLOGY

The Sample

Questionnaires were sent to all faculty on both the 1968–69 and 1969–70 rosters of the School of Education, 135 in all. Eighty-seven completed questionnaires were returned. However, a sizable number on these lists have tenuous relationships to the School—extension members are spread across the state; some administrators have paper and pen appointments, do not identify with the School, and never attend meetings—and the rosters include those on leave. For these reasons, the 64 percent response is an appreciable underestimate of the effective response rate. (The "active and teaching" faculty of this School actually number about 90.) Of those present at either session at which votes were taken (March 11 and April 1), the return rate increases to 70 percent. Of those present at *both* sessions, 74 percent responded, and of those present at all three meetings (26 stalwarts), the response rate climbs to 85 percent. Perhaps more noteworthy, the vote reported in the official faculty minutes and the vote tabulated from the questionnaire are statistically in agreement. Furthermore, the questionnaire response by academic rank was in direct proportion to the rank distributions on the official School rosters.

Thus, the decision to use the responses of those who claimed attendance on the questionnaire as the basic data should produce only minimal and random canceling errors. In short, it seems to be a very high and representative response.

Absentees Become a Quasi-Control Group

An interesting attitudinal-behavioral phenomenon appears when those who say they attended and those who claim absence are compared. The absentees respond so differently on the ballot (becoming, in effect, a control group—though self-selected—against which to measure the effects of the political process) that they must be separated when voting records are analyzed. (For example, some present report they abstained on one or more votes; no one absent ever checked that he would select that option.) Attendance thus becomes the independent variable. The absentees' use as a "control" is enhanced, moreover, by the fact that they do not similarly deviate from attenders in their opinions about faculty voting patterns nor in their causal analyses. Only in their actual voting do they differ.

The Attitude-Behavior Instrument

A covering letter succinctly reported the main events of the meetings so as to refresh faculty memories. The instrument itself merely required checking of appropriate boxes. It asked if each faculty member attended the March 1 and April 1 meetings; how he voted on each of the three motions (or if he was absent how he *would have* voted); how he thought those of each rank and each disciplinary affiliation voted; how confident he felt in these beliefs; and what caused the reversal of the faculty vote (to be indicated by checking a list of thirteen reasons found in the minutes and prevalent in discussions around the School, plus answering an open question). In addition, each respondent was asked to record how he would *now* vote, months away from the heat of those meetings. Edward O. Laumann, Associate Professor of Sociology and co-author of an earlier study using a similar format (Schuman and Laumann, 1967), critiqued the instrument, served as the recipient of the returns, conducted the follow-up, assured anonymity, and the like.[2]

Qualifying Particularities of the School of Education

Finally, two considerations inherent in the School's organizational structure and practice with regard to academic titles dictate a restricted display of the data. First, although the School uses all three professorial titles as well Instructor and Lecturer, the latter two include persons who differ appreciably from those who hold the same title in a literary school department. Rather than being young Ph.D. candidates above the Teaching Fellow's status, Instructors in the School of Education tend often to be faculty of the Laboratory School (elementary and high school)—experienced members of the faculty but more likely than not to be career teachers in the grades. The Lecturers, rather than being visiting or unpedigreed personnel, tend to be people in administrative posts out of and about the University and professors in other schools of the University. So, although their responses will sometimes be used when dealing with totals, Instructors and Lecturers are neither a homogeneous nor a comparable group and will not receive separate analysis and discussion.

Secondly, the structural organization of the School of Education results in several small sub-units (departments) too small in many cases to submit to standard statistical analysis. So they, too, appear in the overall totals but not in the comparative analyses by department. Fortunately, all of the interesting discipline outcomes are best displayed by focusing on the two largest departments—Curriculum and Instruction (with 22 ranked members), and Behavioral Sciences (with 20 ranked members). The former, dealing directly

---

[2] For those acts, and for his helpful suggestions for this manuscript, we extend our thanks. To a group of Center colleagues—faculty, students, and postdocs—who criticized an earlier draft we are also grateful.

TABLE 1. Chronology of Events

Date	Event
1967–1969	Faculty Self Study, Dean's Search Committee, External Review.
1968–1969	Student Organization (SEI) forms.
March 11, 1969	Proposal for Joint Student-Faculty (5:15) Assembly overwhelmingly passed in open vote at Faculty Meeting.
March 18, 1969	Unscheduled debate on the accepted Joint Assembly at a special faculty meeting (called for other matters).
April 1, 1969	Amended Proposal for separate student and faculty assemblies and a joint Forum defeated. Closed vote on By-Law for Regents on the March 11 Assembly defeated.
October 1969	Questionnaire to faculty regarding behavior at March 11 and April 1 meetings.
November 1969	Following a student-faculty retreat and a new Dean and Executive Committee endorsement, a joint student-faculty (12:12) Assembly overwhelmingly approved.
December 1969–January 1970	Closed vote for faculty representatives to the new Assembly defeats advocates of student participation.

with training of teachers, is the unit which most clearly epitomizes the "Ed" School image in the minds of many. On the other hand, Behavioral Science, housing the psychologists and sociologists, as well as the principal research laboratories, is the unit most like an Arts and Science social science department.

The Findings

Because the pattern of events itself is significant, these findings are presented in sequential order. One should keep in mind, therefore, that on March 11 the original proposal for a 5:15 student-faculty School of Education Assembly was passed 42:15; on April 1 a substitute proposal calling for two separate assemblies and a joint Forum was offered and defeated 20:24, and the original Assembly was defeated on formal reading 23:29. Then on October 20, a 12:12 faculty-student *ad hoc* School of Education Assembly passed 72:14, and in subsequent election of faculty representatives, the known pro-student nominees were defeated. Table 1 chronicles the events for future reference.

The March 11 Vote, By Rank

Table 2 displays how each rank reported it voted, how each faculty member thought his own rank voted, and how each rank thought other ranks voted. Professors accurately "predict" their own favorable vote, whereas others regard them as at best split on the idea of student participation

TABLE 2. THE MARCH 11 VOTING, BY PROFESSORIAL RANK (IN PERCENTS)

	Full Professors		Associate Professors		Assistant Professors		All Ranks[b]	
	Aye	*Nay*	*Aye*	*Nay*	*Aye*	*Nay*	*Aye*	*Nay*
"Actual"[a]	67	33	75	25	80	20	72	26
They predict	68	32	89	11	93	7		
Others predict	51	49	81	19	87	13		

[a] As reported by the Questionnaire respondents.
[b] Includes Instructors and Lectures, whose votes on each motion were: 67/33; 60/40; and 38/62.

in a joint Assembly.[3] There is no ready explanation for their remarkable self-insight, unless it be that each full professor trusts that all other professors behave as he does. It is obvious, however, that the folklore of full professor conservatism accepted by other ranks is not in fact as extreme as they believe. Associate and assistant professors, meanwhile, are somewhat more supportive than full professors but think themselves even more favorably disposed toward the joint Assembly than they in fact are. Others accurately predict this progression, though to a more conservative degree. No rank is far from the actual tally. One may conclude only that all ranks favor the proposal but in slightly higher degrees ascending from full to assistant professor.

March 11 Vote, By Discipline

Turning to the reported and predicted vote of the two largest units within the School,[4] Table 3 dramatizes disciplinary differences. Both departments supported the original motion, although the Behavioral Science Department is the more enthusiastic. Predictions generally agree with the vote. Perhaps more important (as subsequent events indicate), predictors see no voting difference between the two departments on March 11.

If this original vote does represent basic faculty attitudes toward the idea of student participation, the results should encourage student politicos. Were it an isolated event, such a conclusion would seem supported by the evidence. Later actions strongly suggest, however, that the sudden and public nature of the proposal and vote exaggerated what appears to be a slight majority favorably disposed toward the idea of a joint Assembly.

[3] "Predict" is used throughout as "render an opinion." In actuality, of course, the questionnaire comes after the fact and calls for recollections. It asks faculty how they voted, why, etc. It also asks how they thought others voted at that time. The assumption made is that their opinion regarding others holds over time and/or their memory accurately distinguishes if changes of opinion have taken place. In this sense they are "predicting."

[4] Only one of the seven other units has more than half as many faculty as the smaller of these two.

TABLE 3. The March 11 Voting: Actual, Reported, and Predicted Voting by the Behavioral Science and Curriculum and Instruction Department (in percents)

		Reported	Predicted
Behavioral Science	Aye	78	71
	Nay	22	29
Curriculum and Instruction	Aye	65	72
	Nay	35	28
Actual Vote: Everyone	Aye	74	
	Nay	26	

$\chi^2 = 0.73$; n.s.
(d.f. = 1. Calculation on "Reported" for B.S. and C. & I.)

The April 1 Votes, By Rank

The substitute motion (two separate Assemblies and a joint Forum) was introduced immediately after the reading of the original joint Assembly proposal, now in By-Law language. Observers relate that some faculty and student leaders knew beforehand that a substitute would be introduced and that it was actually written by the writer of the formal proposal, a powerful leader in his own right. All debate centered on the substitute motion. Those speaking against it (primarily behavioral scientists of full professorial rank) regarded it as a blatant attempt to remove students from decision-making. SEI spokesmen concurred. In the abstract, then, a vote *for* the substitute motion would be linked to a vote against a student-participant Assembly. Table 4 reveals a noteworthy contradiction of rank stereotypes and faculty predictions. The Old Guard voted *against* the substitute, whereas the Young Turks supported it. The predictions, however, run just the opposite.

TABLE 4. The April 1 Voting, by Professorial Rank (in percents)

		Full Professors		Associate Professors		Assistant Professors		All Ranks[b]	
		Aye	Nay	Aye	Nay	Aye	Nay	Aye	Nay
Substitute Motion: Separate Assemblies	Actual[a]	39	61	55	45	67	33	45	55
	They predict	59	41	50	50	31	69		
	Others predict	63	37	54	46	28	72		
Joint Assembly	Actual[a]	41	59	55	45	60	40	44	56
	They predict	18	82	33	67	80	20		
	Others predict	20	80	35	65	76	24		

[a] As reported by the Questionnaire respondents.
[b] Includes Instructors and Lecturers, whose votes on each motion were: 67/33; 60/40; and 38/62.

TABLE 5. The April 1 Voting: Actual, Reported, and Predicted Voting by the Behavioral Science and Curriculum and Curriculum and Instruction Departments (in percents)

		Substitute		Joint Assembly	
		Reported	*Predicted*	*Reported*	*Predicted*
Behavioral Science	Aye	30	32	71	87
	Nay	70	68	29	13
Curriculum and Instruction	Aye	80	69	33	31
	Nay	20	31	67	69
Actual Vote: Everyone	Aye	45		44	
	Nay	55		56	

Substitute: $\chi^2 = 7.58$; $p < .01$
Joint Assembly: $\chi^2 = 4.86$; $p < .05$
(d.f. $= 1$; Calculations on "Reported" for B.S. and C. & I.)

Then, in the second vote upon the original motion, which followed the substitute ballot without discussion, the three ranks assumed a moderate version of their predicted behavior. To reach the 23:29 Aye-Nay configuration from 42:15 outcome on March 11, each rank lost approximately equal degrees of support (about a 20 percent shift, slightly greater among full professors). The extreme change against the Assembly predicted for professors by themselves and others proved to be exaggerated, just as the steadfast support predicted of assistant professors by themselves did not occur.

For the most part, faculty accept the commonly known rank stereotypes rather than projecting their own actions into representativeness. "All others of my rank are like I am supposed to be, but I am not," is what they seem to say.

April 1 Vote, By Department

Table 5 records the substitute and second reading of the Assembly vote for the two largest departments. A very clear phenomenon manifests itself. Similar departments on March 11 are polar opposites on April 1 (cf. Table 3). The Behavioral Scientists, in a 70 percent majority, vote against the substitute motion and in favor of the original student-faculty Assembly. And the faculty as a whole predicts even stronger support than was manifested. Why, when rank by rank support is waning, does the largest department hold firm? Turning to the Curriculum and Instruction Department, one sees the reverse. Eighty percent of that group backs the substitute (which overall failed to gain a majority), and they switch from 65 percent in *favor* to 67 percent *against* the original proposal. Again, the faculty predictions are highly accurate. They apparently have insight into both of these clear deviations from the general voting behavior.

Reasons for the Voting Change, According to Respondents

The questionnaire asked respondents to explain the loss of support for the Assembly. Table 6 lists the 13 reasons for the changed vote, scored

Departments							Statement or Reason
		Ranks					A for issues raised between and/or within meetings
B.S.	C&I	All[a]	Full	Assoc	Asst		B for statements true or false at any time.
1	1	1	1	1	1	A	Although the first vote represented general approval for the idea of faculty-student Assembly, later discussion and events raised questions about the efficacy of the particular bodies which were proposed.
3	4	2	4[d]	6[d]	5[d]	B	Faculty deferred from enacting a major by-law change before installation of the new dean.
6[d]	7[d]	3	3	2	7	B	With students present, a show of hands vote strongly in favor of student participation is understandable. It is also understandable that a later closed ballot did not produce a majority.
2	2	4	4	6	2	B	There are distinctions between faculty and student concerns, and the School of Education Assembly could better speak to faculty concerns without student participation.
4	7	5	2	9	5	A	It was unclear by the time of the April 1 ballot just what the function of the Assembly was to be.
8	6	6	7	4	5	A	Faculty members recognized after March 11 that the faculty-student Assembly would constitute a degree of dilution of faculty prerogative.
10	5	7	6	7	11	A	[e]The controversial Educational Circus (between the March and April meetings) dimmed enthusiasm for student participation.
6	2	8[b]	7	3	2	B	Student organizations which would appoint representatives are not sufficiently representative.
8	9	9	10	4	8	A	The fact that the usual leaders in prestige or persuasiveness did not align themselves on one side of the issue created sufficient ambiguity to lose many who supported the motion earlier.
6	11	10	11	13	8	B	Defeat of the Assembly motion was intended, as students stated, to "take the students out of decision making."
12	13	11	9	10	13	A	Introduction of a counter-proposal confused the issue.
13	10	12	12	10	14	B	The proposed School of Education Assembly would generate rather than resolve conflict between faculty and students.
10	11	13[c]	12	12	10	—	"Other"—[Most frequently these were stronger assertions of one of the other thirteen]
14	14	14	14	13	12	B	Faculty members are generally reluctant to pass major legislation late in the spring.

[a] Includes Instructors and Lecturers and hence makes it possible for rank #2 on "All" to be higher than other sub-groups.
[b] After the first 8 statements, the remaining receive very few votes.
[c] Linking all "others" as one, which they were not.
[d] When ties occurred, the lower of a pair was recorded; when a tie between three, the middle number is reported.
[e] Between March 11 and April 1, SEI staged a rather unstructured affair on issues in education. Distinguished speakers were on hand. A band of guerrilla theatre people unexpectedly appeared. Formlessness approached chaos at times.

according to the importance given each statement by each rank and by the two largest departments. The statements are further divisible into two groups. One set of reasons (A) speaks directly to issues and events that arose between March 11 and April 1. The other group (B) might be categorized as true or false at any time. These are reasons one would expect to be as applicable March 11 as April 1 as October 20.[5]

Doubt regarding the efficacy of the proposed Assembly is the primary concern of every rank. It is commonplace knowledge to political observers that lack of clarity regarding the specific effects, or effectiveness, of a proposed change weakens support. Hekhiris (1967), in studying faculty attitudes toward student participation, finds a similar phenomenon: bickering over particularization increases ambiguity and indecisiveness, thus losing support. If the first vote was approval of the *idea* and the second was to be approval of the specific body, efficacy would indeed be a critical issue.[6] It offers no explanation, however, for the contrasting behavior between the Behavioral Science and the Curriculum and Instruction Departments, nor for the differences between faculty ranks.

The lame duck explanation smacks of convenience. The new dean had been announced in January. Surely the avoidance of major by-law changes would apply March 11 as well as April 1. Also, faculty are not generally known to be so self-effacing about their prerogatives as professionals. Finally, the new dean was on campus between those meetings and left a clear impression that he strongly favored student participation. In fact, he was a key figure in the passage of the Assembly the next November.

The third-ranking reason might be termed the show-of-hands syndrome. It is the only reason dealing with process (as opposed to issues) that receives support. On March 11, the vote was by show of hands, with students present. At least two dynamics may have been at work. First, fence-sitters join others when they see what appears to be a majority of hands going up—and changing would-be negative votes into silent abstainers when the call for "contrary" is requested from the chair, a factor further increasing the percentage of ayes. The questionnaire put the issue a second way, indicating that student presence and the "if you are not with us, you are against us" judgment was the key difference. The faculty—with the exception of one respondent who was aghast that such a thing would be suggested—to a large extent agreed with this latter interpretation.

The fourth-ranking reason is almost verbatim the argument presented by the maker of the substitute motion: "There are distinctions between faculty and student concerns." Such a claim should have been as true or false March 11 as April 1, but perhaps it needed reemphasis. Because it was the substitute motion argument, one would expect to find here the cause for

---

[5] Respondents were not shown this dichotomy.

[6] E.g., changing a By-Law carries with it both long-range and permanent implications. (Although new structures can be dissolved tomorrow with a new vote, faculty bodies do not approach Regents monthly with contrary requests.) In being cautious when facing a not very clear future, faculty are not acting differently from other human groups. The data, however, do not sufficiently probe this reason of "efficacy," and so, the above "explanation" remains hypothetical.

the remarkable difference in behavior between the Behavioral Science and the Curriculum and Instruction Departments. Yet, both rank this argument second. One should keep in mind, however, the projective quality of these responses. Behavioral Scientists may merely be attributing this motive to others, not to themselves. Written comments on Behavioral Scientist questionnaires bear out this possibility. There seems to be an "outsider" quality to these remarks, as if the respondent himself were not of the "faculty" in question.

The two crucial departments do differently support the assertion that student representatives are not representative (#8); the statement about clarity (#5); the controversy caused by the students' Education Circus (#7);[7] and the student claim that the defeat of the Assembly was intended to "take the students out of decision-making" (#10). Behavioral scientists seemed less annoyed by the Circus, and they were not nearly as worried about representativeness. But they did feel the reversal was meant to take students out of decision-making.

Unrepresentativeness of student leaders is relevant to Students for Educational Innovation in a strict sense. Everyone knows five concerned students do not directly represent a diverse collection of well over a thousand graduates and undergraduates, full-time and part-time, on and off campus. But the reputation of SEI among students—and well-known to faculty—was very strong. In the context of its absence as an issue in either the March 11 or October meetings, representativeness also seems an argument of convenience.

Finally, it will be well to keep in mind that taking students out of decision-making is precisely the claim made against the substitute motion by speakers from the Behavioral Science Department.

Summary of Statements

From this table of statements, what things in general caused a three-quarters majority to disappear in three spring weeks? Apparently, confirmation of the *idea* of student participation was not successfully transposed into a suitable format. Also, faculty "remembered" such matters as the clear divisibility of faculty and student concerns, the possible loss of faculty prerogative, lame duck ethics, and the unrepresentativeness of student leaders. In addition, a show of hands with students present influences toward supporting student participation, while having a "Circus," replete with "ungentlemanly" behavior such as guerilla theatre, fresh in mind does not help. These reasons seem substantial and understandable, if tainted with rationalization. But this point is nowhere near the end of the story.

Voting Preference at the Time of the Questionnaire

The final item on the questionnaire asked: "From the perspective of several months removal from those meetings, please check your present

---

[7] Between March 11 and April 1, SEI staged a rather unstructured affair on issues in education. Distinguished speakers were on hand. A band of guerrilla theatre people unexpectedly appeared. Formlessness approached chaos at times.

frame of mind on the subject of a joint faculty-student Assembly." Recall that this question would be answered in October of 1969, six months after the reversal.[8] Thirty percent "heartily endorse" such a proposal. That is the hard-core support. Another 29 percent feel they would "probably favor it." In other words, without the extenuating circumstances surrounding the April 1 ballot, 59 percent support approval of such an Assembly. The difference between that 59 percent and the original 72 percent might logically be attributed to "remembering" serious reservations concerning student participation after March 11. That would have been a logical conclusion, but only partially if at all accurate. Fortunately for interpreters, the sequence of relevant events was still unfolding.

November 1969: The Third Ballot on a Student-Participant Assembly

While the authors were still analyzing questionnaire responses, the faculty met to consider four proposals which had emerged from a recent faculty-student retreat. One was a black student demand to enroll minority students in proportion to state population. Another was to establish an *ad hoc* student-faculty Assembly (with 12:12 parity this time around). Both proposals passed the Assembly by an 82 percent majority. The vote was by secret ballot (requested by blacks so as to secure a "true" measure of faculty positions) but was filled out usually no more than a seat away from a student. How could 59 percent (at best) become 82 percent in the same time period but on two different ballots? For that matter, how could a 44 percent minority (April 1) become an 82 percent *majority* on the same issue differing only in that the second proposal asked for an *ad hoc* body, but with parity, i.e., increasing the student ratio from 25 to 50 percent? Where had all those general concerns, stated only weeks before, gone? It was March 11 all over again, only more so.

Leadership and the Political Process

Looking at this chain of events from the perspective of leadership and the political process—two interrelated factors relatively ignored by respondents—one gathers a much different view. First, the March 11 proposal was not foreseen. For most, the student-participant Assembly was invented in the meeting (though student participation itself was hardly now an issue). Also, there is faculty admission of the effects of the show of hands process. The second reading on April 1, by contrast, was well-planned, from all accounts. The March 18 proposal to place faculty on all student groups was hardly conceived in innocence. Student leaders further report that prominent faculty members approached them during those weeks to persuade them to back the substitute proposal, for they said the Assembly was doomed.

Recall that the substitute was written by the composer of the original by-law. The man who presented the substitute also happened to be the president of the University Senate Assembly and chairman of the Senate Advisory Committee on University Affairs—and not the writer of the motion.

---

[8] When responding, no one was aware that such a vote was just over the horizon.

Germane to questionnaire evidence, this highly respected leader is a member of the Curriculum and Instruction Department. The seconder of his motion maintains membership in the same unit. The clear swing to the substitute in that department begins to become comprehensible. Given the size and high attendance of that department, just this influence can account for failure of the original proposal to again reach the required two-thirds majority.

Meanwhile, leadership opposition to the substitute was dominated by the Behavioral Scientists. Although a clear shift in the evidence does not pinpoint leadership influence in this department, the fact that Behavioral Scientists did *not* shift with even the overall faculty loss of support suggests reference group influence of departmental leaders. Significantly, the voting in these departments is accurately predicted by the faculty as a whole at the same time that they deny leadership impact. One thinks of the old saying that professionals espouse principled arguments as most fitting to their non-political office but are well aware of the infighting.

Looking to the fall vote, it should be noted that the new dean threw his own support behind the Assembly proposal, and no other leader broke ranks. The maker of the April 1 substitute motion, and the writer of that motion for that matter, held neatly in line. Surely the separateness of faculty and student concerns had not vanished as an argument, but, left unexpressed, it seemed to be no longer an issue.

Regarding efficacy and clarity, one might say that the *ad hoc*, as opposed to by-law, nature of the fall proposal relieved minds worried about the global consequences of their vote. That at least was the stated belief of the makers of the motion.

Attendance and the Behavior of Absentees

Two other pieces of questionnaire evidence point to politics as an important causal factor. First, the Behavioral Scientists do not go to meetings in numbers at all comparable with their slightly smaller rival on this issue. Twice as many Curriculum and Instruction faculty attended all three meetings. Part of this phenomenon might be explained by the cosmopolitan/locality distinctions made by Clark (1962). He divides faculty into four typologies based upon two general variables: local versus cosmopolitan orientation, and commitment to pure, disinterested study as opposed to applied, vocational, or professional orientation. "The scholar-researcher" (recall that Behavioral Science is the dominant School of Education research department) is not locally involved, while "the demonstrator," an apt label for the Ed School image, is imbedded in local affairs. A third Clark typology may appropriately describe the Behavioral Scientist (and many others) who does attend meetings and favors such things as student-participant Assemblies:

> The Teacher: the professor who is identified with this college and who is committed to pure, disinterested study; being committed to students and to their liberal education, he is impatient with researchers and believes professionalism and applied work are inappropriate in college. (Clark, 1962, p. 44)

Given the professional nature of the School of Education, one must modify that description somewhat, but it does suggest why at least some Behavioral Scientists show up at faculty meetings and stand firmly for student participation. If the issue were student control of federal grants, a much different attendance configuration might be anticipated. In any case, the advocate of student participation would do well to hustle "teachers" to meetings.

Respondents who did not attend the April 1 meeting also offer a compelling argument for the effects of the political process. The absentees are strongly in favor of the Assembly on April 1, as they were on the March 11 ballot. Yet, they do not otherwise differ from respondents in general in their predictions nor in their causal analyses. They are not a pure experimental control group, for they are self-selected to a certain extent (although some *could* not, as opposed to *would* not, attend that day). Still, if the reasons for the reversal are supported in the same degree by absentees, one must conclude that being in attendance is a critical variable. Those present simply are affected in ways that those absent are not.

The Final Turn of Events—So Far

A last example of the bearing of political process—intended or not (the eminent maker of the substitute motion had a major role in determining the process)—on faculty decision-making is the election of faculty representatives to the *ad hoc* Assembly. The vote took place by mail. Of the ten ranked positions, seven were chosen from the Curriculum and Instruction Department and only one from the largest unit (at the time) in the School—Behavioral Science. It would seem that Mr. Nixon's Silent Majority has its counterpart in faculty deliberations. Student leaders confess that they were asleep to such a reversion to conservatism regarding student participation. Since evidence indicates that those not attending meetings are more, rather than less, supportive of the Assembly, and are for a good part from Behavioral Science, one cannot claim that nonattenders account for the conservative ballot. Perhaps this action says, "Yes, we will submit to pressure to approve a student-faculty Assembly, but in private we will assure that faculty interests are well protected on that body. We really don't 'love' students as much as we say we do."

Whatever the reason for this fourth turn of events, the story is not over yet, nor is the eventual ending clear. It is unknown whether either student or faculty attitudes have been altered by this legislation and litigation, and whether higher education is better or worse for having student-faculty assemblies in the first place.

CONCLUSION AND DISCUSSION

If faculty voting on a controversial issue such as student participation can vary from meeting to meeting without the injection of new insights into its desirability, one must turn to the process itself for explanation. The way in which the vote was taken becomes crucial. Who stands on which side, and even what is the last speech before voting, seem to have great bearing on the outcome.[9] Who attends in the first place stacks the odds. Who is present to observe the vote, and how much can be seen, are also factors. Departmental unity (or self-selected similarity) can tell much of the story. The stage of the professor's career (academic rank) matters. And so does the socialization process of his disciplinary training and association. Confusion about the nature of the proposed change loses support, especially when the new entity is to be of some permanence. Presentation of a counterproposal, even if it is defeated, damages the chances of the original motion. Finally, rational arguments seem to take the back seat to political maneuvering.

Are faculty aware of these political influences? Their reporting of reasons for the April 1 switch argue for the most part against their having political acumen. It seems that the alertness of those few who prepared the counterproposal and the mailed election went relatively unnoticed. Yet, the same faculty who claimed reasons of principle and the specific issue as causes for the reversal also clearly predicted the two departments' behaviors. Was that merely recognition of the Behavioralist versus "Ed" images, or do faculty understand leadership and politics but prefer to claim principle? Because faculty also correctly predict that both departments would endorse the proposal on March 11, the latter explanation gains credence.

It would seem that *both* naiveté and awareness are at work. Like smoking pot, faculty politics seems to be obviously rampant to those who indulge but an inappropriate accusation to those who abstain. The umbrella over both of these extremes, the mystique exuded by the academy, is the self-image that portrays the faculty member as acting essentially by professional concerns of reason and principle.

How do faculty feel about student participation itself? If the questionnaire response and the actual voting tallies are any indication, the odds line up similarly to national party elections. A solid 30 percent favor it regardless of political events, whereas a slightly smaller number are equally dead against it. The broad middle can be swayed either way.

Suggested Further Research

Although our approach and analysis suggest inferences with regard to faculty political leaders and to followers, both the anonymous response and the kind of data collected preclude our advancing warranted assertions. An inquiry into such variables, as well as into the smoke filled room tactics of faculty politicking before meetings, would be an important and valuable contribution to our growing knowledge of faculty. Also, more needs to be known about basic faculty attitudes toward students—and of students toward faculty—so as to better judge what kind of structures and processes stand the best chance of being productive. It appears as if faculty are nearly polarized with respect to their overall trust of students in their midst, not just in the legislative and/or decision-making process.

[9] Favorable remarks preceded the March 11 and November votes. Arguments about the substitute were all that came before the April 1 vote.

RECOMMENDATIONS

If the above analyses prove generalizable to faculties as a whole, the Academy may well wish to reconsider its present governing practices. Certainly, the business of the faculty is teaching and research, not legislating. But if naiveté or intrigue influences academic decisions, especially regarding who is to make decisions in the first place, the main thrust of the university is weakened or at least threatened. One fights off the image of the fox and the henhouse out of reverence for distinguished colleagues, but the above sequence of events surely indicates that knowledgeable leadership is highly influential whether faculty know it or not. Lack of awareness in such a context becomes relatively helpless vulnerability. Also, as students are admitted to academic governance, as seems to be the undeniable trend, it behooves faculty to be at least as alert as student activists to the effects of the political process. If, on the other hand, student or colleague pressure is driving actual views underground, reaching wise decisions—an act requiring consideration of all sides of an issue—is itself endangered.

The presence versus absence of students and public versus private ballot influences carry serious implications beyond the setting of this inquiry. Faculty participation in governance has not been a God-given right. It has painfully, sometimes bitterly, evolved. The secrecy of its voting procedures has been a prime protector of the individual faculty member's freedom to disagree with his dean or chairman. We are still witnessing AAUP cases of promotion denial alleged to be related to more public political behavior not in step with institutional image. Whether or not administrators are by nature and role evil is not the question. They *could* be, and this matters.

Student insurgency further complicates the question of voting style, however. Students are affected by most academic decisions. In this regard, they are the faculty's constituency. As does every other constituency, they feel the legislators of their academic lives should make their votes matters of public record.

In one sense, therefore, faculty are not elected representatives but private professionals concerned about their own and their organization's fate, while in another sense they are legislators governing the lives of students. If they can be intimidated by students or deans or the political process itself, their professional autonomy is violated. This effect argues for the private ballot. On the other hand, if professional and constituent interests do not coincide, one can readily argue for the public ballot as a constituent protection.

The issue is not whether there are exclusively faculty and student concerns. The problem is the improvement of the Academy toward becoming more sensitive to *both* faculty and student concerns. Who decides how life shall be lived and what institutional purposes are to be is altogether too important a matter to be either driven underground or intimidated into brash decision. As long as students remain outside academic decision-making but affected by it; as long as faculty either deny or pretend to deny politics as necessary to their profession while politicos manipulate; and as long as faculty concerns are primarily parochial to their professional interests (a whole further question glaringly confirmed by Max Wise's recent readings of all faculty minutes of six institutions for the past decade); as long as these problems exist, there seems to be no way out of the mercurial academic decision-making climate herein described.

The intent of this study is not to provide a manual for faculty members aspiring to political leadership. (The academic Machiavellian masterpiece remains Cornford's, 1908, a delightful essay that attests to the historical verities of academic life.) It does seem vital, however, that all parties to a debate decide issues on their merits and not because of the dynamics of decision-making itself. But, for those who do hope for a manifesto, let the following go forth: take extensive and deliberate pain to uncomplicate what others confound; clearly refute conflicting testimonials; arrange the strongest leaders behind your cause; and, above all, corral potential supporters and herd them to the meeting grounds. But if the ranks break at the last minute, why, table it.

POSTSCRIPT

The tenor of this analysis may suggest to some a negative impression of faculty. Were faculty state legislators, that assumption might have some justification. The manner of the faculty profession is such, however, that legislation only facilitates, rather than acts as, their principal duty. In their primary roles, faculty open-mindedly and expertly grapple with problems that polarize or intimidate other professions. Even in their current policy-making role, the question of how best to improve sensitivity to students and to meet society's educational needs challenges the creative talents of everyone. To assume that reservation about student participation is merely vested power interest is like judging a faculty member with no blacks in one class of his, *ipso facto*, guilty of racism. From all indications, including the high response to this questionnaire, faculty do care. With full knowledge of such influences as the legislative process, they may become even better equipped to engage the perplexing and pressing problems of the day.

REFERENCES

Bennis, W. G., Berkowitz, N., and Affinito, S. "Authority, Power, and the Ability to Influence," *Human Relations Quarterly*, 11 (May 1958), 143–55.

Cartwright, D. "Influence, Leadership, Control," *in* J. G. March (ed.), *Handbook of Organizations*. Chicago: Rand McNally, 1965.

Clark, B. R. "Faculty Culture," *in* T. F. Lunsford (ed.), *The Study of Campus Cultures*. Boulder, Colo.: Western Interstate Commission for Higher Education, 1962.

Cornford, F. M. *Microcosmographia: Being a Guide for the Young Academic Politician*. Cambridge: Bowes and Bowes, 1908.

Deutsch, M. "An Experimental Study of the Effects of Cooperation and Competition Upon Group Process," *Human Relations Quarterly*, 2 (July 1949), 199–232.

Dykes, A. R. *Faculty Participation in Academic Decision Making.* Washington, D.C.: American Council on Education, 1968.

Freedman M., Kanzer, P., and Carr, R. *Attitudes of Faculty to Student Power and Militancy.* California: San Francisco State College, *n. d.*

Gamson, Z. R. "Performance and Personalism in Student-Faculty Relations," *Sociology of Education*, 40 (Fall 1967), 279–301.

Hekhiris, L. A. "A Comparison of the Perceptions of Students and Faculty at Michigan State University with Respect to Student Participation in University Policy Formulation." East Lansing: Michigan State University, 1967. Ed.D. dissertation.

Kelman, H. C. "Processes of Opinion Change," *Public Opinion Quarterly*, 25 (Spring 1961), 57–78.

Ladd, E. C., Jr. "Professors and Political Petitions," *Science*, 163 (March 1969), 1425–30.

Lazarsfeld, P. F., and Thielens, W. *The Academic Mind: Social Scientists in a Time of Crisis.* New York: The Free Press, 1958.

Parsons, T., and Platt, G. M. *The American Academic Profession.* Washington, D.C.: National Science Foundation, 1968.

Raven, B. H., and French, J. R. P. "Group Support, Legitimate Power, and Social Influence," *Journal of Personality*, 26 (September 1958), 400–409.

Schuman, H., and Laumann, E. O. "Do Most Professors Support the War?" *Trans-action*, 5 (November 1967), 32–35.

Spaulding, C. G., and Turner, H. A. "Political Orientation and Field of Specialization Among College Professors." *Sociology of Education*, 41 (Summer 1968), 247–62.

Stouffer, S. A. *The Behavioral Sciences at Harvard.* Cambridge: Harvard University Press, 1954.

Wilson, R. C., and Gaff, G. "Student Voice-Faculty Response," *The Research Reporter*, 4 (1969).

Yee, R. "Faculty Participation in the 1960 Presidential Election," *Western Political Quarterly*, 16 (March 1963), 213–20.

The Political Attitudes
of Congolese and Lebanese
University Students

14

Theodor Hanf

INSTITUTIONAL SETTING AND SURVEY DATA

This study is based on representative surveys by questionnaire at the four universities of Lebanon and the four most important institutions of higher learning in the Congo.[1] In Lebanon, these are Jesuit Université St. Joseph (USJ), the American University of Beirut (AUB),[2] the Lebanese University (LU), and the Arab University (AU). The Congolese survey included the three universities of the Congo—the Catholic University of Lovanium (CUL) near Kinshasa,[3] the Université Libre du Congo (ULC) in Kisangani, and the Université Officielle du Congo (UOC) in Lubumbashi. Furthermore, the Institut Pédagogique National (IPN), a non-university

---

[1] This chapter consists of selections from a longer paper which is an intercultural comparative study of the political attitudes of university students as they relate to educational and religious factors. Sections were selected which describe the political culture of Lebanese and Congolese students and summarize and compare the two groups on the basis of "enrollment in a university" and "religion." The original study was presented at the Seventh International Congress of Sociology in Varna, Bulgaria, 1970. For more details, see the forthcoming studies by Theodor Hanf, *Studenten und Politik im Libanon. Eine empirische Erhebung* (Bielefeld: Bertelsmann-Universitätsverlag, in press) and Patrick V. Dias, et al., *Les Universitaires Congolais—Enquête sur leurs attitudes sociopolitiques* (Bielefeld: Bertelsmann-Universitätsverlag, 1971).

[2] Additional data on USJ and AUB students are provided by Munir Bashshur in his interesting study "The Two Foreign Universities in the National Life of Lebanon" (Ph.D. thesis, University of Chicago, 1964).

[3] Otto Klineberg and Marisca Zavalloni, *Nationalism and Tribalism among African Students* (Paris–The Hague: Mouton, 1969), passim, offer some data on Lovanium students. Since the sample used for this study was limited to a single class in one faculty, the representativity of this study might be questioned. For a more detailed discussion of the Klineberg–Zavalloni findings concerning Lovanium, see Dias, *et al.*, passim.

institution of higher education, was included.[4] The university settings in the Congo and in Lebanon manifest a number of considerable similarities and parallels as well as important differences.

Both in the Congo and in Lebanon, the universities—compared with those of other developing countries—form the highest level of a rather extensive and highly developed educational system.[5] In both countries, the enrollment at the primary level lies between 85 and 90 percent of all children of school age. In both countries, girls in rural areas are the least enrolled. In Lebanon, these girls come mainly from the rural Muslim regions[6]

At the secondary level, the educational systems of the two countries already differ considerably. In Lebanon, there is one secondary school pupil for 4.3 primary pupils, whereas in the Congo, the proportion is 1:10.5. The differences in enrollment become even stronger at the university level. At the time of the survey, the Congo with its roughly fourteen million inhabitants had about the same absolute number of students as Lebanon with its bare two million inhabitants.

The Congolese and Lebanese universities differ even more as channels of social mobility since the collapse of political parties in 1965. In the Congo, the university is practically the only channel of upward mobility to the influential and well-remunerated positions in the civil service, the economy, and politics. Aside from it, only the army plays a certain role in political recruitment. But in Lebanon numerous other important channels for social ascent exist next to the university, particularly in the economy.[7] The university in Lebanon provides exclusive access only to certain liberal professions (doctors, jurists, engineers, and architects) and to certain higher civil service positions. These facts show that in the Congo the university is much more of an elite-producing institution than in Lebanon.

A basic similarity in the educational and, in particular, the university systems of both countries is their pluralistic structure. In both states, private organizations provide a great share of the educational institutions at all

---

[4] The IPN was selected from among various non-university institutes of higher learning in the Congo because of its numerical importance and especially because of its unique position in training secondary school teachers.

[5] On education in the Congo, see Theodor Hanf, "Erziehungsreform im Kongo," *Zeitschrift für Politik,* No. 4 (1969), pp. 465–75; André Benoit, *Modèles de recrutement de l'enseignement secondaire au Congo* (Bielefeld: Bertelsmann-Universitätsverlag, 1970); Jürgen W. Wolff, *Ein Modell der Bildungsplanung für Entwicklungsländer und seine Anwendung auf den Kongo (Kinshasa)* (Bielefeld: Bertelsmann-Universitätsverlag, 1969). On education in Lebanon, see Theodor Hanf, *Erziehungswesen in Gesellschaft und Politik des Libanon* (Bielefeld: Bertelsmann-Universitätsverlag, 1969).

[6] The drop-out rate in the Congo, however, is far higher than in Lebanon. For the Congo, see Dieter Oberndörfer, Theodor Hanf, and Franz-Wilhelm Heimer, "Möglichkeiten beruflicher Ausbildung im Kongo-Kinshasa" (Research Report for the European Economic Communities, Freiburg, 1967), pp. 11–14. For Lebanon, see Jean Maroun "Le Liban à la recherche d'une politique de l'enseignement" (reneotyped, Beirut, 1966), p. 57; Hanf, *Erziehungswesen in Gesellschaft und Politik des Libanon* (further quoted as Hanf, *Libanon*), pp. 105–6, 119–20.

[7] See Y. A. Sayigh, *Entrepreneurs of Lebanon* (Cambridge; Harvard University Press, 1962).

levels. In both cases, this pluralism is in part due to religious groups and in part to differing external cultural influences, whereby religious groups and external influences are intertwined in different fashions. Lovanium University in Kinshasa (ex-Léopoldville) is Catholic; the Université Libre du Congo in Kisangani (ex-Stanleyville) is Protestant; the Université Officielle du Congo in Lubumbashi (ex-Elisabethville) is a government institution. The Institut Pédagogique National in the Congo, a specialized higher institution for the training of secondary school teachers, owes its foundation and expansion above all to laicistic circles in the Congo (as well as in Belgium and France).

In Lebanon, an educational system of the Franco-Latin type reaches its apex in the Université St. Joseph, a French Jesuit university. The system of education under Anglo-Saxon Protestant influence has its peak in the American University of Beirut, Lebanese government education in the Lebanese University. The Muslim system terminates in the Arab University. However, one major difference between the university systems of the two countries still merits pointing out: while the oldest Congolese university—Lovanium—has been in existence barely one and a half decades, two of the Lebanese universities—USJ and AUB—are already over one hundred years old.

The Surveys

The data used below are extracted from two empirical surveys using questionnaires, conducted among representative samples of Congolese and Lebanese students of the eight institutions of higher education mentioned above. The survey of Congolese students was carried out in 1968 as a team project by Dias, Hanf, Heimer and Rideout.[8] A total of one-third of the Congolese university students were surveyed. The size of the sample, however, varies between 20 and 90 percent at the individual universities, so that statements about the entire student body required some statistical adjustments. But since random samples were picked within each university, the total result can be taken as representative.

The survey of Lebanese students was made by the author in 1961–62. The sample included 10 percent of all Lebanese university students, stratified according to sex, university, department, and religion. Within the various strata of the sample, the random method was applied.

POLITICAL ATTITUDES OF CONGOLESE STUDENTS

Interest in Politics

DISINTEREST AND CONCEALED INTEREST. The first question of the Congo questionnaire asked, "Are you interested in politics?" Already the answers to this question appear to be quite significant. Table 1, part A, shows that about half of the Congolese students claim to be interested in politics. At

[8] See footnote 1.

TABLE 1. POLITICAL ATTITUDES OF CONGOLESE STUDENTS
ACCORDING TO UNIVERSITY[a]

Item	Total	ULC	CUL	UOC	IPN
A. Interest in politics					
Yes	50.9	57.3	49.8	45.9	48.9
Liking for politics	5.0	2.3	3.7	7.1	8.3
Politics leads to success, financial gain, high standard of living	1.2	0.7	1.1	1.2	1.4
Duty of good citizen, for welfare of country, serve country	32.6	35.6	33.5	31.1	34.5
Political involvement inevitable	11.7	9.2	11.8	10.3	9.8
Replace bad leaders	2.3	5.7	0.9	1.9	2.4
No	45.8	37.7	47.6	49.7	50.9
Politics loss of time, no value, other interests	15.8	11.4	14.8	17.2	14.3
Serve country better without	3.1	4.3	2.1	4.3	4.8
Politics is dangerous	4.6	4.6	6.5	3.9	13.1
Politicians are corrupt	10.2	5.2	19.1	15.0	6.0
No Answer	2.3	5.0	2.6	4.4	0.2
B. Most impressive event					
Private	3.4	2.7	4.3	3.5	4.2
Civil war	17.4	29.4	21.2	17.8	22.3
Independence	13.5	9.3	13.4	13.3	15.3
Lumumba murder	13.3	10.7	7.2	16.4	12.5
Frustration, corruption, etc.	9.7	6.6	11.3	8.8	5.6
Pentecost Conspirators' execution	11.6	18.7	12.1	10.4	8.3
Kennedy and King murders	5.0	2.7[b]	5.1	2.7[b]	16.7
Vietnam war	3.5	4.0	4.3	3.0	4.2
C. Social gap between students and citizens					
There is no gap	23.5	29.9	22.8	24.3	23.8
There is a gap	72.2	67.8	72.3	73.1	75.0
Students better qualified	19.9	20.7	15.3	20.1	22.6
Students' higher prestige	5.5	1.1	6.6	5.4	7.1
Students' better finances	10.2	17.2	9.6	10.6	16.7
Differences in mentality	12.3	9.1	12.9	13.1	14.3
D. Favorite politicians					
De Gaulle	25.2	26.4	23.0	27.9	29.8
Mao Tse-tung	18.3	10.3	11.6	25.4	16.7
None	14.9	17.2	15.8	14.6	10.7
Kennedy brothers	12.5	9.1	17.2	10.0	14.3
African non-Congolese politicians	4.9	3.4	6.0	3.9	9.5
Castro, Guevara, Ho Chi Minh	4.4	1.1	4.7	3.0	1.2
Humanitarians (Thant, King, Paul VI)	3.1	5.7[c]	4.2	2.1	2.4
Congolese politicians (Mobutu, Tshombé)	3.4	10.3	5.1	2.7	0.0
Soviet politicians	0.7	0.0	1.2	0.9	0.0
E. Most admired country					
USA	20.1	26.5	21.4	20.9	19.0
Germany	15.3	10.8	16.9	18.3	15.5

TABLE 1. (Cont'd.)

Item	Total	ULC	CUL	UOC	IPN
China	14.1	10.8	10.5	15.9	9.5
France	10.3	13.3	10.5	10.3	14.3
USSR	5.5	8.4	3.6	7.1	9.5
North Vietnam	4.8	1.2	2.6	3.3	1.2
Japan	4.3	2.4	6.9	2.9	3.6
Israel	3.8	6.0	4.3	3.2	4.8
African countries	2.2	1.2	2.4	2.2	1.2
Latin American countries	1.7	3.6	1.0	0.4	1.2
F. Ideology					
Laicists	13.1	11.8	11.4	13.6	13.2
Marxists	12.5	5.7	12.6	13.4	16.8
Maoists	3.6	2.3	4.0	2.7	3.6
Communists	4.2	0.0	3.7	5.4	12.0
Scientific Socialists	4.7	3.4	4.9	5.3	1.2
Animists and ancestor worshippers	6.6	3.5	3.4	5.3	10.8
None	35.2	49.4	33.3	39.6	38.6

[a] The sums do not always add up to 100%, because only the major items are listed.
[b] Only Kennedy.
[c] After King's assassination became known.

first hand, the high number of those not interested (45.8 percent) seems to be astonishing. From the reasons given for this disinterest we can distinguish three groups. First are those who consider politics to be a waste of time (attributed to it no or only little value) and are personally interested in other things (15.8 percent). Some of this group (3.1 percent), moreover, believe that they can serve their country better in a nonpolitical way. Second are those who believe involvement in politics to be extremely dangerous, because political insecurity is very high and because politics prevents regular and stable working conditions (4.6 percent). The third, rather strong group (10.2 percent) justifies its political disinterest by the sad state of Congolese politics. It expresses disappointment in Congolese politicians and attacks their incompetence and corruption in strong language.

We observe a genuine disinterest resulting from their personality or private preferences, among only half of the students claiming to be not interested in politics. The other half, instead, are ostensibly not interested in the kind of politics they see at present in the Congo. Their negative answer implies latent criticism of and opposition to Congolese politics. They are, however, not prepared to articulate this attitude or act according to it in a political way.

OVERT INTEREST. Those who proclaim political interest cannot be clearly divided into different groups. Only 5 percent of the total sample express open enthusiasm for politics and pleasure in political activity. A very small group (1.2 percent) does not hesitate to justify its political interest with the reason that political involvement can be very useful for personal success, for attaining a high standard of living, and for financial gain. The majority, however, give rather idealistic and moral reasons for their interest in politics. Most (32.6 percent) felt that interest in politics is the duty of a good citizen, that the welfare of the country depends on such an interest, and that being politically informed is an essential part of general education. Others (25.5 percent) said they were interested because they want to serve their country, to contribute to its development, to lead the masses of the people out of misery, and to articulate their interests. A small group (11.7 percent) claimed to be involuntarily interested in politics. According to them, politics in any case influences the life of the individual, hence it is better to share in its making. A small group, finally, manifests an oppositional attitude. It is interested in politics "pour remplacer les mauvais dirigeants."

On the whole, one detects a sceptical, reserved attitude toward the present state of Congolese politics among both the majority of the politically disinterested and the interested. Latent, passive discontent is evident in about one-third; active opposition is present only in a minority.

DIFFERENCES BETWEEN THE UNIVERSITIES. Considerable differences can be observed between the individual universities (Table 1, A). The least political interest (45.9 percent) is found at UOC. The two institutions in the capital, IPN and CUL, occupy a median position, whereas ULC leads by far (57.3 percent) in political interest. These differences apparently reflect the different direct contacts with political events. The present generation of students at UOC in Lubumbashi may not have experienced the times of the Katanga Conflict there, and over the last years Lubumbashi has been reduced to a provincial status in terms of politics. The institutions of the capital, instead, are more strongly politicized, a fact that can be attributed to their higher level of information. The student body of ULC in Kisangani (previously Stanleyville), finally, was by far most strongly affected by political events. Because of events during the civil war (1964–66) and the mercenary uprising (1966), this university had to be closed down twice and transferred to other locales in the Congo.

Moral reasons for interest in politics are given particularly at the two Christian universities (CUL with 33.5 percent, ULC with 35.6 percent). Remarkable among the students of IPN is that as many as 13.1 percent reject interest in politics because it is too risky and because as a career it is too unstable. This is probably a consequence of the fact that the most active elements of the faculty preferred administrative and political jobs during the years after independence, whereas the remaining instructors were less inclined to run risks. It is not improbable that the latter strongly influenced the image of the political profession.

Reactions to Political Events

The question about the political or social event that left the deepest impression in the life of each student also permits a number of conclusions about political attitudes. Table 1, part B, shows that only a few students (3.4 percent) mention events out of their private lives. All of the rest mention political events. Far on top of the list are the civil war and its turmoils, mentioned by 17.4 percent as the most important event. Second is the independence of the Congo (13.5 percent), followed by the murder of Patrice Lumumba (13.3 percent). A good number (9.7 percent) mention post-independence frustrations, corruptness of politicians and the entire public life, and prevailing social injustice. A particularly strong impact was also left by the execution of the so-called "Pentecost Conspirators" of 1966, mentioned by 11.6 percent.

It is remarkable that international political events receive only marginal attention. Mostly the assassinations of John F. Kennedy and Martin Luther King (5 percent) and the war in Vietnam (3.5 percent) were mentioned.

On reaction to political events, the individual universities present a relatively uniform picture. The only break in the pattern is that for 29.4 percent of the ULC students, the civil war troubles were the most important event. The probable reasons for this are mentioned above.

On the whole, the answers to these questions show to what a great extent personal life appears to be characterized by political events, especially negatively perceived events. As in the answers to the previous question, one can very clearly observe realism, scepticism, and reserve as basic attitudes toward the politics of the Congo.

The Social Gap Between Students and The Average Citizen

We have already pointed out to what a high degree institutional conditions assign an elitist position to the student within the total Congolese population. The feeling of a social gap between the students and the average citizen is therefore strongly pronounced in the majority of Congolese students (see Table 1, part C). Only 23.5 percent deny such a gap exists. Over half of the sample believe that there is such a gap and that it is considerable. The reasons given are that the student is better able, because of his education, to understand matters of government and to act politically (19.9 percent), or that students have higher prestige (5.5 percent). Others give as main reasons the better financial situation of the students (10.2 percent) or base the gap on differences of mentality (12.3 percent) .

Admiration for Politicians

The students were also asked to name a statesman whom they admired. The answers to this question permit us to define to some extent the content of political opinions and attitudes of the Congolese students. As shown in Table 1, part D, the list is headed by Charles de Gaulle (25.2 percent), followed by Mao Tse-tung (18.3 percent). No less than 14.9 percent expressly state that they hold no politician in particular esteem. This is yet another expression of a negative attitude toward the perceived political world. Among the other politicians mentioned are John F. Kennedy (10.4 percent) and Robert F. Kennedy (2.1 percent). Fidel Castro, Ché Guevara, and Ho Chi Minh together are mentioned by 4.4 percent, and Soviet politicians by only 0.7 percent. Another group (3.1 percent), finally, mentions humanitarian, symbolic personalities like U Thant, Martin Luther King, and Pope Paul VI. African politicians—Senghor, Nkrumah, Touré, Nyerere, Nasser and Hailé Selassié—are mentioned by only 4.9 percent. As will be seen below from the choice of the admired countries, Africa outside the Congo plays only a marginal role in the political consciousness of Congolese students.[9]

There are some differences between the universities. De Gaulle leads at all institutions but scores best at IPN (29.8 percent). The Kennedy brothers are mentioned most frequently at CUL (17.2 percent) and at IPN, whereas at UOC and ULC they are rated low (10 and 9.1 percent respectively). This is remarkable particularly in view of the fact that ULC is *de facto* an American university. At ULC, Martin Luther King is particularly esteemed, because King's assassination became known on campus while the survey was being conducted and this undoubtedly affected the data.

Mao Tse-tung is most admired at UOC (25.4 percent) and also at IPN (16.7 percent), but he ranks considerably lower at the two Christian universities (CUL, 11.6 percent; ULC, 10.3 percent). It is also interesting that Congolese politicians living at the time of the survey were mentioned by only a small minority, who usually picked Joseph Désiré Mobutu and Moise Tshombé. These two politicians were invariably chosen by students who shared their ethnic affiliation.

The Most Admired Country

In the question about the most admired country (see Table I, part E), the United States received first mention (with 20.1 percent), followed by Germany (15.3 percent), China (14.1 percent), and France (10.3 percent). After a definite distance came the Soviet Union (5.5 percent), North Vietnam (4.8 percent), Japan (4.3 percent) , and Israel (3.8 percent).[10]

Except for China and North Vietnam, these are highly industrialized countries. African, Latin American, and other Asian countries were hardly mentioned. Table 2 shows that choices motivated by considerations of economic development far outweigh ideological reasons.

There are only relatively minor differences between the individual universities. The United States is mentioned much more frequently at ULC (26.5 percent) than at the other universities. It gets the lowest percentage at IPN (19 percent), where France is rated higher than at the other universities. These figures reflect the influences exercised upon the different universities by institutions and personnel. China is rated much higher at

[9] This might be partly explained by the fact that during the colonial period there were almost no relations with other African territories—unlike the intense interaction between former French or British territories—and partly by the often not very attractive experience with other Africans as provided by the UN military intervention in the Congo.

[10] These results differ considerably from those obtained by Klineberg and Zavalloni, p. 200. The difference may be explained by the different samples used (see above, note 3), but also by the changes in Congolese student opinion between 1965, when Zavalloni's survey was carried out, and 1968, the date of the present inquiry. The relatively high esteem for Germany found by Dias, et al., however, could be a result of the Congolese students' politeness, since this survey was undertaken by a German institution.

TABLE 2. REASONS FOR THE CHOICE OF THE MOST ADMIRED COUNTRY BY CONGOLESE STUDENTS IN ABSOLUTE NUMBERS

Intelligent, industrious, dynamic people	217	
Economic development	169	
Scientific development, creative, inventive people	142	Developmental
Will to succeed and to overcome underdevelopment, courage, endurance, effort	135	Reasons
Quick development, success in short time	120	
Democracy, freedom of opinion	42	
Revolutionary people, fight imperialism	41	Ideological
Communism, socialism, etc.	37	Reasons

UOC (15.9 percent) than at the other universities. The Soviet Union receives relatively high esteem at IPN (9.5 percent) and quite low esteem at CUL (3.6 percent).

Ideology

Some additional elements of the political attitudes of Congolese students can be extracted from the question about ideology or *Weltanschauung*. Because of the specific conditions at the time of the survey, it was unfortunately not possible to ask directly about the preferred political ideology. This could be done only in connection with the questions about religious attitudes. Nevertheless, the answers do yield a number of relevant data, shown in Table 1, part F. Two clearly defined groups which mention ideologies of a political nature do appear: the laicists (13.1 percent) and the Marxists (12.5 percent). The laicistic group cites a series of catchwords from the vocabulary of classical French and Belgian laicism: positivism, materialism, free-thinking, faith in science, ideological liberalism, enlightened nationalism, etc. The Marxist group is composed of Maoists (3.6 percent), Communists (4.2 percent) and scientific socialists (4.7 percent).

Again there are some differences between the universities. Marxists are least represented at ULC (5.7 percent) and most at IPN (16.8 percent). The laicists are nearly equally represented at all institutions, but somewhat less at the Christian universities than at the UOC and IPN.

Belief in elements of traditional *Weltanschauungen* such as animism and ancestor worship is rarely found at the two Christian universities, but it is astonishingly strong at IPN (10.8 percent).

On the whole, it is remarkable that the divergences between the universities are not very considerable in spite of the different basic attitudes toward these ideological matters manifest in the general institutional setting.

POLITICAL ATTITUDES OF LEBANESE STUDENTS

Political Interest

The political interest of the Lebanese student body is relatively high (81.5 percent), as can be seen from Table 3, part A. The women students

TABLE 3. POLITICAL ATTITUDES OF LEBANESE STUDENTS ACCORDING TO
UNIVERSITY AND SEX

Item	Total	USJ/CES	AUB	LU	AU	Men	Women
A. Interest in politics							
Yes	81.5	76.0	86.4	89.3	90.0	82.7	77.8
No or no answer	18.5	24.0	13.6	10.7	10.0	17.3	22.2
B. Party membership							
(21% of total sample)							
Kataeb	39.3	38.9	23.1	53.1	0.0	44.8	26.9
National Liberal Party	25.1	24.2	30.8	23.6	0.0	25.9	23.1
National Bloc	23.9	33.3	7.7	5.8	0.0	17.2	38.5
PPS	5.8	1.8	23.1	5.7	0.0	5.2	7.7
Progressive Socialist Party	5.9	1.8	15.3	11.8	0.0	6.9	3.8
C. Preferred foreign statesmen							
De Gaulle	27.6	33.6	15.5	31.7	0.0	28.2	25.3
J. F. Kennedy	17.8	22.9	14.1	11.7	0.0	17.9	17.4
Abdel Nasser	15.1	7.4	23.9	8.3	83.5	14.1	18.7
Nehru	9.5	5.3	15.5	18.9	0.0	10.7	5.3
Bourguiba	7.7	10.7	4.3	5.0	0.0	7.7	8.0
Others	21.4	21.1	26.7	25.0	16.0	21.4	25.3
D. Political ideas							
Lebanese independence	45.5	50.9	40.9	54.1	0.0	45.9	44.2
Arab unity	19.8	8.6	21.2	21.6	100.0	19.3	21.2
Democracy & freedom	15.1	17.2	16.7	10.8	0.0	15.5	13.5
Socialism	6.0	6.1	4.6	10.8	0.0	6.5	3.8
World peace	4.7	5.2	7.6	0.0	0.0	2.8	11.6
Others	8.9	12.0	9.0	2.7	0.0	10.0	5.7

manifest only about 5 percent less interest in politics than do their male colleagues.

Among the reasons given for disinterest in politics, it is remarkable that aside from practical reasons ("politics harms studies"), ignorance ("politics is too complicated," "politics is not for girls"), and general hostility toward politics ("politics is nonsense"), the majority of those students who declare no interest in politics (41.9 percent) consider a political discussion inopportune. From the explanations that were frequently added (e.g., "discussion is not good for national unity," "sectarian politics prevents development," "we need economic development for Lebanon, not politics," etc.), we see that at least a part of these "disinterested" students give definitely political reasons for their negative attitude. Thus we can assume that the political disinterest of these students refers merely to certain aspects of Lebanese politics but not to political problems as such.

The degree of political interest differs considerably from university to university. The students of USJ/CES show least political interest (76 percent). At AUB it is much higher, and it rises yet more at LU; it is highest (90 percent) at AU.

Political Commitment versus Party Membership

Table 3, part B, shows us the distribution of the parties at the Lebanese universities. The Kataeb, predominantly a Christian party advocating Lebanese independence from the Great Powers as well as from the Arab neighbors, are particularly strongly represented at USJ (30.9 percent) and at LU (53.1 percent). The National Liberal Party, the pro-western party of former President Chamoun, has its most supporters at AUB, but is also quite strongly represented at USJ and LU. The PPS or Syrian Social Nationalist Party, a non-denominational party fighting for the idea of a Greater Syria, including all countries of the Fertile Crescent, is strongest at AUB and has only few followers at USJ and LU. The moderately leftist Progressist Socialist Party, finally, has a number of members, among the AUB and LU students, but is only lightly represented at USJ. The data about party membership provide us with facts about the political commitment of Lebanese students, which considerably modify the previous statements about interest in politics. Although the AU manifests the highest percentage of students who are politically interested and who identify with a certain political trend, no student of that university indicated party membership. At LU and especially at USJ/CES, instead, the percentage of party members strongly outweighs that of students in full agreement with a party or tendency. The differentiated political interest or incomplete identification with a political trend, which we discovered among the students of the French university, does therefore not prevent considerable concrete commitment in party politics. Conversely, one can conclude that the extraordinarily high political interest and the great degree of identification with a political trend that we found among the students of the Arab University need not necessarily lead to party political activity.

The Preferred Foreign Statesmen

The question about the particularly esteemed international statesman or politician again reveals considerable differences between the student attitudes at the various universities. Table 3, part C, shows the five politicians who are most frequently mentioned—Charles de Gaulle (27.6 percent), John F. Kennedy (17.8 percent), Gamal Abdel Nasser (15.1 percent), Jawaharlal Nehru (9.5 percent), and Habib Bourguiba (7.7 percent). At the French university, de Gaulle ranks far at the top (33.6 percent), followed by Kennedy (22.9 percent). Third is Bourguiba, and Nasser and Nehru are mentioned by only a few. At AUB, Abdel Nasser leads (23.9 percent). The fact that John F. Kennedy is esteemed nearly as high as de Gaulle can probably be attributed to the American character of the university. At the Lebanese University, however, de Gaulle again is far in the lead (31.7 percent). Nasser ranks not much better here (8.3 percent) than at USJ/CES. At the Arab University, however, Nasser occupies a nearly exclusive place with 83.5 percent since the rest goes to numerous politicians. The students of the Arab University mentioned practically no Western statesmen. This question revealed no significant difference between men and women students.

Predominant Political Ideas

Perhaps the clearest and most relevant data for the political attitude of the Lebanese students come from the question about the political idea which could arouse enthusiasm and active support. The total sample mentioned mainly the following ideas: Lebanese independence (45.5 percent), Arab Unity (19.8 percent), freedom and democracy (15.1 percent), socialism (6 percent), and world peace (4.7 percent) (see Table 3, D).

Once more there are considerable differences between the universities. At the French university, more than half of the students stand up for Lebanese independence. Second is freedom and democracy (17.2 percent); Arab unity (8.6 percent) and socialism (6.1 percent) are rated lower. The greatest part of the AUB students (40.9 percent) also favors Lebanese independence, but here the supporters of Arab unity (21.2 percent) rank second, followed by freedom and democracy (16.7 percent), and finally world peace (7.6 percent) and socialism (4.6 percent).

The Lebanese University has the greatest proportion (54.1 percent) of supporters of Lebanese independence. Here also Arab unity comes second (21.6 percent). Equally distributed in third place are socialism and freedom and democracy (10.8 percent). The students of the Arab University, finally, exclusively opted for Arab unity as their preferred political idea.

There is only one difference on this item between male and female students worth mentioning. Whereas only 4.7 percent of the men students list world peace as their most important political idea, 11.6 percent of the women do so.

In summary, we can conclude that the students of each of the four Lebanese universities diverge in their political interests and commitments, in their attitudes to internal Lebanese politics, and finally in their attitudes to the basic political issues of the Lebanese nation.

SIMILARITIES AND DIFFERENCES OF THE CASE STUDIES

Comparison When Using Enrollment at a University

The overall interest in politics is higher in Lebanon with 81.5 percent than in the Congo with 54.9 percent. It can be assumed that the differences between the Congolese and Lebanese political systems are reflected here. In Lebanon we have a liberal parliamentary democracy with an extremely high degree of freedom of expression and political activity; the Congo is a one-party state dominated by the military.

The differences in political interest among the various universities are to be attributed to regional factors in the Congo, the location of the institutions, and particularly to the resulting difference in the students' contact with the civil war events. In Lebanon, instead, the different niveaus and requirements of the universities seem to explain some dissimilarities. At USJ and AUB, where scientific standards and demands of achievement are considerably higher than at the other universities, political interest is somewhat lower.

The differences between the two political systems and the historical experiences during the last decade are also probably a reason for the divergent perception by the Congolese and Lebanese students of *political problems* and particularly *impressive political events*. In the Congo the perception of negative political events dominates. The attitude toward politics is characterized by disappointment, scepticism, and reserve. In Lebanon, instead, the perception of problems is of a more positive and active nature. The problem of national identity is the central point. For one group of students the independence of Lebanon has priority; for another, it is Arab unity. Closely connected with the latter is the question of Palestine as an important political problem, whereas the former is linked with the matter of interior reform.

The *gap* between students and the average citizen is a very significant characteristic of the political subculture of Congolese students. In Lebanon, on the other hand, this problem practically does not arise.

The forms of political commitment also reflect differences between the political systems of the two countries. It was not possible to ask about party membership in the Congo, because at the time of the survey, the single Congolese party was reorganizing its faction at the universities. In Lebanon, however, the students are quite active in party politics. A total of 21 percent indicated party membership; among those are also some who do not fully agree with their respective party line. From this we can conclude that the Lebanese students do not think lowly of the possibilities of influencing politics by political participation.

The same difference between the two countries can again be observed in the fact that in the Congo it was not possible to ask about particularly esteemed local politicians. In Lebanon, however, this question provided valuable elements for a description of the political attitudes of Lebanese students vis-à-vis interior political tendencies and orientations. We obtain three clear group profiles: first, the Lebanese nationalists; second, the Arab nationalists; and third, those who accord priority to the policy of reform which mediates between the first two groups. The Lebanese nationalists clearly predominate at the Université St. Joseph. They also lead at the American and Lebanese universities, although the neutral group also occupies a significant place at these institutions. The student body of the Arab university has an almost exclusively pan-Arab orientation.

Strong similarities between the two countries can be observed in the orientation of international politics, as it is expressed in the question about the most esteemed international politician. In both countries Charles de Gaulle is at the top. In Lebanon, John F. Kennedy occupies second place, but in the Congo, it is Mao Tse-tung. The opposite to Western politicians in Lebanon is not a Communist, but Gamal Abdel Nasser. In both countries there are differences between the individual universities. In the Congo, Western politicians are more often mentioned at the religiously influenced universities, whereas at UOC and IPN, Mao Tse-tung rates higher. In Lebanon, Western and pro-Western politicians lead at USJ, AUB, and LU whereas the students of the Arab University name Nasser as their most admired politician.

Similar parallels and differences between the two countries manifest themselves in the statement about political ideas and ideologies. In the Congo, three groups are observed—a strongly religious group with predominantly pro-Western attitudes, a laicistic group, and a Marxist group. The laicists and, above all, the Marxists are more strongly represented at the universities free from church ties. In Lebanon, instead, two contrasting groups are observed—the defenders of Lebanese independence and the advocates of Arab unity. The Lebanese nationalists are strongest at LU and are also very strong at USJ and AUB. At the latter, there is also a group of Arab nationalists. The student body of the Arab University also turns out to have a completely pan-Arab attitude when using the enrollment variable.

In both countries the divergences are greatest where the university is under a strong religious or ideological influence. In the Congo, this is the case at ULC; in Lebanon, we find it particularly at USJ and AU.

At these universities, however, we also observe a very clear pattern of recruitment. ULC has a disproportionately high number of Protestant students. USJ is predominantly attended by Christians, especially Catholics, whereas at the Arab University, we find an almost exclusively Muslim student body. At those universities where there were less significant divergences in political attitudes—CUL, UOC, and IPN in the Congo, AUB and LU in Lebanon—the recruitment pattern is not specifically characterized by religious affiliation. This indicates that the factor religion and/or *Weltanschauung* merits particular attention.

Comparison When Using Religion

The introduction of the intervening variable "religion" permits us to recognize the similarities and differences between the Congolese and Lebanese students. The number of those who consider religion important is considerably higher in Lebanon (74.7 percent) than in the Congo (65.8 percent). The same applies to belief in a life after death (73.3 percent and 63 percent respectively). Even the number of those Lebanese who believe in all the teachings of their religion is nearly still as high as that of the Congolese (61.8 percent and 65.8 percent respectively). Only 10 percent of the entire student body in Lebanon never visits any place of worship. Hence membership in a religious community in that country also influences to a very high degree religious attitude and religious behavior. In the Congo, this is the case to a much lesser degree. It must, however, be taken into account that in Lebanon the religious communities are at the same time ethnic, cultural, and in part, political groups. Therefore the specifically religious processes of socialization are reinforced in many ways by other socialization processes. The Christian students in Lebanon are more religiously active than the Muslims.

Contrasting the religiously active with the inactive student group in the Congo,[11] and the Christian students with the Muslims in Lebanon,

---

[11] The Congolese students were classified as religiously active, if they considered religion to be important, believed in a life after death and regularly attended religious services; if they answered in the negative, they were classified as inactive.

finally, permits us to observe very different profiles of the student bodies of both countries.

The religiously active group in the Congo manifests a more reserved attitude toward politics. Moral standards play a big role both in the rejection of and in the reasons for political involvement. This group shows a clearly pro-Western orientation in its political images and is largely immune to Marxist and laicist ideologies.

The group of Christian students in Lebanon, instead, is politically much more interested and involved. A considerable portion are members of political parties. There are clear-cut preferences for Christian Lebanese nationalist politicians. In its sympathy for international politicians, this group, like the religiously active group in the Congo, manifests an almost exclusively pro-Western orientation. Its preferred political ideal is Lebanese independence, i.e., the maintenance of the country with its present political system. A great part of this group, nonetheless, desires social reforms and political modernization.

The religiously inactive group in the Congo manifests greater political interest and involvement than the active one. It is divided into two different ideological currents. One is the laicistic current, which is strongly influenced ideologically by Belgian laicistic liberalism and by French radicalism. Not infrequently it tends to be anticlerical. In international politics this group prefers de Gaulle and France, perhaps from the desire for a third force in world politics. Almost as strong as the laicistic is the Marxist current, for which Mao Tse-tung and China are the most important paragons. In part, this group is militantly anti-Western and especially anti-American. Here we also find the most critical comments about the present Congolese regime.

The group of Muslim students in Lebanon is clearly distinguished from the religiously inactive group in the Congo. The influence of their religion, though obviously much less than among the Christians, continues to be strong. Laicistic inclinations are found in a minority of about 20 percent. Like the religiously inactive group in the Congo, the Lebanese Muslim students are by no means pro-Western. Their political ideals and paragons, however, are not found in the socialist-communist camp but in the Arab-Muslim world. Abdel Nasser is their undisputed guiding image, and Arab unity is almost unanimously their first political goal.

Whereas, therefore, the religiously active group in the Congo and the Christian group in Lebanon possess considerable common traits, the religiously inactive Congolese and the Lebanese Muslim groups differ strongly. It is particularly remarkable that for both Congolese groups neither the Congo nor even Africa are to any significant degree guiding examples or even political frames of reference. Instead, we find almost exclusively political ideologies of international and predominantly European origin (or, in the case of Chinese Communism, an Asian offspring of a European ideology).

In Lebanon, instead, the political involvement of both groups of students, irrespective of sympathy or antipathy for ideologies of foreign origin, is focused either on the country itself (in the case of Lebanese nationalism) or on the region (in the case of Arab nationalism). It is here especially that one encounters the limit for parallels or similarities between both case studies, set by the different histories and political cultures of both countries.

We can, with some reservation, say that in the two cases examined, the religion variable has shown itself to be at least as important for determining political attitudes as the enrollment variable in a university.[12] We can, therefore, conclude that religion must be closely linked with the process of political socialization. This study can make no statements concerning the modality of this link. For this, a survey of the secondary and primary schools, which are antecedents of the university in political socialization, would be desirable. But one should be careful not to simply transfer the one-dimensional hypothesis that educational institutions determine political attitudes from the university level to the lower levels of formal education. Instead, it would be desirable to examine a possible nexus between religious and political socialization on the secondary, primary, and pre-primary educational levels, and above all to examine a possible nexus between both of these processes in agents of socialization outside the school. In any case, we can conclude from the comparison of the political attitudes of Congolese and Lebanese students that the religion factor merits greater consideration when studying the subject "students and politics" than it has hitherto generally received.

The results of the two surveys recommend the adoption of a skeptical view of the possibilities to direct or even generated political attitudes through the medium of higher education. Guided or planned political socialization, civic education, nation building, and also propaganda and manipulation through the university seems to be much more difficult or much less successful than many a politician may hope or many a citizen may fear.

----

[12] This proposition will be tested again in a forthcoming comparative study by the author together with Patrick V. Dias, John P. Neelsen, Michael Fremerey, Karl Schmitt, and Heribert Weiland on students' political attitudes in various African, Asian, and Latin American universities.

Generational Gap and Family Political Socialization in Three Arab Societies   15

Halim I. Barakat

We would expect that in non-Western societies also, members of the same family tend to hold similar political views. In fact, the relationships in non-Western, more traditional societies may well be even greater. As a rule family ties are stronger in traditional cultures, and there are not as many other agents of socialization. Only in these rapidly changing societies in which conflict between generations is intense are political orientations not likely to be tied to the family context.[1]

INTRODUCTION: STATEMENT OF THE PROBLEM

Several empirical investigations in Western societies show that the family is highly important as an agency of political socialization. A review of these investigations, such as that of Hyman, would show that there is a very high intergenerational agreement in party identification, political attitudes, and voting behavior.[2] For instance, when both parents have the same party preference, up to 80 percent of the student respondents in the United States agree with them.[3]

The present study is an attempt to assess the importance of family as an agent of political socialization in three Arab societies and to determine what variables influence this process. According to the above quotation from Dawson and Prewitt, relationships between the political attitudes and behav-

The author would like to acknowledge the assistance of his students Margaret Salameh, In 'am 'Mutawwa' and Hind Khalifah in collecting the data on which this paper is based.
[1] Richard E. Dawson and Kenneth Prewitt, *Political Socialization* (Boston: Little, Brown, 1969), p. 111.
[2] Herbert H. Hyman, *Political Socialization* (New York: Free Press, 1959).
[3] Kenneth P. Langton, *Political Socialization* (New York: Oxford University Press, 1969), pp. 52–59.

ior of individuals and those of their parents in non-Western societies may be even greater than in Western societies. Dawson and Prewitt expect this to be true because of strong family ties and relative lack of other agents of political socialization in traditional societies. In the present case, it should be assumed that in the Middle East the family is a very influential institution in political socialization and that the father is the more influential of the parents. In fact, one could argue that in the Arab Middle East, family ties are very strong. These ties constitute the most basic pattern of social organization as well as the most basic source of value orientations. I would go as far as to argue that the family is even more important than religion as a source of the value orientation prevailing in the Arab society. An empirical study by Melikian and Diab showed that university students in the Arab Middle East affiliated themselves with family first, ethnic group second, religion third, citizenship fourth, and political party fifth.[4] A more recent empirical study of a representative sample of students at the American University of Beirut showed that they were less alienated from family than from religion, university, and government. None showed a high feeling of alienation from the family; 5 percent showed moderate feeling of alienation; 32 percent showed little feeling of alienation; and 63 percent were found to be fully integrated in their families.[5] Yet, it is the expectation of this study that there is less intergenerational agreement on political matters in the Arab Middle East than in Western societies. Rapid social change, educational generational gap (i.e., difference in levels of education of parents and their children), norms against parents discussing politics with their children, lack of parents' political involvement, absence of a two party system, mothers' almost total lack of concern with politics, and other factors will be explored as possible reasons for this expected low intergenerational agreement.

The Arab Middle Eastern societies are highly concerned with political matters. One indication of this concern is the observations made by outsiders visiting the Middle East that Arabs are quite often engaged in intense political arguments. It is probably a fact that informal conversations revolve more around politics than around any other topic. Since the end of the First World War, Arabs have been engaged in political debates in cafes, streets, campuses, clubs, etc. Discussion of nonpolitical special-purpose organization might suddenly shift to political matters even in formal and task-oriented meetings.

During the last four decades, Arabs have been ardently concerned about the following political problems and issues:

1. National identity (Meaning of nationalism; what constitutes a nation; what nation or political community they belong to, etc.).

2. National independence and wars of liberation.

3. Palestinian problem.

[4] L. Melikian and L. N. Diab, "Group Affiliations of University Students in the Arab Middle East," *Journal of Social Psychology*, Vol. 44 (1959).
[5] Habib Hammam, "A Measure of Alienation in a University Setting" (M. A. thesis, American University of Beirut, 1969).

4. Forms of government most suitable for Arabs.

5. Socialism, equality, and freedom.

6. Political positions or issues of the left versus the right, and political change in general.

Discussions of these topics rarely take place in the family, and they are least likely to occur among members of different age groups and generations. Parents are most hesitant about discussing both sex and politics with their children. In fact, they worry about their children being involved in or belonging to political parties; they see politics as both consequential (i.e., bringing about reprisals) and rather useless.

The present study aims at checking the following basic hypotheses:

1. The degree of congruence between the political attitudes of individuals and those of their parents in the Arab society may be lower than in Western societies.

2. The family in Arab countries is not equally influential as an agency of political socialization due to differences in rapidity of social change and educational generational gap.

3. Rapid social change is likely to undermine family political socialization.

4. The greater the educational generational gap, the less likely that individuals will tend to politically identify with their parents.

The above four hypotheses are directly related. Rapid social change in traditional societies is likely to result in great educational gaps between parents and offspring. The great majority of parents in such societies have little education in comparison to their children. This educational gap will render parents less influential in transmitting their political ideas and attitudes to their offspring.

Since educational generational gap is much wider in the Arab Middle East than in Western societies, it is expected, in spite of strong family ties, that Arab respondents are more likely to be politically independent of their parents than Western respondents. Furthermore, because this chapter aims at showing the "educational generational gap" as an important intervening variable undermining the family political socialization process, comparisons will be made between three Arab societies that are similar in every relevant respect except rapid social change, and consequently degree of the educational generational gap. The three societies for comparison are Jordan, Bahrain, and Kuwait. All of them are traditional and essentially tribal in social structure. However, much more rapid social change has suddenly started to take place in Kuwait during the last decade and a half. Jordan and Bahrain, on the other hand, started to experience social change earlier but at a comparatively slower pace. Because Kuwait has been experiencing such a sudden and rapid social change, the educational generational gap should be wider than it is in Jordan and Bahrain. Thus, it is predicted that intergenerational agreement on political matters and degree of political identification of children with their parents will be lower in Kuwait than in Jordan and Bahrain, and in Jordan or Bahrain lower than in Western countries.

RESEARCH DESIGN AND METHODOLOGY

To check on the above expectations, three simple random samples of Jordanian, Bahraini, and Kuwaiti students at the American University of Beirut (A.U.B.) were chosen and interviewed in the fall of 1969 and the fall of 1970. There were about 450 Jordanian students in A.U.B. at that time. The great majority of their parents have secondary and university education and belong to the upper and upper-middle classes. A random sample representing these students was chosen by the Computer Center at A.U.B., and the number of respondents came to 40 students.

So far as Kuwaiti students are concerned, there were only about 75 such students at A.U.B. at that time. The great majority of their parents have less than some secondary education. All of them were asked to participate in the survey, and the number of respondents came to 50. There were 54 Bahraini students at A.U.B. during the fall semester of 1970. All of them were invited to participate, and 28 out of them responded.

The respondents in the three samples covered several age groups, both sexes, and a variety of fields of specialization.

The questionnaire was constructed in order to compare Jordanian, Bahraini, Kuwaiti, and Western students and to check on the following specific hypotheses:

1. Intergenerational agreement on political matters among both Jordanian and Bahraini students is lower than among similar respondents in Western societies.

2. Intergenerational agreement on political matters among Kuwaiti students is low in comparison to Jordanian, Bahraini and Western societies.

3. Contrary to findings in Western societies, Jordanian, Bahraini and Kuwaiti students are more likely to agree with their fathers than with their mothers.

4. Contrary to findings in Western societies, even girls are more likely to agree with their fathers than with their mothers.

5. Boys in all samples are more independent of their parents than girls.

6. It is expected that the Bahraini and Jordanian students will show similar rates of intergenerational agreement because of similarities in rate of social change and educational generational gap in their two societies.

7. Upper-class students are more likely to be independent of their parents than middle-class students.

8. Jordanian, Bahraini and Kuwaiti parents are more likely to agree with one another than parents in Western societies.

9. The higher the education of parents the higher the intergenerational agreement.

The interview schedule used in this survey included items of the following nature:

1. Would you rather discuss politics with your father, your mother, both parents, or neither?

2. Which one of your parents do you politically identify yourself with: Your mother, father, or neither?

3. Which of the following political positions best describes you? Which best describes your mother and your father?

	Father	Mother	Self
(a) Leftist, radical, socialist	_____	_____	_____
(b) Liberal, reformist	_____	_____	_____
(c) Rightist, conservative	_____	_____	_____
(d) Indifferent and satisfied with status quo	_____	_____	_____
(e) Other	_____		

4. Which one of the following statements would you choose regarding your general attitude towards your government's policies?

(a) Support the majority of them.
(b) I support some, but not all.
(c) I support few of them, if any at all.
(d) I am indifferent to its policies.

Which one of the above four would your father choose?
Which one of the above four would your mother choose?

5. Which of the following political loyalties best describes yourself, your father, and your mother?

_____ Arab nationalism
_____ Internationalism
_____ Lebanese (or Kuwaiti, or Bahraini) nationalism
_____ Other.

6. Which of the following forms of government would you, your father, and your mother prefer for your country?

	Yourself	Father	Mother
(a) Communism	_____	_____	_____
(b) Capitalistic democracy	_____	_____	_____
(c) Liberal democracy	_____	_____	_____
(d) Socialist democracy	_____	_____	_____
(e) Other	_____	_____	_____

The above research design and items allow for comparisons to be made between groups of respondents occupying different positions on a continuum representing different degrees of educational generational gap. This gap is narrower in Western societies than in Jordan and Bahrain and narrower in Jordan and Bahrain than in Kuwait. The determining condition in this case is diffuseness of education among the older generation (i.e., level of education of parents).

FINDINGS AND EXPLANATIONS

Because the family tends to monopolize the socialization of children in their early years, parents must be very effective in determining their attitudes, values, outlooks, and behavior. As pointed out in an earlier part of this chapter, empirical investigations in Western societies gave ample evidence to support this contention. To give more detail helpful in making comparisons between Western, Jordanian, Bahraini, and Kuwaiti respondents, let us look at a typical investigation.

A study conducted in 1965 by the Survey Research Center of the University of Michigan on a national sample of American high-school seniors shows that when both parents have the same party preference, 76 percent of these students agree with them. Among Republican parents, 68 percent of their offspring prefer that party also. Among Democratic parents, 85 percent of their offspring identify with the Democratic party. When parents differ in their party preference, the father is by no means the decisive force in establishing a child's party identification. The results show that 39 percent of the students agree with the mother, 37 percent with the father, and 24 percent with neither. When the mother is a Democrat and the father a Republican, 44 percent of students identify with the Democratic party, 35 percent with the Republican party, and 21 percent tend to be independent. When the mother is a Republican and the father a Democrat, 29 percent of the students identify with the Democratic party, 33 percent with the Republic party, and 38 percent tend to be independent.[6]

Similar studies conducted in the French, Swedish, and Norwegian societies report similar results, i.e., high intergenerational agreement or high frequency of respondents identifying with the same party as their parents. This frequency was found to be highest in the United States, followed by Sweden and Norway, then France.

These findings provide enough of a basis to justify the conclusion of Dawson and Prewitt that "the family . . . tends to be a conserving rather than an initiating force. More than most other structures, it attempts to preserve and perpetuate traditional practices and modes of thought."[7]

In the light of all that, let us compare the data on the Jordanian, Bahraini, and Kuwaiti students. Do they support the expectations of this study? What kinds of factors are associated with intergenerational agreement? How do we explain the results?

The data presented in Tables 1 and 2 show that the Jordanian and Bahraini respondents are less likely to identify with their parents than Western respondents but more so than the Kuwaitis. This is reflected in the responses to the question connected with whether they politically identify with mother, father, both parents, or neither. Table 1 shows that political identification is not in accordance with Dawson and Prewitt's expectation that the tendency to hold similar political views may be even greater in traditional than in Western societies. As shown in this table, 29 percent of the Jordanian boys reported that they politically identified with their fathers, 12 percent with their mothers, 12 percent with both parents, and 47 percent with neither. So far as Jordanian girls are concerned, 24 percent reported that they politically identified with their fathers, 33 percent with their mothers, 5 percent with both, and 38 percent with neither.

Table 1 shows also that the Bahraini boys tended to identify with their fathers or to deviate from both parents (40 percent identified with father and 46 percent deviated). The Bahraini girls showed even a higher tendency to deviate than the Bahraini boys. When they did not identify with their

---

[6] K. P. Langton, pp. 52–59.
[7] R. E. Dawson and K. Prewitt, p. 124.

TABLE 1. STUDENTS' POLITICAL IDENTIFICATION WITH PARENTS (IN PERCENTS)

Nationality	Sex	Political Identification With:				
		Father	Mother	Both	Neither	Total
Jordanian students	Boys (N=22)	29	12	12	47	100
	Girls (N=18)	24	33	5	38	100
Bahraini students	Boys (N=15)	40	7	7	46	100
	Girls (N=13)	20	13.5	13.5	53	100
Kuwaiti students	Boys (N=25)	32	0	0	68	100
	Girls (N=23)	43	0	0	57	100

mothers, they tended to deviate rather than identify with their fathers.

The Bahraini boys were more likely to identify with their fathers than the Jordanian boys, but they showed similar tendencies toward deviation from both parents (i.e., 47 percent of the Jordanian boys and 46 percent of the Bahraini boys identified with neither of their parents). The Bahraini girls showed the highest deviations (53 percent) among the Jordanian and Bahraini respondents.

As expected, the Kuwaiti students showed the least tendency to politically identify with their parents. There was no identification at all with the mother in this respect. As shown, 32 percent of the boys identified with their fathers and 68 percent deviated. The Kuwaiti girls were even more likely to identify with the father than boys; 43 percent of them identified with their fathers and 57 percent deviated.

The data in Table 1 confirmed the first three hypotheses listed in the section on research design and methodology. The data on the Bahraini and Kuwaiti students confirmed hypothesis 4 (i.e., girls were found to agree with their fathers rather than with their mothers), but the data on the Jordanian students did not confirm this hypothesis because the girls showed some tendency to identify with their mothers more than with their fathers.

Similarly, the data on the Jordanian and Kuwaiti students confirmed hypothesis 5 (i.e., boys were more likely to deviate than girls), but the data on the Bahraini students failed to confirm it because the girls in this sample showed more tendency to deviate than the boys.

By way of comparison, the data on the national sample of American high-school seniors showed that 39 percent of the boys identified with the same political party as their fathers, 33 percent identified with their mothers, and 28 percent with neither. So far as American girls in this sample are concerned, 30 percent identified with their father, 47 percent with their mothers, and 22 percent with neither.[8]

[8] K. P. Langton, p. 67.

TABLE 2. POLITICAL POSITIONS OF STUDENTS RELATIVE TO THEIR PARENTS
(IN PERCENTS)

| Nationality | Sex | Political Position Identical to | | | | |
		Father	Mother	Both	Neither	Total
Jordanian students	Boys (N=22)	14	5	36	45	100
	Girls (N=18)	16	16	32	36	100
Bahraini students	Boys (N=15)	13	7	33	47	100
	Girls (N=13)	33	0	0	67	100
Kuwaiti students	Boys (N=25)	28	0	0	72	100
	Girls (N=23)	40	0	0	60	100

The comparison of the two sets of data shows that there is a greater tendency toward political independence from parents among Jordanian and Bahraini than among American respondents. As reported above, 47 percent of the Jordanian boys and 46 percent of the Bahraini boys deviated, in comparison to 28 percent of the American boys. The greatest deviation was shown by the Kuwaiti boys (68 percent) and the Kuwaiti girls (57 percent).

This significant difference is not necessarily a true difference. Rather, it may be an artifact of differences in the procedure of measurement. The question posed to the Jordanian students is of a more general nature than the question posed to the American students. However, when a more specific question is posed, the responses remain almost the same as those made to the more general question.

The results based on the more specific question, which is connected with definite political positions (i.e., being leftist, liberal, rightist, indifferent, etc.) and best described the respondents and their parents, are shown in Table 2. Fourteen percent of the Jordanian boys held the same political positions as their fathers, 5 percent as their mothers, 36 percent as both, and 45 percent as neither. Sixteen percent of the Jordanian girls held the same political positions as their fathers, 16 percent as their mothers, 32 percent as both, and 36 percent deviated. The data on the Bahraini students is quite similar, except that no Bahraini girls held the same political positions as their mothers (who do not seem to have any), and thus they were more likely to have the same political position as their fathers (33 percent) or to deviate (67 percent).

Again, the Kuwaiti students showed the highest tendency to deviate: 72 percent of the boys and 60 percent of the girls did so. The percentages of deviation among students from the three Arab societies under study (i.e., 45 percent of the Jordanian boys, 47 percent of the Bahraini boys, and 70 per-

TABLE 3. BAHRAINI STUDENTS' SUPPORT OF THEIR GOVERNMENT
POLICIES IN COMPARISON TO THEIR PARENTS (IN PERCENTS)

Sex of Respondent	Students' Attitudes Toward Their Government Policies Are the Same as:				
	Father	Mother	Both	Neither	Total
Boys (N=15)	33	0	37	40	100
Girls (N=13)	0	8	46	46	100

TABLE 4. BAHRAINI STUDENTS' PREFERENCE OF FORM OF GOVERNMENT
RELATIVE TO THEIR PARENTS (IN PERCENTS)

Sex of Respondent	Prefer the Same Form of Government as:				
	Father	Mother	Both	Neither	Total
Boys (N=15)	27	0	33	40	100
Girls (N=13)	16	0	46	38	100

cent of the Kuwaiti boys) were found to be significantly higher than the percentage of deviation in the American sample, which is about 24 percent.

Thus, the responses to the general and specific questions were not found to be different. On the contrary, they turned out to be similar in the case of the Jordanian and Bahraini respondents, and almost the same in case of the Kuwaiti students. Furthermore, the data based on the other specific questions connected with political loyalties, preferred forms of government, and support of their government policies show similar trends. To illustrate, Tables 3 and 4 on intergenerational agreements on government policies and preferred forms of government are included here. They show similar tendencies to deviate from the political positions of their parents.

It might also be of some interest at this stage to refer to the significance of parents' agreement on political matters as a factor contributing to the influence of the family as an agency of political socialization. The majority of the Jordanian parents in our sample (65 percent) held the same political positions. When both Jordanian parents held the same position, 63 percent of their children were found to agree with them. When parents differed, 39 percent agreed with their fathers and 15 percent with their mothers. Further comparisons between the American and Jordanian respondents could be made. In both sets of data, boys tended to identify with their fathers and girls with their mothers (though American girls did so more than Jordanian girls). Similarly, in both sets of data, boys were more likely to deviate than girls. On the whole, the Jordanian fathers had more influence than Jordanian mothers. In other words, the Jordanian respondents were more likely to politically identify with their fathers than with their mothers. This was not the case among American respondents. The father in the United States was by no means the decisive force as in the Arab society. As pointed out earlier, when one parent was a Republican and the other a Democrat, the American mother exerted greater influence on party loyalties of their offspring than the father.[9]

In short, the above data verify the basic expectation of this study that intergenerational agreement on political matters among Jordanian and Bahraini students is lower than among American students. So far as Kuwaiti students are concerned, the data show that 28 percent of the boys hold the same political position as their fathers, none as their mothers, and a great majority (72 percent) as neither. As for girls, 40 percent hold the same political position as their fathers, none as their mothers, and 60 percent as neither.

Thus, deviation (72 percent of the boys and 60 percent of the girls) is the dominant tendency and is much higher among the Kuwaiti than among the Jordanian, the Bahraini, and the American respondents. In fact, these findings are almost diametrically opposed to the findings in the United States.

Another striking result is the complete absence of the Kuwaiti mother as a transmitter of political loyalties. The few Kuwaiti students who held the same political positions as their parents stated that they identified only with the father. Even among the girls, none identified with the mother. Some Jordanian respondents commented on the margins of their questionnaires that their mothers agreed with whatever their fathers said. Others commented that their mothers were indifferent to politics. Still others commented that they were not sure of what political views their mothers held. Kuwaiti students commented that their mothers were completely politically passive or that they were not supposed to talk politics.

This does not mean that the respondents are not close to their mothers. For instance, when Kuwaiti students were asked about the extent of their closeness to their parents, 40 percent said they were equally close to both parents, 37 percent said they were closer to their mother, 14 percent to their father, and 9 percent to neither. What is interesting about these findings is that even among those who said they were closer to their mothers, none showed any tendency to politically identify with them. Nevertheless degree of closeness to parents must have some influence on deviation (see Table 5). Out of those who said they were closer to mother, 27 percent held the same political positions as their fathers, and 73 percent deviated. In comparison, 43 percent of those who said they were closer to father held the same poli-

TABLE 5. RELATIONSHIP OF CLOSENESS TO PARENTS TO POLITICAL POSITIONS OF KUWAITI STUDENTS RELATIVE TO THEIR PARENTS (IN PERCENTS)

Closeness to Parents	Political Position is the Same as:			
	Father	Mother	Neither	Total
Closer to mother (N=18)	27	0	73	100
Equally close to both (N=19)	32	0	68	100
Closer to father (N=7)	43	0	57	100
Close to neither (N=4)	0	0	100	100

[9] Ibid., pp. 52–68.

tical position as he did, and 57 percent deviated. Of those who said they were equally close to both parents, 32 percent held the same political positions as their fathers, and 68 percent deviated. Finally, all those who said they were close to neither deviated.

In short, the results show that intergenerational agreement on political matters among Kuwaiti students is much lower than among Jordanian and American students. The general trend is independence from parents rather than political identification. Although there is no identification with mother whatsoever, it does not mean that fathers are influential in transmitting their political views to their offspring. The new generation of Kuwaiti students does not seem to be politically socialized in the family in spite of its strong ties and the relative lack of other agents of socialization.

The questions that need to be raised at this stage are: How do we explain the above findings? Why is it that Jordanian and Bahraini respondents are less likely to politically identify with their parents than Western respondents? Why is it that the majority of Kuwaiti students in our sample are politically independent of their parents? The importance of answering these questions becomes clear when we realize that family ties constitute the basic social structure and pattern of social organization in Jordan, Bahrain, and Kuwait.

Though the stress in explaining the above findings will be on the existing educational generational gap, a number of other variables and conditions will be identified as possible determinant forces.

During the last decade and a half the socioeconomic conditions in Kuwait have been changing very rapidly. Compared to the twentieth-century exposure of their children Kuwaiti parents seem as if they were raised in the Middle Ages. The whole way of life in Kuwait has had to adapt to numerous challenges. The new generation of Kuwaitis, like the "People of the Cave" in the Arab legend, awakened after centuries of deep sleep and suddenly found themselves face-to-face with all the technical and socioeconomic complexities of the twentieth century. All of a sudden, the old generation became something out of the distant past. A wide and deep gap separated the two generations. This gap is reflected very clearly in the differences in the levels of education of parents and their offspring. University education is now available to both sexes. In the case of our respondents, the data show that only about 12 percent of their parents have secondary education or higher. The great majority (88 percent) have some secondary education or less. This educational gap must have undermined the role of parents as agents of political socialization and, thus, prevented the offspring from identifying with their parents. The data presented in Table 6 support such a conclusion. As shown, the majority of the Kuwaiti students (67 percent) whose fathers have secondary education or higher tended to identify with them. Quite the opposite, the majority of the Kuwaiti students (73 percent) whose fathers have some secondary education or less tended to disagree with them. Is other words, 33 percent of the former group in comparison to 73 percent of the latter group tended to deviate from the political positions of their parents. The educational generational gap is narrower among the Bahraini and Jordanian than the Kuwaiti respondents. For instance, about 40 percent of the parents of

TABLE 6. RELATIONSHIP BETWEEN PARENTS' LEVEL OF EDUCATION AND THE POLITICAL IDENTIFICATION OF THE KUWAITI STUDENTS (IN PERCENTS)

Father's Level of Education	Political Identification With:			
	Father	Mother	Neither	Total
Secondary education or higher (N=6)	67	0	33	100
Some secondary or less (N=44)	27	0	73	100

TABLE 7. RELATIONSHIP BETWEEN PARENTS' LEVEL OF EDUCATION AND THE POLITICAL IDENTIFICATION OF THE BAHRAINI STUDENTS (IN PERCENTS)

Father's Level of Education	Political Identification With:				
	Father	Mother	Both	Neither	Total
University education (N=17)	36	10	18	36	100
Secondary education or less (N=11)	18	5	12	65	100

the Bahraini students have some university education. The data presented in Table 7 show that there is a negative relationship between educational gap and political identification with parents. Those whose parents have university education are less likely to deviate than those whose parents have secondary education or less.

Thus, the greater the educational generational gap, the lower the intergenerational agreement on political matters. This generalization might tell us why the Kuwaiti respondents who identified themselves as middle-class tended to be more politically independent of their parents than those who identified themselves as upper-class (see Table 8). The educational generational gap is greater among middle and lower classes in Kuwait. This difference between the middle class and upper class is much less in Jordan because education was not limited to the upper classes as in Kuwait. Consequently, whereas the relationship between the social class of parents and political identification with them is negative among Kuwaiti students, it is positive among the Jordanian students (see Table 9).

In the remaining section of this paper, a brief description of three other factors that are thought to undermine family political socialization in the Arab Middle East will be made. These other three factors that seem of special relevance in this context are:

TABLE 8. RELATIONSHIP BETWEEN SOCIAL CLASS AND POLITICAL IDENTIFICATION WITH PARENTS AMONG KUWAITI STUDENTS (IN PERCENTS)

Social Class Identification	Political Identification With:				
	Father	Mother	Both	Neither	Total
Upper class (N=17)	47	0	0	53	100
Middle class (N=29)	24	0	0	76	100

TABLE 9. RELATIONSHIP BETWEEN SOCIAL CLASS AND POLITICAL
IDENTIFICATION WITH PARENTS AMONG JORDANIAN STUDENTS
(IN PERCENTS)

| | Political Identification With: | | | | |
Social Class Identification	Father	Mother	Both	Neither	Total
Upper class (N=9)	12	25	0	63	100
Middle class (N=31)	29	21	11	39	100

1.   Low rate of membership in political parties relative to Western societies. Arab parents are much less likely to belong to political parties than their counterparts in the West. In spite of the apparent developing political consciousness in the Arab society, politics has been considered a dirty game, especially to members of the old generation. Besides, there has been an intense feeling among the people that involvement in politics leads nowhere. Feelings of powerlessness rather than efficacy have been dominant. Because of such feelings parents could not play an important role in political socialization. Furthermore, none of the Arab societies under study has a two party system.

2.   The prevailing norms in the Arab society discourage discussing politics with children. In response to the question connected with whether they would discuss politics with their fathers, mothers, both parents, or neither, the great majority of Kuwaiti boys (88 percent) and all the girls said they would rather discuss politics with neither (see Table 10). This is not so among the Jordanian and Bahraini respondents. Only 18 percent of the Jordanian boys and 15 percent of the Jordanian girls said they would rather discuss politics with neither. None, even among the girls, said he preferred discussing politics with his mother. Almost similar responses were

TABLE 10. WOULD YOU RATHER DISCUSS POLITICS WITH FATHER, MOTHER,
BOTH PARENTS, OR NEITHER? (IN PERCENTS)

| | | Would Rather Discuss Politics With: | | | | |
Nationality	Sex	Father	Mother	Both	Neither	Total
Kuwaiti Students	Boys (N=25)	12	0	0	88	100
	Girls (N=18)	0	0	0	100	100
Jordanian Students	Boys (N=22)	41	0	41	18	100
	Girls (N=18)	45	0	40	15	100
Bahraini Students	Boys (N=15)	60	0	13	27	100
	Girls (N=13)	46	9	30	15	100

given by the Bahraini students though they showed more tendency to discuss politics with the father than both parents.

3.   The mother plays a very passive political role in the Arab society. This should be an important factor undermining family political socialization.

CONCLUSION

This was a comparative study of the influence of the family as an agency of political socialization in Western societies and three Arab societies. Though the family in the Arab Middle East is the most influential agency of socialization, there seem to be (1) a great difference between Jordanian or Bahraini students on one hand and Kuwaiti students on the other so far as degree of political identification with their parents, and (2) only a little intergenerational agreement on political matters relative to Western societies. This is opposite to the expectations of some political sociologists in the West that the relationships between the political attitudes and behavior of individuals and those of their parents in traditional non-Western societies may well be even greater than in Western societies. The present empirical investigation of Jordanian, Bahraini, and Kuwaiti students at the American University of Beirut showed that intergenerational agreement on political matters among Kuwaiti students is much lower than among Jordanian and Bahraini students. Similarly, intergenerational agreement among Jordanian and Bahraini students is significantly lower than among similar Western respondents. These findings are explained most effectively in terms of educational generational gap, norms discouraging discussing politics with children, and the passive political role of mothers.

The Young Pioneers

16

AN AGENCY OF POLITICAL SOCIALIZATION
AND EDUCATIONAL DEVELOPMENT

William M. Cave

There have been few political systems throughout history that have made such prodigious efforts to influence directly the political socialization of its youth as the Soviet regime. Almost from the inception of the post-revolutionary order, Soviet leaders have sought to channel the activities of youth in a systematic, orderly, and constructive manner commensurate with the goals of the Soviet social order. To facilitate this Herculean task, such youth organizations as the Octobrists, the Young Pioneers, and the Komsomol were created to ensure the desired sociopolitical orientation and training deemed essential for building a communist society. Although all three have contributed importantly to the political socialization of youth, the Young Pioneers command special attention because of their unique role as an educational and political social system articulating closely with the larger Soviet social order.

The primary aims of the Young Pioneers are the development of character and the teaching of moral values. The Soviet youngster is nurtured in collectivist values so that he will always be willing to subordinate his personal interests to the welfare of the group. He is taught to obey his parents and teachers, to respect physical labor, and to encourage his fellow Pioneers and classmates to study with diligence. It is anticipated that many of the Young Pioneers will eventually be graduated into the ranks of the Komsomol where more intense political indoctrination leads ultimately to Communist Party membership.[1]

This chapter represents an adaptation of a chapter written by the author on the "Young Pioneers" appearing in a book entitled *Education and Development in Central Asia: A Case Study on Social Change in Uzbekistan*, by William M. Cave, William K. Medlin, and Finley Carpenter. (Leiden, E. J. Brill Press, 1970).

[1] Robert T. Holt and John E. Turner, eds., *Soviet Union: Paradox and Change* (New York: Holt, Rinehart & Winston, 1962), p. 166.

The organization of Young Pioneers is closely integrated with the Soviet school system. Each school has a full-time staff member who is responsible for directing the activities of the Pioneer. The Young Pioneers are housed in structures called "Pioneer Palaces" which, upon close examination, take on properties and characteristics analogous to the school.

Soviet policy in education is based upon the assumption that the Communist Party can shape human consciousness to desired specification through a centrally planned program of indoctrination and supervised group activity.[2] The Soviet concept of education is thus seen as a highly manipulative one. Further, the emphasis on the planned and systematic nature of this political socialization process via the educational system represents an unusually potent and effective force. All parts of the politico-educative system lend themselves to functional analysis in terms of the manner by which they contribute to the socializing objective. This analysis includes not only the various school experiences but also the numerous supplemental activities which are integral parts of a unique political and social reinforcement system. Within this socializing milieu, Soviet youth organizations are assumed to play a vital role.

In the analysis that follows an attempt is made to cast the behavior of the Young Pioneers within the context of social system theory delineating their unique properties and specialized roles as political and educational social systems.

The Emergence of the Pioneer Palace as a Social System

As the early history of the Pioneer movement revealed, high expectations were created regarding its significance as a politically conscious and socially useful organization. Entrance into the Young Pioneers was intended to be selective, embellished by emotive and emblematic symbolisms indicative of an elite association. As Harper points out, it was originally conceived to be an arm of the Party under the guidance of the Komsomol, articulating closely with the Soviet school as well as the indigenous community.[3] Based in part on the prototype of the Boy Scout, it possessed an implied puritanical quality, but differed in the order of priorities assigned to its activities. As an institution designed to fulfill specific functions in a rapidly developing industrial society, it merits serious attention both as an *agency of political socialization* and an *extension of the Soviet school*. It is partly in concert with these two major roles that the Pioneer Palace emerges as a clearly identifiable social system articulating closely with the school and other social institutions while manifesting some unique, subcultural properties of its own. Its political order is authoritarian, analogous to that of the Soviet school, with a well-defined administrative hierarchy along with a professional staff to plan the activities and supervise its membership.

Pioneer Palaces are virtually ubiquitous in the Soviet Union and gen-

[2] James Bowen, *Soviet Education* (Madison: University of Wisconsin Press, 1962).

[3] Samuel N. Harper, *Civic Training in Soviet Russia* (Chicago: University of Chicago Press, 1929).

erally have impressive facilities for carrying out their programs of character development and indoctrination. Almost every city has a major building that has been converted into a Palace, and in the rural areas the Pioneers are usually housed in a collective farm school. Some of the Palaces (such as the Anichkov Palace in Leningrad and the Lenin Hills Palace in Moscow) border on elegance. The ubiquitousness of the Palaces attests to the high premium placed on their value as a socializing agency by Soviet authorities as well as their importance in the general educational scheme.

A "we feeling" permeates the social climate of the palace and, indeed, carries over into other secondary associations. A compact nexus of social relationships exists which may be observed in the numerous group experiences provided as well as in the interaction process witnessed in the activity circles.

This "psychic" aspect of the Pioneer community is one that draws particular attention to the symbolism of the kerchiefs, badges, and the oath as expressed through the sentiments of its members. Special occasions heighten this psychic phenomenon and give credence to its universality. Such events as the May Day festivities and Lenin's birthday, among others, evoke unrestrained excitement and serve to intensify the "we feeling." During these celebrations, the Young Pioneers are literally on public display—marching, performing, and proudly exhibiting the results of their avocational, artistic, political, social, and scientific learnings. One may observe the Soviet public's enthusiastic response to the efforts and enterprises of the Pioneers, which brings an element of pride to the ranks and tends to increase their consciousness as a separate and distinct social organization. In this manner, group cohesiveness is fostered and intensified. Likewise, under these emotionally integrating experiences, the approximation to the "ideal" Soviet model is more readily attainable. This model is one in which youth are portrayed as "young Leninites" possessing the ideal human traits of a communist society. "The Pioneer organization nurtures in young Leninites the best human traits of communist society: unbounded love towards the fatherland, diligence, tenancity, and persistence in achieving goals, lofty benevolence, courage and cheerfulness."[4]

The Pioneer Oath, which every member takes under relatively solemn and ritualistic circumstances, calls attention to the loyalty as well as the moral and ethical behavior expected of each member toward the state. The oath not only appears in highly visible places in the Palaces but is conspicuous in strategic locations in the schools as well.

A characteristic mode of social interaction is discernible both in the extramural activities of the Palaces and in the various subsystems that emerge. The recognition accorded the Young Pioneers assures them of their worth and importance to the Soviet state. The restrictive age-group membership ascribes to it some exclusive property in spite of its massive character. The Pioneer organization is clearly for children; and although adult authority is ever present, its deportment is certainly no more "despotic" than its counterparts in comparable Western social systems.

[4] Holt and Turner, p. 165.

The Soviet leaders have created a "community of youth," buttressed it by a complete system of reinforcement, and harnessed its adolescent energy by providing a multiplicity of constructive activities and experiences that are consonant with the goals and objectives of the state. The Pioneer Palace is a unique social system, the ramifications of which are likely to be felt in all sectors of the Soviet educational orbit.

POLITICO-EDUCATIVE PROPERTIES OF THE PIONEER PALACE

From both a political socialization and an educational perspective, the Pioneer Palace fulfills two seemingly contradictory functions, both of which contribute vitally to the overall educational scheme. These two generalized functions are: (1) the inculcation in youth of Soviet political ideology and morality; and (2) the discovery, cultivation, and development of the special interests, abilities, and talents of youth. The former would require commitment to the group and the state; the latter would emphasize creativity and individuality, hardly the necessary attributes for collective obedience. However antithetical these two functions might appear, Soviet officials maintain they are both necessary to produce individuals who correspond to the blueprint of the "new Soviet man" and, at the same time, are capable of being trained to meet the increasing demands of the Soviet economy. The "new Soviet man" is depicted as disciplined, working steadily and consistently, puritanical in conduct and motivation.[5] Khrushchev pointed to some of the qualities of the new man in his report to the 22nd Party Congress on the Party Program:[6]

> The generation of communism must be molded from childhood; it should be cared for and tempered in its youth; we must see to it that none are crippled morally, that is, become victims of incorrect upbringing and bad examples. If young plantings of fruit trees are damaged in any way, a great deal of work is needed to have them come up right, and even then these efforts are not always successful. The same may be said of the generation. . . .
>
> The molding of the new man with the new ethic is a most important duty of the Soviet school, family, and society. The training of all children, adolescents and youths and girls for life and work in a communist society requires that greater attention be paid to moral upbringing. . . .
>
> The moral code includes the basic standards of behavior. After these standards become assimilated and are practiced in everyday behavior, they become moral qualities, attributes of the personality, and characterize the moral make-up of people. The aim of moral upbringing is to convert the moral standards and principles into the main personality traits of the new man."

The key to the moral and political upbringing of children was seen in the organization of their activities and active participation in collective

---

[5] Raymond A. Bauer, Alex Inkeles, and Clyde Kluckhohn, *How the Soviet System Works* (New York: Random House, 1956), p. 162.

[6] Harry G. Shaffer, ed., *The Soviet System* (New York: Appleton-Century-Crofts, 1965), p. 290.

enterprises. The focal points for these activities were assigned to the school and the Soviet youth organizations. Hence, the Young Pioneers emerged as a crucial institution in the molding of character and the reinforcement of the moral code leading to the creation of the "new Soviet man."

The following illustrate those properties and/or roles of the Young Pioneers in fulfilling the high expectations of the Soviet hierarchy as a major socializing force in the emerging social order.[7]

The Collectivizing Nature of the Pioneers

The sociopolitical organization of the Young Pioneers represents the exemplification of the *kollektiv* concept in action. According to Soviet definitions, any group constitutes a collective if that group functions as a social unit with approved leadership in a cooperative and cohesive manner and operates under socially acceptable values toward productive ends. It may differ in size but should not be too large or unwieldy—e.g., a fifty-member group is too large for effective leadership and good interaction among the members. Units in the system of collectives are designated as the link (up to 10 members), the squad (two to four links), the troop (all the squads in a social unit, such as a school), and the brigade composed of several links usually organized for socially useful labor activities. Each collective unit is headed by a member of the group or in the case of larger units, by a specially appointed senior person responsible to Party or Komsomol authorities. Unit heads are nominated by senior Pioneer supervisors from local Party headquarters or the Party cell representative (there is one in every school). The "nominee" undergoes a period of trial and finally is "elected" to the position. The germ of future political responsibility and accountability is evident here.

Activities carried on in the Palaces may be viewed as experiments in group living. The Pioneers provide, through the medium of the circles, an opportunity for experiences in interpersonal relationships. Through the collectivization of interpersonal relationships, the twin ultimate aims—self-discipline, and the desire to work for group ends—may be more fully realized. In these various group situations, whether they occur in the Palaces or in the school, a great deal of emphasis is placed on active participation. In observing a history discussion circle in the Tashkent Pioneer Palace, it was noted that the group was disciplined to listen attentively to every point and every opinion rendered among the group, a habit indicating emphasis directed toward individual contributions to the group.

Although much has been written concerning the subordination of individual wishes to the needs of the group, it is difficult to confirm such a phenomenon empirically in the absense of longitudinal observations. Perhaps in the formal, organizational meetings such a process is readily

---

[7] The observations made of the Pioneer Palaces and referred to in this chapter were recorded from field visits made to Soviet Central Asia in the spring of 1962 and 1964 by the author and two colleagues from the University of Michigan. Pioneer Palaces were also observed in Georgia, Kiev, and Moscow in addition to the Central Asian Republic of Uzbekistan.

identified. However, from numerous observations of the Pioneer activities in the Palaces, schools, and on the collectives, there is little evidence of *complete subordination* of the individual to the collective. The function of the Pioneers as a collectivizing agency seems to be important for the following reasons: (1) It provides a source of friendship formation and creates *comaradrie* settings vital to the young adolescent. It is entirely possible that diadic and triadic patterns emerge from these settings, opening the way for an extensive network of *informal* relationships that may carry over into the school as well as other social contexts. Although admittedly speculative, it is difficult to visualize how the formation of cliques can be avoided, particularly when the majority of the activities are self-selective and based on individual interest. (2) It gives the young Pioneer a sense of belonging. In the words of the Samarkand Pioneer Palace Director: "There is a place for everyone, even for those who are not members." The assumption that all who participate are subject to influence seems to be implied in the director's statement. (3) Since the test of normalcy is applied to participation in a collective, the collectivizing nature of the Pioneer movement provides accessibility for youth to satisfy the societal "rites of passage and intensification." The important point here is that the Soviet adolescent may meet the societal requirements while pursuing a rewarding, enjoyable set of activities. (4) The collectivizing nature of the Pioneers provides an ideal laboratory for the training of youth leaders. Experiences in a multiplicity of leadership roles (e.g., link, squad, troop, discussion leader) can be gained through participation in both the socially useful projects and the Palace activities. The former come under the guidance of the Komsomol; the latter are organized under the aegis of the Director of the Pioneer Palace and cater to a much more impressionistic age group.

THE PIONEER PALACE AS AN IDEOLOGICAL ENCAMPMENT

To even the most casual observer, it borders on the impossible to escape the ideological overtones that are so characteristically a part of the atmosphere surrounding the Pioneer Establishments. From the uniformality of the red kerchief to the symbolisms and pictorial representations strategically located throughout, there is an incessant flow of Soviet propaganda which seeks to instill in the young Pioneer loyalty and devotion to the state, recall the glory of the Revolution, and exalt the virtues and deeds of the "great Lenin." Although many of the activities appear relatively free of such anointments, the Pioneer is constantly reminded of the Code and his obligations to it. The Pioneer Oath, with illustrations, generally can be found decorating the walls of the Palaces, and in the Pioneer room in the schools. The oath, which each youth recites upon becoming a member of the organization, signals the intense loyalty to homeland and allegiance to the revolutionary tradition symbolized by Lenin which authorities seek to inculcate among the young.

The encampment simile may be further illustrated by observations made of the activity teachers' and adult leaders' behavior as they interact with the children. In the main, they reflect a kind of puritanical model, characterized by an air of firmness, a passion for orderliness, and an uneasy grace. Of course, there are wide variations in personalities, but their deportment within the confines of the establishment manifests striking similarities. The tendency toward consistency in youth models, however, is important since it tends to reduce the likelihood of disparities existing between latent and manifest levels of behavior. In other words, the Pioneer teachers and adult leaders are more apt to approximate the ideal conception of Soviet behavior. In this manner, deviancy is less likely to occur, reinforcement for proper conduct is maximized, and sanctions are much easier to maintain. There is very little of what might be termed "horseplay" in the Palaces, although the subtle restraints do not seem to curb the enthusiasm of the participants. Certainly the presence of adults in their midst accounts, in part, for the good behavior of the children, but there is also a noticeable *esprit de corps*, a feeling of oneness, that acts also as a deterrent to the shirking of one's duty and responsibility. This seems to be spontaneous and, therefore, real. The Soviet youth leaders make very effective use of this phenomenon.

At the same time, one observes in the Pioneer program a certain strain and uneasiness on the part of the adult leadership (*not* the teaching staff) with respect to the emerging value orientations of the youngsters and the social system developing within the Pioneer Palaces, homes, etc. It appears that what the Pioneers themselves (including many nonmembers) seek in their activities and associations is often at odds with the official concerns of the Pioneer Party leaders. Although it is not easy for the outside visitor to observe the strictly ideological-doctrinal activities, our observations indicate that much of this kind of activity is "staged," nonspontaneous, and routine from the standpoint of the children. Although there appears to be considerable reverence for Lenin as a leader and model for the young generation, it is also evident that the changing context of Soviet society and the difficulty in making an ethnic-cultural linkage between the individual native and the Russian Lenin often render these political-type Pioneer activities less than "real."

This interpretation helps to explain the somewhat urgent nature of the adult leaders' attitudes toward the youth program, expressed in constant cuing during mass-ideological activities, a near "barrage" of propaganda symbolisms and slogans, frequent "pep" rallies, and increasing attention to selecting young Pioneer leaders. Officially acknowledged delinquency provides additional context for these patterns.

The difficulties involved in controlling the behavior of a mass organization are legion. Yet, activities do serve as excellent distracters, and when they are fun and rewarding, controls are much easier to impose. Under such conditions, ideological "sidetrips" are apt to be met with a minimum of resistance. At the same time, these incursions are also likely to be diffuse and certainly less intense than if there were a small, elite group of native Uzbeks with whom the leaders were dealing. The major complaints registered by some Soviet officials regarding the present mass character of the Young Pioneers have been precisely along these lines—that the organization has become unwieldy, making it difficult to carry on effective ideological or indoctrinal programs.

THE YOUNG PIONEERS AS A SUBSTITUTE MORAL AND SPIRITUAL SYSTEM

Next we may turn to a major function of the Young Pioneers—the inculcation of Soviet political ideology and morality, and the specific manner in which the Young Pioneer organization fulfills this function. That this is a recognized major role of the Young Pioneers is clearly stated. The Young Pioneers are defined as

> . . . a mass political children's organization which . . . brings up children in the spirit of love and devotion to the Motherland, friendship between nations and proletarian internationalism; it draws Pioneers and school children into public life, develops in them a conscientious attitude towards study, discipline, love of work, and curiosity; it brings up children to be all-around developed individuals, conscientious, healthy, courageous, full of joy of life and unafraid of difficulties, future builders of Communism. . . .[8]

Early in the formation of the Soviet state its leaders recognized the need for a substitute system of morality, one that would be predicated on the ideals of a communist society. The target of the new moral code was Soviet youth; the agencies through which the code was to be taught were the schools, the Komsomol, the Octobrists, and the Young Pioneers. The latter organization, the Pioneers, was ideally suited for such a task since its membership represented a highly impressionistic age group as well as a potentially "socially-useful" group.

From their very initiation into the organization when they publicly declare the Oath, Young Pioneers are expected to behave as morally responsible and ardent patriots dedicated to the building of a communist society. Their day-to-day conduct comes under review.

Admission is a solemn affair, often planned to coincide with some national event or festival. Each new member recites the Pioneer Oath, copies of which may be found hanging on the walls of Pioneer Palaces and houses as constant reminders. Then the highly symbolic three-cornered red scarf, representing the unity of the Pioneers, is tied around the neck of each new member, clearly identifying him with all other Young Pioneers in the Soviet state.

"I, a Young Pioneer of the Soviet Union, before my comrades give this oath, to love the Soviet Union, to live, to study and to fight according to the teaching of Lenin and in the way which the Communist Party teaches."[9] This oath, affirmed by each Young Pioneer, contains the basic precepts of Soviet political ideology and morality into which the Pioneer organization indoctrinates its members.

[8] William Clark Trow, ed., *Character Education in Soviet Russia* (Ann Arbor, Mich.: Ann Arbor Press, 1934), pp. 89–95.
[9] G. Manlin and A. Sokolovskii, *Ty—pioner. Pervaia Kniga Pionera.* (Gor'kii: Gor'kovskaia Pravda, 1960), p. 45.

The first principle is the cultivation of patriotism. "I, a Young Pioneer of the Soviet Union . . . give this oath, to love the Soviet Union. . . ."[10] Each Young Pioneer is required to know the hymn of the Soviet Union and that of his republic. Among other things, the Young Pioneers are responsible for the mobilization of all the school children for state holidays and other major patriotic occasions.

Further, "the finest Pioneer palaces are housed in the former residences of leading families of the pre-revolutionary aristocracy. This architectural symbolism probably still impresses upon the Soviet children who have access to these, the best of the Pioneer facilities, the national leadership's justice and solicitude for the popular welfare."[11]

Included in this cultivation of loyalty and devotion to the state is the identification of the youth with the Communist Party: ". . . to live, to study and to fight . . . in the way which the Communist Party teaches." Thus the symbolism of unity in the three-cornered red scarf. So too is the official recognition and praise accorded the Young Pioneer at public ceremonies by Party leaders to give the youth a sense of belonging, importance, and commitment to the Communist Party.

Also a party of this cultivation of intense pride and loyalty for the state is a glorification and praise of the Revolution and the great Lenin: ". . . to live, to study and to fight according to the teaching of Lenin. . . ." There is a Lenin corner in every Pioneer house, along with a statue or portrait of the supreme Soviet father symbol.

And finally the Young Pioneers attempt to instill a "communist conscience" into each member. The Young Pioneers are told that "a conscious, responsible, accurate, and exact performance by each pupil of his school responsibilities, his assignments in social practical work, and the rules of the internal school regimen should become 'a matter of his honor.'"[12] To this end peer group influences and pressure are relied upon heavily in both the punishment and reward system of the Young Pioneer members. Each member knows that he is held accountable to the collective for his behavior: "I, a Young Pioneer of the Soviet Union, before my comrades give this oath . . ." It is constantly stressed that a Young Pioneer must set a moral example for all youth.

In its literature, in talks given by youth leaders and teachers, and in some of the special activities, the Pioneer organization provides additional teachings to those of the schools on the philosophical and spiritual values that the Party and government support. Cause and effect relationships are seen in materialistic contexts, illustrated for young people in an attractive way through manipulating modern scientific and technical progress so as to prove the finality of material relationships. At the same time, moral and social values such as conscientiousness, love of labor, aesthetics, healthy habits, genuine enjoyment, civic spirit, patriotism, fearlessness, and similar qualities are actively taught through the many Pioneer functions. An

[10] Ibid., pp. 46–47.
[11] Holt and Turner, p. 165.
[12] Trow, pp. 68–70.

attempt is apparently made, too, to have the young person realize these virtues as personal attributes that will make him a worthy person in his own right and for society at large. On the basis of very limited access to situations in which this kind of training was carried on, it is not possible to evaluate the success of Soviet efforts. It can be said, nonetheless, that very little evidences were *noticed* of contravention of the various precepts that enshrine the Pioneer model.

The actual assessment of changes in ideological perspective is a complex task and often proves inconclusive. Furthermore, it is acknowledged that field observations have important limitations, particularly in the ideological realm. If nothing else, however, the presence of large numbers of young people under one roof, pursuing a host of constructive activities and projects and relating to one another in quasi-controlled environment, does seem to lend itself to indoctrinal influence patterns, which youth authorities attempt to use effectively in hastening the political socialization process.

The Pioneer Palace as an Extension of the School

The Young Pioneers have often been likened to American voluntary youth organizations. To a limited extent, this comparison is justifiable. Both are geared primarily to adolescent age groups, come under the aegis of adult supervision, and offer an array of recreational and avocational pursuits. Both are infused with ideological overtones and claim moral and ethical outcomes as complementary goals. Although a concern for character building is expressed by both, the comparison usually ends here. Rarely are American youth associations seen as extensions of the school, and never explicitly as political socialization agencies. Generally the opposite is true, in that they tend to be dichotomized from the school and are often viewed as competitive.

Conversely, the Pioneer Palace is firmly entrenched in the Soviet school, sometimes physically and almost always sociopsychologically. The prime purpose of the Pioneers is the shaping of socialized forms of behavior consistent with Soviet ideology and the development of special knowledge and skills that reflect the interests and abilities of the individual child as well as contribute to reaching officially stated goals. Those skills and knowledge are in addition to those developed in the regular school programs. In short, the movement aims at character building according to Soviet values and at the development of special skills and aptitudes according to individual interests. Efforts of the Pioneers supplement and reinforce the Soviet school so that state-controlled factors of influence can operate upon a broad base. The Pioneers represent, therefore, not only an extensive learning agency but also one which is systematically reinforced and supported by the Soviet social order.

As in the school, character training represents attempts to establish social organizations that operate as collectives from small groups to large complexes wherein the rules of collective labor are practiced in a variety of contexts. The important environmental forces are social in character.

Emphasis is placed upon inculcation of peer group control, and it is brought about, in general, by formalizing rules of behavior and by rotating leadership among the children to administer the policies prescribed by central authority and modified by the local organization to fit the special requirements of the indigenous community. Although such modification may be peripheral, provision for it apparently has the psychological effect of stimulating the development and execution of local programs. As a result, it is common to find that a given Pioneer organization and its subunits exhibit pride in their special achievements afforded by the limited autonomy. Competition between collectives has more sanction than that between individuals.

In general, the structure of the Pioneer environment parallels that established in the school in the sense that special facilities for learning are provided, including teachers to instrument the objectives. Equality of opportunity is particularly stressed in the Pioneers since one of the central functions is to develop human potential that cannot be adequately or comparably stimulated in the regular schools.

Each activity is clearly defined by a set of objectives, and whether the process involves physical skill, a laboratory experiment, or steps in problem solving, the instructional staff sets examples of model behavior to illustrate in concrete terms the proper procedures. The widespread emphasis upon learning suggests why the school model is reflected in youth organizations.

Characteristics of the reinforcement and punishment system in the Pioneer organizations are highly similar to those in the Soviet schools. Active punishment is used as a last resort, whereas emphasis is given to the rewards (often honorific) that occur as a result of compliance with the spirit and letter of the rules. Punishment is manifest largely in the form of threat. For example, expulsion from the organization (as from school), one of the most severe punishments, is implied clearly each time a panel of peers reviews a case involving a serious breech of behavior or policy. Actual expulsion, however, is not a frequent event and has been carefully handled over the years:

> One must approach expulsion from a Pioneer organization very cautiously. In order to evaluate the conduct of a Pioneer it is necessary to study in detail the causes which led the Pioneer to act in the way he did. One must try to eliminate these causes, to draw him into interesting work, to talk with him, to win him over, and to tell him of the harm resulting from his acts. Even the much milder reprimand should be applied only in extreme cases, but that much more frequently than expulsion. The latter should follow only after all other educational measures which might be employed have been found to have no influence.[13]

The school model may also be identified when one analyzes the psychology of group processes that have evolved in the Pioneer organization. As in Makarenko's much cited work, these processes have emerged largely as a result of empirical trial-and-error techniques rather than from the application of deductions from behavioral theory. For example, the size of the link, the smallest collective, seems to be the result of "cut-and-try" methods. The

[13] Ibid., pp. 74–75.

purpose of the link is to provide a social context for each member so that his peers act to monitor and otherwise influence his action in accordance with policy. The following quotation reflects some of the psychological properties of control: "For the best conduct of the entire work of the brigade it is broken up into links of ten children each. The links are formed on the basis of age, maturity, and friendship"[14] (Statute of Pioneer Organization). Organizational techniques are laid down: "For greater elasticity and efficiency it is important for an organization not to be bulky; that is why the division is separated into these links, each one made up of a small number of children. It is thus possible to do more effective work, to meet individual questions, and adapt procedure to varying interests and to children at different stages of development."[15] To implement this concept there are three age groups: a younger, middle, and older link, so that each link may be homogeneous in terms of interests and abilities.

The psychology of leadership advocated as most effective in the Pioneer organization contains the following characteristics:

1. The leader is supposed to help and to advise instead of dictate.
2. The leader must work to earn the respect and love of the children by acting as an elder comrade.
3. He should be sensitive to the moods, dreams, motives, and interests of each child.
4. He ought to encourage Pioneer participation in self-management so that direction from above theoretically becomes minimal.
5. The leader should spend much time with the children, talking about their interests and experiences so that they feel free to share their secrets with the leader.

Several methods of control are exercised to influence children who are not well-disciplined. They include: (a) conference between the leader and the delinquent member; (b) discussions in public meetings, division councils, and links; (c) suspension or expulsion from the division; (d) public censure, rebuke, reproof; (e) diversion of attention with interesting tasks.

Pioneer groups seem to have a strong influence on individual members. Exercise of control is expressed as a combination of adult leadership and peer group operations, involving a combination of positive rewards, threats, and punishment. Rewards are used to help the child identify with a cohesive group that adopts and executes a set of clear-cut values expressed in behavioral terms. Another principle that is obvious is that Pioneer activities take a considerable portion of the child's time so that the probability of choosing deviant forms of action is somewhat minimal. A third principle that is pervasive throughout the school, Pioneer organizations, the community, home, and other foci of action is that a strong attempt is made to limit the alternatives of decision-making to constructive activities. Constructive alternatives, of course, are those so considered in the light of Soviet ideology and policy which reflect both immediate needs of the industrializing society and

[14] Ibid., p. 75.
[15] Ibid., pp. 75–76.

goals of the Government. In this way, the political socialization of youth is subtly assured.

Although it is empirically impossible to state the extent to which the movement, with its personnel, successfully performs *all* these functions, it is obvious that the Pioneer network is a politically potent mass organization. The intensity and conviction of its participants are unknown quantities, but the fact that they are there indicates that society has come to reckon with the Pioneer program and to involve itself in certain degrees in this unique social system.

THE FACILITATION OF SOCIETAL MOBILITY

The propensity of political and educational social systems to support prevailing schemes of social stratification has been noted in a number of studies. Despite their avowed claims of equality and openness in their formal educational structures, the Soviet education and political systems seem to be no exception to this finding. Education occupies a position of high prominence among Soviet economic priorities, and subsequently, the attainment of higher levels of education and training bears a marked relationship to mobility in Soviet society.

The role of Soviet youth organizations in the facilitation of social mobility is difficult to assess. First of all, the accepted mode of upward mobility is fraught with considerable ambiguity. Hence, the precise manner in which normative patterns of mobility shape the youth organizations, the school, and other socializing agencies (directly and indirectly through their effect on values which implement social control) is not clear. The lack of clarity is due partly to the political nature of the youth organizations. Perhaps more important, the ambiguity may be the result of conflicting ideal-typical normative patterns of upward mobility in Soviet society which are reflected in its social systems and have political determinants.

In a paper suggesting a framework for relating cross-cultural differences between systems of education to prevailing norms of upward mobility, Turner used different organizing "folk" norms to account for the differences.[16] He termed these folk norms *sponsored* mobility and *contest* mobility, respectively. Sponsored mobility refers to the tendency of a social system to *select* out or *recruit* for future elite status those individuals chosen by an already established elite. Elite status is therefore *given* on the basis of a criterion of supposed merit. Upward mobility thus requires sponsorship and is granted on the basis of whether the candidate is judged to have those qualities deemed desirable to perpetuate the elite group.

Contest mobility, on the other hand, is seen as an open system in which elite status is the prize, and is *taken* by the candidate's own efforts. Upward mobility is therefore not sponsored by an established elite; hence, the elite does not solely determine those aspirants who shall or shall not attain it.

[16] Ralph H. Turner, "Sponsored and Contest Mobility and the School System," *American Sociological Review,* 25 (December 1960).

Curiously, the Young Pioneers' organization reflects both of these norms. Sponsorship can be detected through both the talent-discovering and political-indoctrinating functions of the Palaces. In the former, it is not uncommon for highly talented youth to be referred to or directed toward activities which would enhance further development of their talents. Teachers are often the prime referral agents for such a transaction.[17] In addition, there are adult Young Pioneer representatives in all the schools who may be even more vital in the selecting process.

In the case of the latter function, recognizing and encouraging future leaders who possess those qualities deemed necessary for ultimate party membership have always been an acknowledged objective of the Palaces. Many of the activities require dutiful, loyal, and conforming behavior which are prerequisites to entry into the Komsomol. The Pioneer Palace thus represents an excellent breeding ground for the identification of future Soviet leaders.

On the other hand, competition and individualism are also encouraged. One must therefore expect at least a modicum of "open contests" in which the individual is rewarded for effort, enterprise, and risk-taking. It is interesting that much of what Soviet ideology has to say about success—hard work, persistence, enterprise, etc.—correlates more directly with the governing objective of contest mobility in that elite status is provided for those who earn it and contribute the greatest to the welfare of the state. The notion of sponsorship by established elites leading to ascribed status positions represents an anathema to Communist ideals. Yet, both of these folk norms exist within the confines of Soviet youth organizations.

The political implications of these conflicting folk norms as they may be applied to the facilitation of upward mobility are perhaps best illustrated by the visibility of the two major power factions in Soviet society—the party elite and the scientific community. Both groups exemplify these conflicting ideal-typical normative patterns of upward mobility in a most dramatic macro-manner, whereas the social system of the Pioneer Palace depicts those patterns in microcosm.

Although education is certainly not the only avenue to upward mobility, the chances are that, with the growth of Soviet technology and the increasing social differentiation of its social structure, educational levels will likely be an even more valid predictor of vertical mobility in the future. It will, however, continue to be infused with political overtones which, in turn, will likely have a demonstrable effect on social mobility patterns in the Soviet order.

SUMMARY

The politico-educational properties of the Pioneer Palaces indicate a pattern of Gesellschaft-like social relations in which interaction tends to be somewhat impersonal, norms rational, and relations used instrumentally. As

[17] Urie Bronfenbrenner, *Two Worlds of Childhood: US and USSR* (New York: Russell Sage Foundation, 1970).

in most mass organizations, the absence of prolonged and intimate associations prohibits the unveiling of many facets of the human personality and leads to a high degree of functional specificity. This is often useful in the management of tension in that members of the Pioneers need reveal only a small portion of themselves while pursuing activities in the Palace. This takes on added importance when one considers that, due to the lack of predictability, together with the rapidity of change in the social arena, the Gesellschaft-like social relations are generally subjected to greater stress than their Gemeinschaft counterparts. However, the more complex Gesellschaft-like structures have numerous mechanisms by which their members are controlled in the interests of the social system. In addition, the extreme interaction pattern of affective neutrality seems also to reduce the strain on the social system.

The following represent the more salient political and educational aspects of the Pioneer Palace which lend credence to its role as an important agency in the political socialization process:

1. It exerts a virtual monopolistic control over organized, outside-school youth activities within the prescribed age range, thus delimiting the alternatives for adolescent behavior and reducing the likelihood of social deviancy. Such a "built-in" sociopolitical control mechanism makes it possible for a more permissive stance regarding behavior to be taken within the Pioneer organization.

2. It serves as an important medium in capturing the allegiance of youth. The data suggest that this objective is not likely to be attained merely through the indoctrinal aspects of the Pioneer programs and the "ideological forays" attributed to its circles. Rather, it may be argued that the appealing nature of Palace activities, the great desire on the part of youth to "belong," and the enthusiastic, *official* interest shown in the organization of Young Pioneers tend to increase the benign visibility of the state and, hence, share in capturing the allegiance of Soviet youth. Furthermore, the social interaction patterns of the Palace openly court the acceptability of all who desire to participate and will abide by the rules.

3. The Young Pioneer organization operates on the assumption that fundamental personality changes can be effected through directed personal and collective experiences. Thus, no stone is left unturned in the persistent attempts to influence the Young Pioneer along socially desirable avenues. Efforts along this path may be seen in (*a*) the accessability to the individual via his involvement in activities of high interest; (*b*) the control mechanisms of the collective; and (*c*) the reinforcement contingencies of the social system.

4. Its unique relationship to the Soviet school provides for learning continuity and a basically attractive accentuation of the socialization process. Not only are school aims reinforced by the activities of the Palace, but also behavioral areas less apt to be successfully dealt with by the school can be stressed and developed. The Pioneer Palace thus continues the socializing functions of the school.

5. It functions as a laboratory for the development of leadership skills.

More than any other youth organization, the Pioneer Palace affords the individual the opportunity to *lead*—to test out, develop, and experience the role of leader in a helpful and rewarding environment. At the same time, it affords unique opportunities for certain native, "non-Soviet," sociocultural forms to develop and generate influence.

6. It far exceeds the social and moral parameters of the typical youth organization in that it reflects a keen interest in the intellectual and vocational aptitudes of the participants. The channeling of talented and skillful youth (native and Russian) into commensurate activities tends to increase the personal awareness of their potential and leads to an earlier crystallization of career thoughts. In this manner, the state benefits from the early discovery and cultivation of human talent, and the individual may be catapulted into a potential career line based on his interests and unique attitudes. In short, the Pioneer Palace assists the school in the "sorting and selecting" process.

7. The social climate of the Palace encourages the social interaction of Soviet youth with diverse ethnic and social backgrounds while it contributes to the distinctiveness of nationality and subcultures. There seems to be a marked tendency to discourage the formation of "cliques" and yet to support a certain amount of ethnocentricity in encouraging participation of native and minority cultural groups in art, music, history, and literature. This phenomenon is an illustration of congruency in institutional roles in that both the school and the Palace act to perpetuate the nonthreatening traditional elements of the indigenous culture, thus minimizing discontinuity in its cultural patterns. Native identities are likely to persist and develop new forms in such situations.

8. It provides a constructive outlet for adolescent energies, helping to reduce the inevitable discord between the adult and adolescent worlds. Activities tend to minimize conflict, permitting the articulation of diverse (dominant, native, minority, etc.) value systems in the absence of a stress situation. In this manner, it functions as a "safety valve," managing tension and reducing the strain on the system.

Finally, the Pioneer Palace demonstrates the capacity to place a premium on excellence and performance, with, yet, an almost equivalent emphasis on participation and involvement for its members. Like the school, it exhibits a wide range of behavioral outcomes. Such a range is conducive to the development of skills and performance among talented youth, and it encourages the pursuit of interests and avocations among the less talented. Under these circumstances, motivation toward desirable goals may cease to be a major problem, while the political socialization process is further enhanced.

The Inquiring Activist 17

CITIZENSHIP OBJECTIVES FOR THE 70s

Byron G. Massialas

One wonders how long it will take American educators who deal with citizenship training, or, for that matter, with any aspect of schooling, to realize that we have entered a new era. This era is generally characterized by a demand for radical system change—change in the governance of the schools, in the curriculum they offer, and in the relationships between the teachers and the taught. Actually there are no aspects of education that have not come under attack by student groups. The charges most frequently made by these groups are that the school provides a program that is obsolete and irrelevant and that does not present a realistic picture of society; that the organization of the school and of each individual classroom stifles creativity and reflection; and that the school, instead of being a training ground for democrats, is an authoritarian establishment transmitting, either by design or default, authoritarian values.

That educators have not yet entered the new era in citizenship is beautifully illustrated in the activities of the Committee on Assessing the Progress of Education. The Committee, comprised of many prominent educators and lay representatives, sought to develop objectives in many educational areas including citizenship, science, and writing. In the words of Ralph W. Tyler, one of the architects of National Assessment, the program is intended to "furnish information to all those interested in American education regarding the educational achievements of our children, youth, and young adults, indicating both the progress we are making and the problems we face."[1] The Committee, working with a number of advisory panels, produced in 1969 its "Citizenship Objectives." The publication of the Citizenship Objectives was followed by reports that provide partial assessment

---

[1] National Assessment of Educational Progress, *Citizenship Objectives* (Ann Arbor, Mich.: Committee on Assessing the Progress of Education, 1969).

results[2] and commentary.[3]

Aside from the question of whether or not the whole idea of national assessment and the methods used in obtaining results are compatible with the concepts of educational diversity, the booklet on specific citizenship objectives raises the issue of whether the concept of citizenship merging from this committee's work is relevant to the conditions and needs of youth in modern society. Let us take a closer look at the statement and see what our most distinguished educators tell us we ought to know and value in order to become "good citizens."

The *Citizenship Objectives* identify and develop ten broad goals as follow:

1. Show concern for the welfare and dignity of others.
2. Support rights and freedoms of all individuals.
3. Help maintain law and order.
4. Know the main structure and functions of our government.
5. Seek community improvement through active, democratic participation.
6. Understand problems of international relations.
7. Support rationality in communication, thought, and action on social problems.
8. Take responsibility for our personal development and obligations.
9. Help and respect their own families (Ages 9, 13, 17).
10. Nurture the development of their children as future citizens (Adults).

Under each goal there are several subgoals which vary according to age. There are four age groups to which these goals are directed—9-, 13-, and 17-year-olds and adults. What image of citizenship emerges from the goals and subgoals? At best it is the citizenship of the obsolete past where everybody lives in a beautiful world, where people and governments are responsive to the wishes of the individual, and where everyone behaves or is expected to behave according to the Ten Commandments. The objectives basically contradict most of what we know about human nature and society, how children learn, and the kind of participatory behavior that is realistic and should be expected from youth. Furthermore, the objectives reflect middle-class values and conveniently exclude the poor, the black, and the activists from their reference groups.

Goal 1E expresses the desire that individuals be "loyal to country, to friends, and to other groups whose values they share." The interpretation of this goal for the 9-year-olds includes the following: "They are willing . . . to devote much of their own time and effort to friends, family or larger groups. . . . They feel allegiance to their country as expressed in the Pledge

---

[2] National Assessment of Educational Progress, A Project of the Education Commission of the States, Report 2, *Citizenship: National Results—Partial* (Denver and Ann Arbor, Education Commission of the States, July 1970).

[3] National Assessment of Educational Progress, Report 2, *Citizenship: National Results—Partial, Observations and Commentary of a Panel of Reviewers* (Denver and Ann Arbor, Education Commission of the States, July 1970).

of Allegiance, respect for flag and other symbols." On this objective the 13-year-olds are expected to demonstrate the same behavior as the 9-year-olds. Under 1F the following statement is presented as desirable: "[They] understand and oppose unequal opportunity in the areas of education, housing, employment and recreation." This objective, however, does not apply to either the 9- or the 13-year age group; it applies only to those whose age is 17 or above. Now this is a strange logic to apply to youth (ages 9 and 13)—power of loyalty to family and country, but not power of intelligence to deal with the critical issues of society. The inclusion of the stated behavior in the first instance and the exclusion in the second instance clearly indicate the biases of the authors of the "Citizenship Objectives" about learning and what is worth knowing and feeling. They assume that a young person can learn to be loyal to country (loyalty is a given and nowhere is it defended) but cannot learn how to analyze the critical issues of our times. This assumption contradicts much of the work of contemporary psychologists (e.g., Jerome Brunner, Jacob Getzels, Philip Jackson, and Herbert Thelen) who point to the enormous capacity of children and adolescents to understand and critically analyze the world around them. Also, as Bloom indicates, since most of the powers of intellect are developed at a very early age (possibly the pre-school and early elementary age), it is indefensible to exclude even the groups under 9 from serious discussions of the role of the citizen. Deliberate exclusion of this group violates the rights of children to be raised as early as possible to be reflective thinkers in a democratic society. Since no reflection on the nature of allegiance to country is required in the citizenship objective (it implies, instead, a primordial allegiance to nation), one wonders how desirable this goal of unreflective support is for a modern political order, because it could lead to a system where only a few rule and the rest are their obedient and loyal citizens.

Objective 3 is to "help maintain law and order" or what one might call the "Spiro Agnew" philosophy of citizenship. The objectives in this section show total unawareness and unconcern for the conditions prevailing in the schools and in the larger society. The goals are written as if Berkeley, Columbia, and Chicago never happened; the Vietnam War never existed; and racism has not been a problem of the highest order since America was founded. Let us look closer at some of these objectives.

Objective 3 expresses the desire for youth to "understand the need for law and order." Although understanding is presumably sought, the statements for each age group are prefaced as follows: "Age 9. They know that laws can help protect all individuals . . . ." "Age 13 . . . they recognize the dangers of unfettered violence and gang warfare." "Age 17. They know that law and order serve to: maximize individual liberties and safety; restrict and define punishment; limit the political power of individuals and groups with economic or military strength. . . ." The verbs used in making operational the goals of law and order are "to know" and "to recognize." One would expect that understanding would include the ability to analyze, to synthesize, to evaluate, and the like, as per Bloom's taxonomy. But, "to know" and "to recognize" assume finality, i.e., that the proposition stated as a behavioral goal is *a priori*, correct, good, and acceptable. To accept without question that laws and rules can "help protect all individuals from unfair treatment" is indefensible as a citizenship goal. The Jim Crow laws in the South protected only a group of people, whereas they denied protection to others (often the majority of the people). In the Union of South Africa, the law supports apartheid, thus violating the Charter of the United Nations and the Declaration of Human Rights. In Hitler's Germany, the law supported the Nazi atrocities. Often the law favors those who have the power and the economic capability to study it and take advantage of all the loopholes in it. One can make a long list of cases where the existing law as well as the way it was enforced did not safeguard individual rights and liberties. Given these contingencies, a much more defensible behavioral objective would have been stated as: "They *examine* (or *probe into*) the extent to which laws and rules can help protect all individuals. . . ." "To examine" assumes that the individual is capable of finding out for himself what the real value of the law is. He is not forced to accept someone else's position. In the end the individual might very well find out that law when administered fairly does protect individual rights and liberties.

The "law and order" section of the objectives generally aims at preparing passive citizens who are told, starting at a very early age, what the "right" or "wrong" behavior is. It is revealing that the students' duties and responsibilities, but not their rights and privileges, are stressed. The students are asked to "comply with public law and school rules," "help authorities in specific cases," and "report facts truthfully to authorities." Ethical standards are mentioned, but whose standards they are and how they are arrived at are not discussed. In the absence of any explicit method of arriving at defensible "ethical standards," one can only assume that the adult, white, middle-class standards which underlie all goals hold. For the 9-year-olds the standards include compliance with "school regulations on fighting, dress, behavior on school grounds and in hallways, cheating, tardiness, attendance, and language." For the 17-year-olds, standards of behavior include compliance with "school regulations on parking, fighting, dress, smoking, behavior on school grounds and in hallways, display of affection to opposite sex, cheating, tardiness, attendance, and language." The longest list of "do's" and "don't's" is offered to the 17-year-old. The authors of the "Citizenship Objectives" obviously think that 17 is a dangerous age and that individuals need the guidance of the school to perform adequately. What is conveniently forgotten is that this age group is generally asked to fight wars which were not of their own making. They are old enough for fighting in the wars but not old enough to manage even the most personal matters such as dress or dating.

The objectives stress the importance of participating in student government and school elections. But any observer of the American or world educational scene knows that this type of participation is ineffective and actually prevents students from having a voice in the management of the school. Student councils are at best glorified debating societies whose decisions are either vetoed or ignored by the administration. To consider that internalization of the value of participation in school affairs through the traditional vehicles as a desirable citizenship objective is to fail to examine all the available evidence to the contrary.[4] We know from the work of Marc Chesler and others that participation in traditional-type school clubs and student bodies does not make much difference in the operation of the school. What really makes a difference is organized political action on the part of the students that results in political confrontation, political negotiation, and political compromise. The evidence from the schools and universities suggests that direct action tactics are quite effective in changing both the tempo and the direction of decision-making in the schools. The "Citizenship Objectives," by perpetrating old myths about student participation, fail to respond realistically to the conditions of the present and the future.

The fourth section of "Citizenship Objectives" seeks to have students know the "main structure and functions of our governments." This section is indeed a classical textbook approach to the study of governments, i.e., stressing that the governments always operate in the interests of their citizens, that laws are made through the procedures specified by the Constitution, and that there is a clearcut division of power among the various branches and levels of government. Both the 13- and 17-year-olds are told the "proper" ways to influence governmental policies, which are, in addition to voting in an election, writing to public officials and the mass communication media and joining political parties and other organizations. All of this activity is conducted "by the book," and everybody happily participates in a system which miraculously provides instantaneous feedback and is responsive. What is excluded from all this is an accurate assessment of the importance of the informal, behind-the-scenes manipulations to gain control of the governmental power to make authoritative decisions. The informal political process which is not in the Constitution or in the civic textbooks is underemphasized in the objectives whereas the structural and formal components of government are overemphasized.[5] Throughout, there is a tendency to equate American ideals with American political realities, thus performing a disservice to the American youth which is supposed to attain such critical powers as to "seek full understanding of the several sides of an issue . . . ," "ask questions . . . probe for more complete answers . . . ," "question the authority or evidence for doubtful assertions," ". . . recognize grossly illogical statements," etc. One wonders how youth is to develop full understanding of several sides of an issue when only one side of American public life (the white, middle-class side) is presented to him. It should not be surprising then to find that students rebel against the larger society that posts lofty ideals for itself but never attempts to implement them.

It is amazing that a statement of citizenship objectives for the seven-

---

[4] Marc A. Chesler's work in riot-prone schools is relevant here. See his article "Shared Power and Student Decision-Making," *Educational Leadership*, Vol. 28, No. 1 (October 1970), pp. 9–14.

[5] The "Citizenship Objectives" present almost the same idea of American government as that of the most popular civics textbooks published in recent years. For an analysis of these textbooks, see the author's "American Government" in C. B. Cox and B. G. Massialas, eds., *Social Studies in the United States: A Critical Appraisal* (New York: Harcourt, Brace & World, 1967), pp. 167–95.

ties would be so unrealistic and flat. More amazing, however, is the fact that many American public school boards and administrations are convinced of the worthiness and defensibility of these goals, thus allowing their students to be tested on them.[6] The available partial assessment results support the proposition that students have distorted and quite unrealistic views of our society and their role in it. In general they believe they can influence political decisions by engaging in the activities often mentioned in their civics texts—voting in an election or writing a letter to a Congressman. One can only anticipate the frustration of these young people when they discover that the real world is not the one described in their civics or history textbooks. Sooner or later youngsters discover that the textbook world is for the classroom and for the teacher and that it definitely should not be (and cannot be) applied to the outside. For the outside world, what one learns from friends and from observing actual life is most appropriate.

For some youngsters there are traumatic transitions that must be made from the classroom with its Polyanna look on life to the harsh world—from the ideal to the practical. Some youngsters make this transition fairly easily. For some it is painful and may result in exhibiting defiant or deviant behavior. The majority get used to playing two roles: one in the school or family, the other with friends in the real world. For many the duality of roles (which in many respects are in conflict with each other) will persist in adult life. When they become parents themselves, the roles will again be performed: one with their children (i.e., this is a rosy world) and the other with the system (i.e., how do I fool the city assessor and get a break in my real estate tax). This great gap between the ideal and the real and the conflicting role performances are thus perpetuated from one generation to the next.

CITIZENSHIP OBJECTIVES AND THE BELIEFS OF YOUTH: ARE THEY COMPATIBLE?

The discrepancy between the ideal and the real which is illustrated in the analysis of the "Citizenship Objectives" is well-documented in the studies reported in this book. Let us try to briefly recapture the main findings from these studies and point to their educational implications.

Goldstein, who reviewed elementary social studies textbooks as well as selected curriculum guides used by major school districts, confirmed the observation that neither source provides children with a realistic view of the world. The U.S. government is always depicted as a "benevolent Santa Claus" which has the interest of people at heart and "selflessly is fighting for freedom." Black America is generally not represented. Social problems such as unequal distribution of income, problems of housing, of ethnic minorities, and the like are left out. Only middle-class white America is given a prevalent role in the textbooks and curriculum guides.

[6] There were 100,000 respondents in the partial assessment completed in February 1970. See *Citizenship: National Results—Partial, op. cit.*

We know from psychological studies and the work by Hess and Torney that the ages of early childhood and elementary school are extremely important in one's development of basic orientations toward one's environment. Yet the learnings that are stressed in the school and in the classroom at this level are learnings that do not hold in the real world. Under the influence of the school, children are expected to learn the ideals of the political system although later on they have to unlearn all this and find out for themselves how the system really works. Some of these children, cushioned by their teachers and parents against the outside world, will grow up without knowing that societies have problems and that there are ways one can go about resolving them.

The studies reported by Statt and Glenn give us an empirical base to examine how children acquire citizenship values and to look into the content of these values. Statt, basing his findings and interpretations on Piaget's developmental psychology, shows that high status American children as compared to Canadian children of similar backgrounds are more ethnocentric or "geocentric." American children seem to know more about the international system than Canadian children. The observation that the rituals and symbols of nationalism (the Pledge of Allegiance, the display of the flag, etc.) were much more apparent in the American school than in the Canadian school is certainly in line with what we know about American classrooms. Although Statt does not attribute any direct cause and effect relationship to the presence of these symbols on one hand, and children's ethnocentric tendencies on the other, there is something to be said about the general milieu that produces this. Statt suggests that the entire society is responsible for these tendencies. Certainly, one cannot overestimate the press of society's norms on children's attitudes toward and views of other people. But as all of the authors contend, the school, which could have taken a leadership role in this area, is actually reinforcing these "geocentric" predispositions. The teachers, the textbooks used in class, the organization of the schools and the general nonparticipatory environment all contribute their share to children's parochialism and ethnocentrism. Since it has been shown that most educators assume that young children cannot think for themselves, schools do not provide any option and require that kids learn and value the ideals of the adult middle class.

Glenn clearly shows how young children have been socialized into accepting the textbook tenets of good citizenship—to be loyal and obedient to the government and to show respect for authority. The rural or inner-city children much more than the suburban children learn the hard way that the government does not really care for them and should not be trusted. Also these children have a more limited view than their suburban counterparts of their ability to understand how government operates and to influence its decisions.

One of the most significant findings in the Glenn study is the transfer value of school participation. The children who participate in classroom activity, as opposed to those who do not, feel more politically efficacious themselves, or perceive their families and neighbors to be able to influence the governmental machinery. This finding, which certainly needs to be replicated and further elaborated, suggests that feelings of efficacy and participation within the school may bring about feelings of participation or actual participation in the larger political system.

When it comes to means of bringing about political change, elementary school children's ideas coincide with those of the civics textbooks and with the "Citizenship Objectives" that we reviewed in the preceding section. Writing a letter to the President and voting in an election appear with monotonous regularity as the best means to change government. Very few children favor the activist's ways to bring about change. One wonders how coincidental it is that the activist approach to change (e.g., direct confrontation, protest, or demonstration) is also conspicuously absent from the official civic education programs in the schools.

Shifting the focus to secondary school youth, Ellen Shantz reports some very interesting findings from a suburban school. At the level of political *interest,* students score relatively high. When it comes to political *action,* however, even on such things as discussing public affairs with friends or going out of the way to find appropriate reading materials on politics, students score relatively low. It is this discrepancy between the abstract and the actual (i.e., between the expression of interest in politics and the actual participation in the political process) that confronts the educator willing to create the conditions for responsible and critical citizenship. The individuals who have these tendencies are the political spectators, i.e., the ones who usually join the ranks of Mr. Nixon's "Silent Majority." As we see throughout this book, the general conditions prevailing in the schools contribute to the creation of the "Silent Majority"—the gutless individual who hides behind the anonymity of the masses and is not willing to take a public stand on what he believes in.

Billings provides us with excellent insights into the makeup of a black activist. The black activist exhibits more sensitivity to the realities of the system—he knows, for example, that traditional institutions within the school (e.g., student government) do not bring about change. Change comes as a result of aggregation and interest articulation—a principle that scholars of political behavior and system change have firmly established. The black activist youth, unlike the rest of the youth of their age, learn this important principle on their own. It is a trial-and-error process which sometimes may lead to very severe personal and group punishment and painful experiences. But through these processes they soon find out that confrontation politics— against the teachers, the administrators, and generally the oppressive white world—work out. They soon realize that a small group of committed activists have the potential power to close the school and, through this, to bring about needed change. Although Billings does not deal directly with this, he suggests that the distinguishing feature of the black activist (as opposed to the white activist) is his sense of efficacy—he believes in the ability of the black to control his destiny and influence his own future. Thus black power concepts replace older concepts of civil rights groups as the most effective means to alter a society characterized by racist policies as well as segregationist individual attitudes.

Ehmann, in a way, confirms the propositions advanced by Billings regarding the political efficacy of black students. Black students do not seem to be affected very much by classroom discussions of social issues. Possibly they learn the issues involved and the means for political action in peer groups or in "street-corner society." The white students, on the other hand, respond well to direct discussion of controversial issues in the classroom as far as their political efficacy is concerned. The same general findings are produced by Levenson who indicates that blacks who are exposed to a civics course have a lower sense of participatory responsibility than those who did not have such exposure. As Ehman points out, the overall effect of issues discussion (presumably in an open classroom climate) reinforces and promotes feelings of efficacy among students of high-school age. Students who had more than five semesters of social studies seem to show significant increase in their sense of political efficacy as opposed to students who had fewer than five semesters of work in the field. Since four semesters of social studies are normally required in the senior high school, the extra work taken is usually electives. These electives, which traditionally have not been taken seriously by the teachers, the publishers, or state departments of education and accrediting associations which control curricula, may have a built-in factor which frees the political capabilities of students. Whether the factor rests with the teacher responsible for the course, the materials used in it, or the students who are attracted to enroll in it is an open question and certainly merits extensive investigation in the future.

Levenson produces evidence which corroborates the notions that run throughout the book on the politically passive role of the teacher in discharging his classroom responsibilities. Teachers generally stress obedience, not participation, are quite reluctant to deal openly with political controversy, and do not take appropriate measures to guarantee the free and intelligent discussion of socially significant issues. Given this overall performance of teachers and the quality of the textbooks they use, the finding that civics courses are very poor predictors of participatory behavior among students is not difficult to explain. Levenson's article provides the necessary data to substantiate the claim I make later that unless the teacher consistently emphasizes controversial issues and encourages the students to participate directly and intelligently in exploring and resolving these issues, the number of civics courses (or any other courses) taken at school will continue to be unrelated to the development of efficacious and active citizens.

Moving into a cross-national framework, Farnen and German offer valuable information on the political beliefs of youth in five Western societies—the United States, Sweden, West Germany, England, and Italy. Overall, there are no fundamental differences in youth's attitudes toward their governments—in the five countries under study, young people are generally supportive of the government, and they feel efficacious in changing it. It is most interesting to see how many of the results of studies of youth in the United States apply to the other four nations as well. As in the United States, for example, the impact of the civics curriculum on the political socialization of youth in the four countries is negligible. Students do not become more efficacious or knowledgeable as a result of having been taught about the governmental machinery or the history of political institutions. There are many possible explanations of this, some of which are as follows: (a) The materials presented to youth are often repetitive. U.S. History, for example, is normally taught to American youth three times—at the fifth, eighth, and eleventh grades. It is basically the same story told in narrative fashion for three full years. (b) The program of studies or the individual courses are too general—they attempt to cover a little bit of everything; as a consequence the student cannot concentrate and deal in sufficient depth with any topic. (This seems to be the inference drawn from a study in Sweden.) (c) Since social issues are largely ignored or glossed over, the civics program provides information which is not relevant or realistic. (d) The content of the subject is dull and unimaginative. Most civics and government books in Europe and in the United States do not provide motivational devices to get students truly interested in the subject—there is very little creative involvement either through visuals, games, or case studies. In England where there have been some concentrated efforts to deal directly with social conflict and other provocative topics, there are some positive results in the political attitudes of youth. However, the official curriculum in England as in all the other countries is still history-dominated in both content and method. (e) As mentioned repeatedly by several authors, classroom instructional strategies have a great deal to do with political socialization of children and youth. A classroom characterized by expository teaching styles rather than by conditions where students participate in generating and testing their own ideas does not contribute to positive political attitudes. The organization and administration of the school have also a great deal to do with political outcomes as we see when we examine the findings of Wittes and Blackburn and Lindquist. As German and Farnen indicate, there are other factors such as age, socioeconomic status, and membership in extra-class organizations that may make a significant difference in how youth respond to political questions. This is why it is extremely difficult to make generalizations about the influence of the schools—there are many other institutions that may reinforce or negate its efforts.

As indicated by Heggan, the Colombian educational system is like the European and the United States systems in that it presents youth with idealized versions of political life. Heggan, who did not rely exclusively on questionnaires but interviewd students and visited classes, found out that Colombian schools were quite successful in instilling in youth love for their leaders and acceptance of democratic values. This was especially true of first-year high-school students. It is interesting though to see that although positive orientations toward the leaders and the country were expressed, there were no cognitive bases to support these orientations. Students demonstrated faith in and support for the system but could not provide defensible reasons—either grounded in logic or in the operations of the real world—to substantiate their faith. Students operated under the naive notion that citizens acting individually could affect the political order. Parties, pressure groups, communications media were not mentioned as playing an important role in Colombian political and social life. This indicates that indoctrination rather than reflection is the dominant mode of politicizing young people in schools. This mode has a striking resemblance to the mode inherent in the United States' "Citizenship Objectives" which we discussed in the first section of this chapter. This mode assumes that young people, although not able to think for themselves, should develop life-long attachments to political leaders and existing political institutions. Of course as students reach the higher grades, they begin to see how the political world operates and they witness the discrepancies between the ideal and the real. Heggan's observation that the greatest change in participatory interest among students takes place in those areas that are excluded from the formal curriculum is extremely important and applies to other countries as well. The moral of this is that the schools, if they cannot deal truthfully with the political life of a nation, should get out of civic education altogether and let children and youth acquire their political know-how on their own.

The study reported by Lewis is one of the very few we have from African countries south of the Sahara. The majority of the students that Lewis studied seem to feel that they can effectively participate in family or school decisions. It is interesting, however, to observe that when participation in conflict situations is introduced the school participation rate drops from 65 percent to 54 percent. One wonders how low the expectations for participation would be if real controversial issues were presented—i.e., student discipline, dress codes, teacher competence, and grades. The schools in Sierra Leone would probably be no exception to the general rule that students can participate in trivial matters but not in important ones. Even at that, however, it is important to note that more students indicated participation in decision-making in peer groups than in school or family. If, as Lewis indicates, it is reasonable to assume that participation in nonpolitical groups such as family, school, and peers may transfer into strictly political activity, and if the peer group is the most responsive, then we may wish to promote systematically the formation of peer groups and the availability of a range of decision-making experiences in them. This observation and corresponding recommendation is made by Wittes as well.

Although Sierra Leonians are pretty confident that they can participate in nonpolitical group decisions, they do not share the same level of confidence regarding governmental responsiveness to the demands of the average citizen. Generally the youth felt that public officials were not interested in the problems that people had. The strongest sense of efficacy (in governmental as well as in nonpolitical participatory activity mentioned before) was registered among students with an urban background from a relatively high socioeconomic class. In this respect Sierra Leonians, again, were no exception to the pattern observed in Western societies, i.e., that the more educated, the more urban, and the higher the socioeconomic status of the student, the higher his sense of efficacy to influence decisions in the political system.

Wittes explores different organizational arrangements of secondary schools as perceived by students and develops four different typologies—

ranging from diffuse schools where the sources of decision-making and power are not clearly seen (the completely laissez-faire situation) to differentiated schools where the decision-making process is clearly defined in terms of the various persons who by virtue of their positions participate in it. In political language this type might be called a legal-rational system. In the first type the overall power level is perceived as being low, whereas the opposite is true in the differentiated school. The research that Wittes has done gives us new insights into the kind of school system that is conducive to student feelings of participation both in the school and outside it. Although not all the hypothesized relationships held, some of the findings confirmed many ideas about optimal school environments for student participation. For example, the students who do have successful interpersonal relations (low discrepant individuals in the peer group) and who perceive the organizational structure of their school as being differentiated have a higher internal sense of personal control than those who are not integrated well in the peer group and are identified with a type of school other than differentiated (especially diffuse or local control types).

Successful peer group membership and clearly established but equitably divided power roles in the school are related to an individual's belief that he can control his own life. The implications of this finding are very important for the school—first, in the kind of organization that is desirable for maximum participation and, second, in the kind of support to peer groups that needs to be given. If a legal-rational system of governance exists and if students as well as faculty are truly participating members of a group of peers, then the political efficacy of all is bound to increase. This may produce an environment where learning about political participation takes place as part of the formal curriculum and actual practice in participation accompanies the formal learning. Although a great deal more needs to be done to establish many of the relationships suggested above, it is reasonable to expect that a total (not partial) participatory milieu in the school will have the best chance to produce the citizen who can cope well with the social problems of the seventies.

The cleavage between political youth and traditional schools is dramatically illustrated in the case study by Blackburn and Lindquist. The evidence presented on university level decision-making supplements the research findings of all authors in this book which indicate that: (a) schools are not meeting responsibly the demands of youth, and (b) there is a great disparity between what is taught as the ideal and what actually happens within the boundaries of the school.

Although the above are generalizations that hold for all levels of education, there are also unique findings that make the case study very important. For example, the cleavage between the old and the new manifests itself not only between teachers and students but between different groups of teachers. In our case there is a basic split over student participation in decision-making between two major departments—the Department of Curriculum and Instruction and the Department of the Behavioral Sciences in Education. As Blackburn and Lindquist point out, the members of the first department represent the "Ed School" image (i.e., the teachers of teachers), whereas the members of Behavioral Sciences are primarily researchers who apply the concepts and methods of the social and behavioral sciences to the study of educational problems. Although it is easy to stereotype Ed School people, many of the negative faculty attributes of their most representative department (i.e., Curriculum and Instruction) are supported by the available evidence. Many of the charges leveled against teacher trainers in schools of education are true. Such charges as emphasis on the trivial rather than the important in "methods" courses, little or no faculty familiarization with the scholarly findings of the academic disciplines, systematic avoidance of social issues on controversial professional problems, a forced separation between the theoretical and the practical, a stress on untenable "professional" course requirements and obsolete rules regarding teacher certification, and, conversely, denial of program flexibility are to this writer generally justifiable, since they describe accurately prevailing practices. The Curriculum and Instruction professor is the true personification of the Education Establishment that much has been written about. Although the behavioral scientists have their faults also (i.e., in this case they underestimated the importance of physical presence at the faculty meeting deciding on extent of student participation), they do have a much more open and forward look on many of the issues of education than do their colleagues in curriculum and instruction, and they are prone to apply systematically the findings of the social sciences to the process of education. It is certainly no coincidence that most of the major breakthroughs in recent years have come from behavioral and social scientists—Piaget, Bruner, Bloom, Hess, Gagné, Cremin, to name but a few. There are virtually no breakthroughs issuing from the teacher education—"curriculum specialists" groups. In spite of all this, the old teacher-educator is still in control in many of the large schools of education around the country. Where one of the group does not occupy the main power position, the group makes sure that the dean would be sympathetic to its philosophy. In the case study reported here, the new dean, who had just come from a position with the government, was instrumental in making some changes (e.g., the issue on student participation in school governance), but his basic educational philosophy was in line with "Establishment" philosophy.

The great reluctance on the part of many faculty members to engage students in decision-making in many respects contradicts what these same professors advocate in their education courses. One of the main themes of education, which both establishment and anti-establishment faculty espouse, is participation of the child in his own learning experiences, thus forming a "democratic classroom." In this type of classroom everyone—not just the teacher—is given the opportunity to express his views. Unfortunately, many of those who preach those doctrines are not inclined to apply them to their own situation. Their classes are usually characterized by a dull lecture-type discourse on irrelevant topics, and the locus of power in the organizational structure of their school rests with the few privileged ones. The rest of the faculty is either silent or when vocal and in opposition to the status quo, is conveniently removed from all major decisions. The teachers-in-training, who are usually middle-of-the-road youngsters in comparison with students in other departments, being reinforced by the "School of Education" model, become the future teachers of America. No wonder that these teachers are neither sensitive nor concerned with the real issues confronting the nation's youth.

The chapters by Barakat, Hanf, and Cave not only provide us with insights into the Bahraini, Kuwaiti, Jordanian, Lebanese, Congolese, and Soviet-Uzbek societies but also point to agencies other than education that influence the political socialization of youth—family, religion, and youth organizations.

Barakat dispels some myths about the assumed political compatibility between parents and children in Arab societies. Contrary to commonly held beliefs among Western scholars, Arab students in the two countries under study show as much or greater generational political differences as American students. For example, there is a trend toward more independent political thought among the Jordanians than among the Americans. However, the Jordanians more so than the Americans identify politically with the father rather than the mother. The Arab father still plays a dominant role in the family whereas in the American family the father and mother share influence roles. Among Kuwaitis the generational gap is more apparent than in the other two groups—72 percent of the boys and 60 percent of the girls identify with neither parent. In the Kuwaiti family the mother appears to conform to the model of the woman as the passive partner, a model that prevails in many developing countries of the Middle East.

The relatively great intergenerational differences among the Kuwaitis are explained, in part, by educational factors. Where the education of the parents does not even approximate the education of the offspring, the generational differences are sharp. This is shown rather clearly in Kuwait where, due to the sudden affluence of the country as a result of the exploitation of available oil reserves, the availability of formal education has been increased dramatically in less than the span of one generation. In most of the Western societies the educational gaps were bridged slowly, over a relatively long period of time, thus making the results (i.e., the political beliefs of the offspring) not as strikingly different from those of their parents. As Barakat indicates, the educational gap between Kuwaiti parents and their children and the apparent political differences reflect the chasm between their two worlds—one of the nineteenth century, the other of the twentieth. Barakat's study also shows the importance of examining carefully the cultural setting of a society and the main institutions that are part of that society in order to understand and explain the citizenship values of the young. Just transplanting assumptions about and evaluation instruments of the political beliefs of youth from one society to another is simply not adequate—cultural differences need to be considered carefully in conducting cross-national comparisons.

The study reported by Hanf penetrates quite deeply into the political and social fabric of the Congo and Lebanon. His findings are important and they further indicate the necessity to look into factors that lie outside the school but are politically relevant. Lebanese students seem to be more sensitive to political issues and have a higher interest in politics than Congolese students. Although the selective recruitment patterns of the respective universities may explain this difference in political interest, a study of the prevailing political conditions in each country may also partially explain the results. For example, in the Congo there is an absence of multi-party politics, whereas Lebanon is characterized by a multitude of parties (many of them formed on religious-ethnic basis) to which 21 percent of the interviewees belonged. (Here an interesting comparison with the corresponding age group in America can be made—American college students rarely belong to a political party.) In the Congo the individual feels separated from the government—his political efficacy is somewhat low and his political cynicism appears to be high. In contrast, the Lebanese seem to be sensitive to the major political problems of the nation (e.g., the issue of Palestine, the discrepancy between being loyal to an independent Lebanon as opposed to a United Arab Nation) and they have a rather positive and "activist" attitude toward the solution of these problems.

It is also quite interesting to see that the two systems share a number of things in common but that there are also differences. For example, students in both countries, evidently since both were under French influence prior to independence, have a strong affinity toward deGaulle. Identification with the other leaders, however, varies both between and within countries. Generally the Christian universities favor Western political leaders, whereas the opposite is true for the non-Christian. Active participation in religious activity (especially among Christians) is important in predicting political interest and commitment among Lebanese students. The opposite pattern holds for Congolese students.

The study by Hanf again points to the difficulty in isolating the relevant factors in the political socialization of students. As the two cases illustrate, when ethnicity, religion, and school are intermingled, the research may not tap the relative significance of each. More detailed and penetrating studies are needed to explore further the insights presented by Hanf.

Cave provides many insightful observations on the role of the Young Pioneers in the socialization of Soviet youth. Unlike its American counterparts, the youth organization in the USSR is integrated into the activities of the school and has an explicit political function. The combination of influences from the school and from the Young Pioneers provides for a very powerful environment in which youth are motivated to develop politically relevant behaviors. This situation contrasts sharply with the prevalent pattern in the United States where the purposes of youth organizations and peer groups not only are unrelated to those of the school but are quite antithetical to and contradict the school's political and social goals.

It is quite interesting to note that many of the things that the authors of this book recommend for the schools from which their research emerged —the need for surfacing the creative and leadership abilities of youth, for developing a sense of community and an esprit de corps, for giving youth the opportunity to deal with the real world in their own terms—are things that Cave presents as being currently incorporated in Pioneer organizations. On the other hand, however, some of the indoctrinational aspects of these organizations are not compatible with the main idea that the contributing authors of this book advocate, which is basically the creation of an atmosphere in the school where youth examine reflectively the political and social systems in which they live and offer and implement through action recommendations for system change.

Toward a Radical System Change

The evidence suggests that the school, whether in a Western country or a non-Western one, has not performed a leadership role in the political process. In the politicization of children and youth the school maintained an attitude of passivity and compliance. The school generally took its directives from the power groups in the community and traditionally sanctioned or promoted an education that was racist in content. It also enforced certain conditions that negated individual initiative and freedom. The schools aiming at "training for citizenship" introduced strict discipline and unquestionable respect for authority. We have already seen how the "Citizenship Objectives" published in 1969 still continue to reflect this traditional orientation which considers education as disciplining students.

The school and community reinforced each other in their approach to citizenship education. For example, until recently the U.S. judicial system supported the schools in interpreting their notion of good citizenship. The courts generally upheld the action of school boards to expel students or dismiss teachers for showing disrespect for authority.[7] The courts historically helped schools impart in American youth patriotic feelings—patriotism usually interpreted in emotional terms, concentrating on violations of compulsory flag salute, Pledge of Allegiance, etc. The suppression of individualistic behavior by the schools was also ratified by some courts.

The Tinker case, however, provided a major departure in this traditional alliance that existed between the courts and the schools.[8] This particular case involved a group of students who were suspended from school because they violated an anti-armband regulation that was instituted by the principals of the Des Moines schools. The Supreme Court of the United States ruled that the rights of speech and expression (First Amendment of the Constitution) applied to secondary school students. The wearing of the armband was construed to be part of free speech. The majority decision stated that "state-operated schools may not be enclaves of totalitarianism" and that "school officials do not possess absolute authority over their students." The decision further pronounced that students may not be regarded as "closed-circuit recipients of only that which the State chooses to communicate." Rather, the school should provide the student the opportunity to become a participant in the educational process. This would possibly lead to "an enlightened citizenry possessed of the critical powers necessary

---

[7] Richard L. Berkman, "Students in Court: Free Speech and the Functions of Schooling in America," *Harvard Educational Review*, Vol. 40, No. 4 (November 1970), pp. 567–95.

[8] Tinker v. Des Moines Independent School District, 393 U.S. 503, 89 S. Ct. 733 (1969).

to sustain a democracy."[9] Reduction of the traditional authority of teachers and administrators would actually strengthen education in its role for citizenship training because "the nation's future depends upon leaders trained through wide exposure to that robust exchange of ideas which discovers truth 'out of a multitude of tongues, rather than through any kind of authoritative selection.' "[10]

In spite of the ruling mentioned above, there is a great deal more to be done on the larger society's part to bring about needed change in the schools. However, the schools themselves, in order to be functional (i.e., instill an activist outlook—an outlook which prompts youth to involve itself directly in political and social change) should introduce radical and complete changes in their operational procedures and in their curriculum. Here are some possibilities:

1. The traditional form of school governance needs to be drastically changed. The separate and unequal streams of decision-making, one for students, one for faculty, and one for administrators, with administrators invariably having veto power over all the decisions, must be immediately replaced by a democratic procedure. The traditional student councils and faculty assemblies have not provided for participatory behavior. In these meetings only trivial matters are discussed, and the main protagonists (students, administrators, and teachers) never come face to face to discuss issues. The important decisions are all made in the principal's office.

A new format of school governance would be predicated on the assumption that there are no areas of decision-making in which students cannot participate. Once this decision-making group becomes operational and is institutionalized, its procedures and the roles assigned to various members of the group are communicated to all (students, parents, teachers, district school officials) and are made explicit. Student handbooks which include the duties and obligations of students as well as their rights and freedoms should be written for each school. Similar handbooks for faculty and administrators should be available. Thus individual rights of all the participants in school decisions are promoted and safeguarded. This operational procedure helps to bring about a system of mutual responsibility and accountability.

Although the exact form that such a decision-making group takes could not be spelled out in the abstract, it should provide a tripartite arrangement where power is shared by all concerned. This can be accomplished through a six-member executive board where students, faculty, and administrators are represented by two members each. This executive board makes all policies in the school and serves as court of appeals—any decision can be appealed by any member of the three groups. The same tripartite representation can also be accomplished in policy-making committees (e.g., curriculum, personnel, student activities) which are appointed by the board to handle problems in a specific area. The rules made by these groups are strictly adhered to by all. The principal has no veto power.

2. In addition to an organizational structure in the school which promotes

[9] Berkman, p. 581.
[10] Tinker v. Des Moines, p. 739.

participation in decisions, there is need to deal with the process of decision-making in formal school instruction. Whether the subject is home economics, mathematics, sciences, art, or civics, thorough and penetrating discussions of student involvement in the political life of the school and of the nation should take place. The legal rights of students and faculty should be carefully reviewed. Available handbooks should be examined and their implications for decision-making in the classroom, in the school, and in the community should be explored. Documents produced by organizations such as the American Federation of Teachers, the National Education Association, the American Association of University Professors, the American Civil Liberties Union, and material published by school boards, as well as decisions issued by the courts, can provide the basis for intelligent classroom discussion.[11] Particular cases where individual rights were involved, preferably in the students' own school, should be used as the case material to which the principles from the readings mentioned above should apply.

Some math, language, or science teachers may question spending classroom time discussing decision-making and individual participation in it. What they need to understand, however, is that decision-making takes place whenever human beings come together—whether in a mathematics class, a science laboratory, a gym, or a school choir. The topic is as relevant to the mathematics classroom as it is to the civics or humanities classroom. Also, as research indicates, unless decision-making is studied and practiced in all of the aspects of schooling, the school's influence on the individual will be minimal. As it was pointed out before, as the individual grows older he needs a more and more powerful environment to change basic value orientations that were formed early in life. A powerful environment means that all components of the school should reinforce each other.

What the mathematics and science teachers need to understand is that the problems of our time are not basically problems of math and science. The problems are human problems which need to be addressed in human rather than mechanical terms. If there is any way that the principles of mathematics and of science can apply to the resolution of human conflict, this should be clearly done in the classroom—with real students dealing with real problems. To assume that math and science provide their own inherent relevance is no longer defensible.

3. There is an urgent need to deal explicitly and in an intellectually honest way with the pressing social issues of our time. Whether it is the Israeli and fedayeen problem in Lebanon, the separatist movement in Canada, the question of Northern Ireland in the United Kingdom, or the problem of racism in the United States, schools in the respective countries need to address themselves to social and political controversy. Given a climate of academic freedom, students and teachers must study and reflect upon the main problems of society—the use of drugs, war as an instrument of national

---

[11] See for example, Student Rights Project, *Student Rights Handbook* (New York: New York Civil Liberties Union, n.d.); *Rights and Responsibilities of High School Students* (Board of Education, City School District of the City of New York, September 1970); Jean Strouse, *Up Against the Law: The Legal Rights of People Under 21* (New York: New American Library, 1970).

policy, unequal distribution of income, injustices in the interpretation and execution of law, unreflective population growth, etc. In a survey conducted in 1970 for Rockefeller's Task Force on Youth, 55 percent of the college students interviewed believed that the United States is basically a racist nation.[12] Over one-fourth of the respondents also believed that "today's American society is characterized by injustice, insensitivety, lack of candor and inhumanity." Fifty-six percent of the students also indicated that the military needs fundamental reform.

The problems to which these expressions of belief refer are not normally within the established school offerings. Given their importance to the individual and the society, these social problems need to become a part of the formal school curriculum. Each subject should have its social issues components. For instance, biology could deal with the bio-medical aspects of family planning; science with pollution; home economics with abortion; social studies with race relations; language-arts with the inhumanity of man to man; foreign languages with cases of extreme ethnocentrism, etc. Whatever the vocational and occupational aspirations of the students, critical analysis of social issues is both intellectually and psychologically defensible. Dr. Chandler McC. Brooks who headed a group of physicians organizing a visiting scholar series at Brooklyn's Downstate Medical Center criticized the narrow specialization of the doctors and made a plea for including social issues in their program of studies. He stated: "As we learn to conquer some of our infectious diseases, some of the physical disease, even some of our genetic diseases, we have got to go into some of our social distresses—the problems of crowding, contamination, economic injustice, anxiety, insecurity, because these cause sickness."[13]

4. Civics and history courses need to be drastically revamped. Ninety-five percent of the content of these courses such as descriptive accounts of the "100-Years War," how a bill becomes a law, the naming of the U.S. presidents or the European monarchs must be deleted. The chronological and narrative history starting with Mesopotamia and, at best, finishing with the Congress of Vienna of 1815 must be given up completely. The enumeration of various branches of government in each level and the description of the various structural components should also be set aside. Instead, civics and history ought to deal in depth with generalizable case studies taken from any relevant historical period or region of the world. These programs ought to stress the skills of inquiry—given a springboard, students ought to be able to hypothesize about existing relationships or be able to take a position regarding a value conflict. The hypotheses and value positions must be clarified and explicitly grounded. Also, these programs should be multidisciplinary and have a cross-cultural focus. Value clarification and analysis of social issues should become focal.

An attempt to develop high-school programs meeting the above criteria was recently made in a work entitled "World History through Inquiry."[14]

[12] "Student Social Criticism Rises," *Tallahassee Democrat*, December 19, 1970, p. 5.
[13] *St. Petersburg Times*, December 21, 1970.
[14] Byron G. Massialas and Jack Zevin, *World History through Inquiry*, 9 units (Chicago: Rand McNally, 1969 and 1970).

The program uses original materials and case studies to treat in depth certain problems and issues—political elites, social stratification, problems of unequal distribution of income, racism, war and peace. The materials are organized in 60 to 90 page units under such titles as "Social Structure," "Man and his Environment," "Cultural Exchange," "Political Systems," "Religious-Philosophical Systems," etc. The way the materials are presented invites students to develop ideas on their own and to deal critically with pressing social issues. The program is future-oriented, encourages students to manipulate data, and makes a direct attempt to get them to surface their own values and examine them openly.

The ideas and the rationale upon which this program was based are sharply developed by Alvin Toffler in *Future Shock*.[15] Under the heading "Education in the Future Tense," Toffler makes a plea that education be data-, skill-, future-, and value-oriented. He proposes that we design "contingency curricula" which are "educational programs aimed at training people to handle problems that not only do not exist now, but which may, in fact, never materialize."[16] The person of the present and the future must be able to deal with alternative value choices. As Toffler points out, " . . . the person who lacks a clear grasp of his own values (whatever these may be) is progressively crippled. Yet the more crucial the question of values becomes, the less willing our present schools are to grapple with it." Thus we need a dramatic shift in our school programs—from exclusion to inclusion. We need to deal with values directly and in justifiable ways. But although accepting problems of value to be part of the formal curriculum, schools should not try to indoctrinate students in accepting the values that a particular community or a group of school teachers holds. Teachers and supporting communities should accept the notion that no particular values are taught—values are critically examined in the open forum of ideas. The teacher, although he may take a stand in the classroom on a particular value problem, always takes the position of "defensible partisanship." He is partisan not to a particular ideology or set of values but to the process of examining values in the open and providing explicit grounds in support of positions. Given the unrealistic picture of society that our students get in the classroom, there needs to be a total and complete shift to create a school environment where students deal with the real world of the present and the future. For example, instead of providing obsolete information on the structural components of government (e.g., the number of federal agencies in a given department or the number of readings a bill needs to go through before it goes to the President for his signature) students ought to be presented with all the psychological and sociological evidence of how political leaders make decisions, how various pressure groups influence them, and what the actual power of the average citizen is. In addition to analyzing the behavioral information on decision-making, students ought also to be given the opportunity to apply some of the principles learned in a formal setting to negotiating a new policy with the decision-makers in their school,

---

[15] Alvin Toffler, *Future Shock* (New York: Random House, 1970).
[16] Ibid., p. 365.

to taking group action in a community issue, or operating as a pressure group to influence local politicians. Through these processes students begin to understand their government better and to feel competent in changing it.

5. The evidence suggests that students become more politically efficacious when the classroom operates in the true spirit of inquiry. In such a classroom the teacher or the student may provide the springboards for discussion. The students, however, develop ideas and positions and test them against available evidence. Ideas or positions are challenged constantly by all. The student soon learns that grounds in support of positions or hypotheses are important. The better grounds one has, the more likely that his ideas will be accepted. The student also learns that it is easier to debate, adjudicate, and, when necessary, compromise social ideas if the ideas are expressed in clear and communicable language. When ideas are well-defined, disagreements may disappear, since often these disagreements result from confusion over the use of terms and certain expressions.

The teacher needs to create the psychological conditions that will support true inquiry. He rewards students for creative work and always encourages or praises them for their participation in discussion. The teacher always needs to challenge students to defend and clarify their ideas. Through his style and manner of presentation, the teacher makes clear from the very beginning that all statements or claims to knowledge are to be examined and then accepted or rejected in the open forum of ideas. He develops and constantly reinforces the notion that neither authors of books nor teachers and students are immune from questioning and detailed probing.

In our research we find that classrooms generally fall into three categories—the expository, inquiry-nonprobing, and inquiry-probing classes.[17] In the expository class, the teacher does most of the talking—his students have very little or no chance to present and test their own ideas. In the inquiry-nonprobing class, students participate a great deal, but the teacher does not challenge these ideas by asking for the grounds that support them and for clarification of their meaning. In the inquiry-probing class, the teacher and the students continuously probe into the evidence that purports to provide the grounds for certain propositions or value judgments. They also probe into the meaning of these propositions.

The differences among students resulting from participation in these three types of classrooms are striking. The inquiry-probing teacher is liked the most by the students. Students in the inquiry-probing classroom gain more cognitive understanding of the world and feel more competent in changing it than in the other types of classrooms. The student in the inquiry-probing class has a better grasp of his cognitive powers than do the students in the other types of classes. He is more prepared to face the problems of the future than his counterparts in the expository or inquiry-nonprobing classes.

---

[17] B. G. Massialas, Nancy Sprague, and Jo Ann Sweeney, *Structure and Process of Inquiry into Social Issues in Secondary Schools*: Volume III (Ann Arbor: University of Michigan, 1970). (Research performed pursuant to contract OEC-7-061678-2942 with Office of Education.)

Conclusion

This book examined the conditions that promote a sense of or actual participation in decisions among youth. We emphasized the conditions within the school and we examined the role of administrators, teachers, peers, the formal curriculum, the school organization, and extracurricular activity. In addition to these, we looked into some of the important agents that relate to the political socialization of the child, such as the family and religion. We found, generally, that when the individual is given the opportunity to participate in decisions whether in school, in the family, or with friends, he develops a high sense of efficacy—he feels he can change the system. This individual is also motivated to learn more and to become a productive member of his society.

This book has also examined the objectives of citizenship in the United States and selected countries of the world and found them to be completely unrealistic and inconsistent with basic human rights and the movement away from the nation-state to concepts of world culture. Citizenship objectives must drastically change to reflect accurately the present and future conditions of the world. These objectives must be behaviorally based and must have as their central purpose the development of the activist—the individual who can take direct action based on his critical assessment of the social problem at hand. Only when the inquiring activist is the predominant product can educators claim that schools have come of age—they have become agents of social change rather than perpetrators of uninspiring traditions.

Author Index

Subject Index

DATE DUE			